EUROPE'S NEW RACISM

Europe's New Racism
Causes, Manifestations and Solutions

Edited by
the Evens Foundation

evens foundation

Berghahn Books
New York • Oxford

First published in 2002 by

Berghahn Books
www.BerghahnBooks.com

© 2002 Evens Foundation
Reprinted in 2005

All rights reserved.
No part of this publication may be reproduced in any form or by any means without the written permission of Berghahn Books.

Library of Congress Cataloging-in-Publication Data
Europe's new racism : causes, manifestations, and solutions / edited by the Evens Foundation.
  p. cm. -- (Culture and politics/politics and culture ; v. 1)
Includes bibliographical references and index.
ISBN 1-57181-332-2 (alk. paper) -- ISBN 1-57181-333-0 (alk, paper : pbk.)
1. Europe--Ethnic relations. 2. Racism--Europe. 3. Europe--Social policy. 4. Immigrants--Europe. 5. Europe--Race relations. I. Evens Foundation. II. Series.

D1056 .E966 2001
305.8'0094--dc21

2001037825

British Library Cataloguing in Publication Data

A catalogue record for this book is available from the British Library.

Printed in the United States on acid-free paper.

ISBN 1–57181–332–2 (hardback)
1–57181–333–0 (paperback)

Table of Contents

Editorial Preface   vii

Part One: Models and Perspectives

Developments in Theories of Racism   3
Nora Räthzel

Understanding Institutional Racism   27
Marc Verlot

Hate Speech, Violence and Contemporary Racisms   43
John Solomos & Liza Schuster

The Role of International Law   57
Natan Lerner

Racism and Poverty in a Human Rights Perspective   71
Bas de Gaay Fortman

Does a Supranational Europe Stimulate and/or Combat Racism?   85
Robert Maier

Part Two: Different Contexts

Refugee and Asylum Policy Influenced by Europeanisation   105
Gudrun Hentges

Ethnic Relations in Local Contexts: beyond a dualist approach to identities and racism
Maykel Verkuyten — 131

Economic Globalisation and Racism in Eastern and Western Europe
Béla Greskovits — 143

Part Three: Avenues to Remediation

The Role and Forms of Education
Giovanna Campani — 165

Racism, Devolution and Education in the European Union
Jagdish S. Gundara — 187

What Interculturalism could bring a Solution to Racism?
Rik Pinxten & Marijke Cornelis — 211

Biography of All Authors — 233

Index — 237

About the Foundation — 246

Editorial Preface

Cultural identity, whether real or imagined, has become an important marker of societal differentiation. The series 'Culture and Politics/Politics and culture' focuses on the interplay of politics and culture and offers a forum for analysis and discussion of such key issues as multiculturalism, racism and human rights. This first volume discusses new racisms in Europe.

The debate on this subject is timely and important. Indeed, all over Europe we now witness new forms of exclusion, of racism and of new extreme right primordialism. Culture and cultural differences are haunting political discourse on the notions of citizen, refugee and immigrant.

It is of the utmost importance that the democratic regimes within and around the European Union should start to react against these tendencies in order to defend democracy. However, in order to develop policies that combat racism in a convincing and efficient way, it is necessary to have a good understanding of the phenomenon first. We hope that this book will add to the existing literature in a significant way.

A first group of articles offers models and perspectives on new racism in Europe.

Räthzel engages on a wide-ranging exploration of changes in emphasis and format of present day theories on racism. Although it is beyond the scope of one chapter to be clear on all conceptual intricacies of this field, the author did a great job in thinking through the recent manifestations of racism on this continent. *Verlot* analyses what institutional or structural racism is installing itself in the European context. The way institutions allow for or maybe invite new exclusions is the subject of this type of research. *Solomos and Schuster* focus on the particular format of hate speech that has become widespread in new racist tactics. In the context of Human Rights agreements and institutions of international law a particular alertness is invited, as *Lerner* illustrates in his contribution. *De Gaay Fortman* links racism to poverty and hints at remedies enhancing the implementation of Human Rights.

New forms of racism manifest themselves in different contexts: *Maier* analyses in what ways European structures and initiatives that go beyond the national ideological boundaries are coping with new racism. The inefficiency and perverse effects of well-meant policies are scrutinised.

One growing subcategory of human beings who have been subjected to discrimination in a harsh way over the past decade is that of refugees. With the fall of the Berlin wall and the implosion of the former Soviet Union, the urgency of the 'refugee problem' and hence of asylum policy, have only increased, as is detailed by *Hentges*. The development of majority versus minority perspectives within and beyond national structures is the focus of analysis in *Verkuyten*'s article. He describes the role of ethnicity and power in local identity dynamics. *Greskovits* looks at the developments in eastern European countries. Globalisation substitutes for national politics to some extent, as the economic forces induce societal adaptations in this era.

Although we are convinced that solutions are urgently needed, modesty forces us to be cautious in this endeavour. No simplistic solution will pass the test of time. Nevertheless, we invited some scholars to develop their line of thought, which would point to one or the other way to counter racism and suggest avenues to remediate racism. *Campani* proposes to make a clear choice in educational policy: either for multicultural or intercultural education or for antiracist education. The political implications of each choice are discussed. *Gundara* discusses the developments of devolution within nation states, as it is met by the practice of subsidiarity at the European level. He emphasises the role of education pointing at the responsability of schools in community building. Finally, *Pinxten and Cornelis* sketch recent ideological developments in Europe. They show how new communitarianism and the choice for freedom and modern citizenship are emerging as mutual alternatives. The way the so-called 'Third Way' positions itself in this arena is up for discussion.

The book offers a set of insights and analyses, not a final conclusion or a blueprint. We hope the book and the series may enhance the discussion on culture and politics, both within academia and beyond.

Ellen Preckler Christine Castille Corinne Evens

Part One

Models and Perspectives

DEVELOPMENTS IN THEORIES OF RACISM

Nora Räthzel

Introduction

In the following, I shall discuss some of the main ways in which racist practices and ideologies have been theorised. I understand racism as part and parcel of the political institutions, political practices, and everyday cultures in western nation states. Therefore, this account concentrates on theories explaining racisms as situated in the centre of western societies rather than as a marginal phenomenon, for instance as practices and ideologies of right extremist, fascist groups. If I follow a more or less chronological structure, this does not imply that 'older' theories of racism or older forms of racism have been replaced by newer ones. They may have only been pushed to the margins of theoretical debates. Some forms of racism may no longer be dominant in public domains but may still be alive in much of everyday thinking and practice. In case there is any doubt, this account is not comprehensive and it is unavoidable that important contributions to theorising racism will be missing.

Refuting the Concept of 'Race'

One of the results of the second world war was the founding of the United Nations as a means to secure peace by replacing violent clashes between states with peaceful negotiations. A suborganisation of the UN was UNESCO, committed to education and research. One of its first aims was to study and understand racism, the ideology that had legitimated the genocide of Jews and Gypsies in Germany.

As Robert Miles tells us (1989), the term racism first entered the English language as a translation of Magnus Hirschberg's book, *Rassismus*, originally written in German (1938). His book refuted the claim that there are discrete human races, hierarchically ordered, thus challenging the backbone of German fascist ideology. Races were defined biologically, using existing or ascribed phenotypical characteristics as indicators for psychological 'traits' and supposed intellectual and moral superiority/inferiority. This 'race-theory', known in theories of racism as 'scientific racism', originated in the nineteenth century. It defined the 'Aryan race' as superior to all other 'races'. The Jews, defined as an 'Asiatic people', where at the bottom of this hierarchy. Some racist theories constructed Jews as mixed with blacks, the black Jew thus becoming the ultimate threat to the survival of the 'superior' white culture (see Gilman's analyses of Chamberlain and other representations of blacks and Jews and black Jews in Germany, 1992: 24ff).

During the 1950s and 1960s UNESCO assembled, on four separate occasions, groups of scientists of international reputation who were asked to summarise the scientific evidence concerning the nature of 'race'. The so-called 'scientific racism' was refuted as scientists proved that there were no different races.

A recent rejection of the idea of different human races comes from genetics. 'In fact, we find that any population, however small, has enormous genetic variation; on average, one finds 85 percent of the total human variation within populations and only 15 percent between. To a very superficial examination, races exist, in the sense that some groups of individuals are distinguishable and relatively uniform for a few superficial traits. That there exist 'pure' races is a pure myth, generated by the fact that most Europeans are white, sub-Saharan Africans black, many Asians brown, and a few further traits may help to distinguish more finely the geographic origin of individuals. There is no equal uniformity under the skin. Genetic differences among populations and races, however defined, are small or trivial compared with those within populations. Another myth which dominated the nineteenth century thought is that interracial hybrids are inferior, and that race admixture is to be avoided at all costs. The degree of genetic differentiation in the human species is so small that it is impossible that racial admixture is genetically dangerous' (Cavalli-Sforza 1999).

It is certainly useful to have this scientific evidence countering the idea of different human races. However, to assume that racism can be fought by refuting the concept of race implies a view of racism that sees it as a result of rational, though false thinking. Racist behaviours and feelings, however, are not a result of false consciousness or the wrong information. They are embedded in societal and individual structures. This should become clearer in the course of this article.

The UNESCO achievement of showing that racism has no scientific foundation was important, but the notion of hierarchically organised human races was mainly discredited by the genocidal racism practised by German fascism. In France and Germany for instance, the term 'race' is hardly ever used in public discourse today. This is not the case in the English speaking countries. Sometimes within quotation marks, but often without, 'race' is used quite matter-of-factly. The reason given by the authors that follow this practice is that it is used as a social construction not as an empirical fact. Some scholars, like Robert Miles (1989), have argued against the usage of 'race' as an analytical category, warning that it reproduces what it criticises.

The fact that the 'old' racism was discredited for public usage does not mean that it has completely disappeared. In everyday life the idea of different 'races', perhaps not involving the element of hierarchical order, prevails. Now and again theories emerge giving the concept of biologically different 'races' validity. There are different traditions of theorising racism which I want to highlight, very briefly, using the United States, Germany, France and Britain as examples.

In the US, a body of theory developed that analysed the enslavement and oppression of people of African origin in the United States as racism. The Black Power movement, organising against this oppression, introduced the term into the political and theoretical debate (Carmichael/Hamilton 1968). Oliver Cox (1948/1976), a black Marxist, wrote the first book on racism which analysed it in the context of capitalism and colonialism. For him, racism was a rationalisation of exploitation.

Subsequently, ideologies legitimating colonialism, the slave-trade and South-African apartheid by defining peoples in Africa, Asia and Latin-America as 'inferior races', were analysed as expressions of racism. This history of racism founded a tradition that defines racism as a theory and practice of white people aimed against black people. Most British theory of racism has argued within this framework, with the exception of writers such as Robert Miles (1989) and Phil Cohen (1988), who have criticised this one-sidedness, arguing that this meant equating one instance of racism with racism in general.

In Germany, racism has largely been identified with anti-Semitism and thus with the so-called 'scientific racism'. That is why, until the end of the 1980s, racism towards migrant populations was not defined as such. It was argued that calling the discrimination of migrant workers racism would offend Jews and Gypsies, as it would equate genocide with the discrimination of 'foreigners'. Another argument has been that calling exclusionary and discriminatory practices against migrants racist would provoke resistance against discussing and changing them. In public debates and in theoretical accounts the terms 'hostility against foreigners' and 'hostility against strangers' are more frequently used than the term 'racism'. In France, the definition of racism has been similar to that in Germany as Max Silverman and Nira Yuval-Davis explain:

> Until fairly recently, anti-Semitism was the major paradigm for the understanding and analysis of racism in France. This is, in part, due to the powerful tradition of anti-Semitism itself in modern France ... The rise of the so-called 'Jewish question' at the end of the nineteenth century was symbolic of the struggle at that time between ... advocates of the so-called political/civic model of the nation ... and those of the opposing ethnic model, founded on essentialist and deterministic notions of blood, earth and race. (Silverman and Yuval-Davis 1999)

Yet, two very influential theories of racism based on the politics and experiences of colonisation have been developed by French scholars. Frantz Fanon analysed the forms of daily racism and its effects on blacks:

> I was responsible at the same time for my body, for my race, for my ancestors. I subjected myself to an objective examination, I discovered my blackness, my ethnic characteristics; and I was battered down by tom-toms, cannibalism, intellectual deficiency, fetishism, racial defects, slave-ships ... (1986:112)

Albert Memmi has been most influential in the English speaking world for his book on the coloniser and the colonised (1967) where he analyses, among other things, how history becomes naturalised in images of the colonised Other. Feminists have used his work to understand the construction of women as the Other. Memmi wrote the article on racism in the French Encyclopaedia Universalis, where he defines racism as a justification of privileges and of the aggression towards the victimised. His book on racism, published in France in 1982, was only translated into English in 2000.

The New Racisms: Cultural Racism, Differential Racism

Martin Barker (1981) was the first in Britain to claim that a new racism had emerged, that, for instance, the Powellit racism in Britain was based on a notion of cultures (not of races) that were seen as essentially different and unassimilable. Barker therefore called the new racism, *cultural racism*.

Miles (1993), argued that Barker had restricted his analysis to speeches of members of the Conservative party and ignored fascist groups and the everyday discourse. In both cases the 'old racism' prevailed. Additionally, Miles criticised Barker for not discussing racism in relation to nationalism, thus ignoring the fact that the legislation of the government in the 1980s rested on arguments already used in 'classical racism': 'by removing the right of entry to, and settlement in, the United Kingdom from certain categories of British subject, the state established new (racist) criteria by which to determine membership of the 'imagined community' (ibid. 74).

In France, Balibar (1988a) and Taguieff (1987) also argued that there is a new racism. Their argument was perhaps more readily accepted in the French context as there emerged a group of intellectual circles calling themselves, and being called, *La nouvelle droite*. One of its philosophical leaders is Alain de Benoist.

The theories of the new right can be seen in the light of, and as responses to, new forms of anti-racism in the 1980s. A new generation of migrant communities began to develop forms of political and cultural identification which expressed their lives in the receiving countries. They fought racism by asserting their difference, using their cultural heritage as a source of strength and self-assurance. In France they created the slogan *droit à la différence* demanding the right to be different *and* to have the same rights as the 'native' populations. Such a demand was caused by the republican notion of equality which claimed that equal rights required the abolition of religious and other 'particularistic' belongings from the public realm and their confinement to the private.

Taking up the *droit à la différence*, the new right argues that in order to preserve the variety of cultures, people from different cultures need to stay in their respective places. The French culture, has the same right to preserve its difference as any other, and this difference is threatened by the presence of other cultures in the country. As it argues in favour of differences, Taguieff called this new racism, *le racisme différentialiste*. Like Barker, he claims that the new racism does not speak about hierarchies, but just about differences and the necessity to respect them. I would like to present some formulations of this new right in order to show the way it uses anti-racist terms. In an article about the New Millennium, published in *Junge Freiheit*, a German journal of the New Right for young people, Benoist writes:

> We will have to know whether it will be possible to re-organise and harmonise the living communities, or whether the steamroller of standardising globalisation will flatten the variety of cultures and peoples forever (my translation from the German in www.jungefreiheit.de, July 2000).

Expressed like this, this sentence could easily be written by a multiculturalist on the left. In this article, the threat to difference is not seen as caused by migrations but by 'the economy'. Things sound differently in another article, arguing for what in Germany is called *Ethnopluralismus* and in France le *différentialisme culturel* by the new right:

> Against the egalitarian world we set pluralist mankind, which possesses different skin colours in different parts of the world. Their respective mental manifestations, conditioned by inheritance, reflect the different ways of feeling of a soul that makes other psychic strings sound... Our rootedness is territorial, human and cultural (Benoist quoted in Krebs 1981, pp. 23, my translation from German).

Here we see a clear link between phenotypical traits, inheritance and different 'feelings of a soul' which could be termed culture. Differences become naturalised, perceived as static, and 'rooted' in what the old racism used to call 'soil' and is here reformulated as 'territorial'.

It is comparatively easy to draw a line between such articulations and the old racism that ordered the world into hierarchised races. Other statements, arguing on a more philosophical level, can easily be mistaken as coming from a left or liberal position:

> The right to difference is a principle and has a value only as a generalisation. In other words, I can only defend my difference legitimately as long as I recognise and respect the difference of others. As soon as this right is instrumentalised and your difference is opposed to that of others, instead of admitting that the difference of others is no threat to your own but in fact reinforces it; as soon as you consider difference not as something which makes dialogue possible but as something which validates its rejection, when consequently, you posit difference as an absolute, whereas it exists by definition only in a relation, you fall back into tribal nationalism, into belonging as pure subjectivity. (TELOS, Winter 1993 – Spring 1994, Numbers 98 and 99. Special Double Issue. No page numbers, downloaded from the internet)

That this philosophy is used to argue for separation and against migration should make everybody think twice who believes difference per se could be liberating or subversive. What is lacking in the above definition of difference though, is an acknowledgement of relations of domination determining which differences are 'playful' and which, 'are poles of world historical systems of domination' (Haraway 1990: 203). In addition, reducing relations between individuals or groups to a relational difference without at the same time accounting for people's sameness, reifies differences and eludes people's mutual interconnectedness. While differences exist only in relations, it is also only in relations that they can be transcended without being denied.

Along with the naturalisation of culture and difference goes the naturalisation of racism. Using the catchphrase 'threshold of tolerance', it is argued that individuals cannot bear the presence of more than ten percent of 'strangers' without becoming aggressive. One wonders then, how the so-called strangers can manage not to be in a permanent state of aggression as they are constantly surrounded by more than ninety percent of 'strangers'. Maybe they are the superior races after all.

There is no space here for a more detailed analysis of the theories and strategies of the new right (see Lange 1993, Venner 1994). Perhaps one of the most important challenges of the new right is that its celebration of different cultures makes it difficult for anti-racist scholars and activists to retain this concept as a liberating one.

The appropriation of the notion of culture and the *droit à la différence* by the racist right has increased the problem of accounting for cultural differences and for communities of migrant origin (or for ethnic minorities) to have their differences recognised, *without* being imprisoned in static constructions of culture and accused of a communalist parochial ethnicity. This is especially true in France and Germany.

In Germany, the rejection of the notion of different cultures or different ethnicities has to be understood mainly as a reaction against the German history of applying a static culturalist notion to define the German nation and to exclude those who are seen as not belonging. A recent (October 2000) revival of this is a discussion about the German 'guiding culture' to which the migrants are asked to assimilate if they want to belong. As some scholars argue, this cultural definition of the nation led directly to German fascism. For many anti-racist scholars, the lesson from this history is to avoid what they see as the ethnicisation and culturalisation of communities.

The rejection of the category of ethnicity in France follows the Republican tradition. The citizen is seen as a political subject, defined as an abstract individual, belonging to the public sphere, his or her specific ways of living, culture, religion being confined to the sphere of the private. The modern individual is seen as defying all attempts to confine him to a specific culture, a collective (Finkielkraut 1987). This may sound sensible enough. The problem is that by rejecting the notion of ethnicity it becomes difficult to identify forms of racism and to tackle them. Cultural differences, seen as merely parochial essentialisms, are not respected (see Silverman 1992).

In Britain, culture and ethnicity are widely seen not as static, primordial traits but instead as flexible, ever changing, diverse and complex ways of life, constantly negotiated and re-organised. Yet, especially after the so-called 'Rushdie-affair', there is also the fear of 'irreconcilable' differences between, for instance, fundamentalist Muslim groups and other groups of either migrant or native origin. In general, the discussion in Britain (and partly also in the United States) does not focus on whether cultural and ethnic identities are useful or not, but instead on the question of how to avoid essentialist notions of culture and ethnicity (for example: Hall 1991, 1996, 1997, Back 1996, Gilroy 1993).

Theories of racism are not only about explaining how and why racisms occur but also about the way in which they can be fought. One way is to deconstruct racist constructions of the Other and, foremost, to demand rights and a legitimate space in society for minorities who are the targets of racism. When demands for that space, for the right to take part in shaping the rules according to which a given society works, are countered by constructing difference in a way that requires separation, there is a need for an alternative theoretical understanding of differences.

In my opinion, the conceptualisation in Britain of culture and identity as ever-changing, flexible processes, though important, does not sufficiently take into account the fact that flexibility and hybridisation can be instrumental in, instead of counter to, reproducing the opposing binaries of the majority Self and the minority Other. This will be discussed further below.

Implicit Racisms

Most early attempts to understand the so-called 'scientific racism' (and also many more recent ones) focused on explicit expressions of racism. They saw racism as a specific ideology and practice confined to particular groups in society or, as in the case of fascist Germany, to the ruling group which then influenced the masses. In these accounts, racism is always regarded as a conscious, deliberate practice and ideology.

Feminist analyses of racism and colonialism have shown that women, although hardly present in the public realm and also the victims of discrimination, have taken, and still take, an active part in supporting and reproducing racism, colonialism and fascism (Ware 1992, Koonz 1986). Other studies have investigated the ways in which belonging to the dominant group shapes the lives and self-conceptions of women and can make them an (often unconscious) supporting part of a racist system (Frankenberg 1993, Rommelspacher 1994, Räthzel 1994).

The studies of the participation of women in racist practices were one result of the broad and ongoing discussion initiated by black women in Britain and in the United States about the way in which 'second wave' feminism had ignored the experiences, demands and oppressions of black and (black and white) working class women, and thus become complicit in the perpetuation of racism and class oppression (Carby 1982, Amos and Parmar 1984, Davis 1983, Hooks 1981, Hull and Scott 1982). These analyses demonstrated how even the oppressed can sustain racism in their own struggle for liberation. They showed the extend to which racist thinking and feeling is part and parcel of western cultures and is internalised even by those who are more likely to be on the receiving end of power relations. Black feminists did not limit themselves to criticising white feminists. They developed theories of black feminist thought (e.g., Collins 1990) and a great many works emerged – too numerous to refer to here – looking at the experiences of women of colour, their oppressions and their resistances.

With the focus on racism of the everyday, we find a proliferation of definitions and explanations of racisms. If there are different kinds of racism at different times, political conjunctures and places, it becomes less important to discuss whether there is a new racism or not. Every expression and practice of racism has to be situated and analysed within its specific time and spatial context. Equally, it is important to distinguish between different kinds of racism occurring within different strata of a society. For instance, attitude studies showing that racism is especially prominent amongst those with comparatively low levels of education, rely upon the evidence of responses to a handful of simplistic statements which the designers of questionnaires define as indicating racism. More sophisticated forms of discrimination and racism cannot be measured with those instruments (for a study on racism of the elites see Wodak and van Dijk, 2000).

Another question, which appeared during the late 1970s and has been discussed ever since, is the relationship of racism to other forms of oppression like sexism and class subordination (Davis 1983, Anthias and Yuval-Davis 1992, Zack 1997). Because racism and sexism are both processes and ideologies of 'naturalisation',[1] some authors have included all forms of naturalisation, e.g., sexism, homophobia, oppression of the disabled, into the concept of racism (Guillaumin 1972). Others have talked about the double or triple oppression of women (as women, women of colour, working class women, see Smith 1983). This has been criticised on the grounds that the articulation of different forms of oppression changes their character. Instead of adding up, Deborah King (1988) has proposed to see oppressions as multiplying.

I cannot report in detail on how these relationships have been analysed. Instead, I would like to present three theories of racism in modern western societies (racisms exist in other societies too, but they are not the focus of this article) which aim at understanding racism within broader concepts of the modern nation state, the world economy and modernity in general.

Racism and the Nation State – Racism and Nationalism

Racism, in Balibar's view (Balibar 1988b,c), has three histories, three forms: anti-Semitism, colonialism and racism against the black population in the United States. There are racisms of the interior (against minorities –or majorities like in the case of South Africa) and racisms of the exterior (against colonised peoples). Racism goes further than nationalism, because the construction of a 'race' transcends the borders of nations (the white, black, brown, red 'races', the Caucasians, etc.).

Racism is a kind of a philosophy of history. It makes the invisible origins of destiny visible. It is a form of classifying human beings by developing criteria according to which one can decide *if* they are human beings and, if so, what kind of human beings. Classification has to precede hierarchisation. Such classifications are forms of 'naturalisation'. Social and historical differences are transformed into natural differences deriving from a natural origin.

As we have seen above, it is quite common to define racism as a form of naturalisation of the social. However, in the face of new developments within the natural sciences this definition may be outdated. The concept of nature has changed. It is seen and treated as a field of constant intervention, especially if we consider genetics. One could argue that science does more to change nature than it does to change social relations. One might say that today, in neoliberal times, it is the market that has acquired the status of nature as something unchangeable and even uncontrollable.

Racism, Balibar suggests, is a universalism: It is based on the universal character of the human species (the so-called races), the universal laws of origin and destiny, the universality of aggression against strangers, and the universalism of a preferential altruism.

The 'necessity', from the point of view of the nation state, to construct a 'Volk' is connected to the fact that no nation has an 'ethnic basis', but all construct themselves upon one. Therefore, the nation has to create a 'fictional ethnicity'. Racism creates this 'fictional ethnicity' on which nationalism, the 'imagined community' of the nation, is based.

This leads to a decisive (re)definition of the modern state. While many liberal theorists emphasise the egalitarian character of the modern state, Balibar points out that it is not the 'modern state' that is (officially) egalitarian, but the modern nation state. Only the members of the 'national community' are considered as equal and can thus enjoy 'equal rights' – at least formally. The borders of the nation state are the borders of 'equal rights'.

An example of this is the international and national legislation against racism. Those nation states which sign international treaties emphasise their prevailing right to treat non-citizens differently without having this defined as a case of racism (see Lerner, this volume).

Racism, Balibar concludes, provides a construction of a pure race for the construction of the nation. This inevitably leads to a constant contradiction between nationalism and racism. Racism strives for the pure member of the nation. Not even all members of the majority can meet these standards. There are legal definitions of who is a national. These legal definitions never quite meet the racist criteria (see the hatred of the neofascists in Germany against the 'ethnic Germans'). The race is *always* smaller than the national community.

Racism is a form of transcendence, of constructing an aesthetic ideal human being, constructed as body and mind. Here, sexism and class-exploitation enter. The ideal human being in racist discourses is always an ideal man, a man that can seduce women and dominate others. Women are confined to the role of assisting in securing the domination of the 'superior race'. Domination of the 'lower classes' and domination of women are the emblems of the ideal incorporation of the superior race. Yet, nationalism wants to be a populist movement, precisely transcending the borders of classes.

For Balibar this is the reason why racism tends to define the 'proper race' negatively, by defining those who do not belong to it: the minorities, the migrants, the Jews, the immigrants, the Gypsies. By defining their features as undesirable, the desirable features of those who belong are implicitly defined.

The incongruity between a nation and a race also works to transcend national boundaries. A race is not only smaller, it is also bigger than the nation state. The imperialism of nation states was legitimated by a higher principle which was said to lead their actions: the necessity to spread the higher moral and cultural values of the civilised 'humanity' (race), referred to as 'the white man's burden'.

The International World Economy and the Constructions of Race, Nation and Ethnicity

Wallerstein (1988) combines the analysis of economic and political interests to explain the development of racism, or rather, the existence of categories like 'race', 'nation' and 'ethnic group'. They are used to mark the continuity of a phenomenon. Because of its continuity, that phenomenon has the power to influence everyday attitudes and can serve as a basis for present demands.

The temporary dimension is central to the concept of 'people' The past serves to either legitimate or de-legitimate the present. Therefore, it is constantly being changed according to the demands of the present. At the same time, this changing cannot be admitted, otherwise the past would lose its legitimising function, which relies on its construction as something eternal, written in stone. It does not make any difference, though, if the present is explained and the past is constructed with reference to a genealogy (race), to historically located socio-political groups (nations) or to cultural groups (ethnic groups). So why are there three categories, asks Wallerstein.

Each of these categories, he argues, are connected with one of the basic structures of the capitalist global economy: Race refers to the horizontal division of labour in the world economy, to the antinomies of centre and periphery; Nation refers to the political superstructure of this historical system – the sovereign nation states; Ethnic group refers to the household structures within nation states which make sure that large sectors of unpaid labour are maintained.

Wallerstein suggests that with the differentiation of centre and periphery and the domination of the former over the latter, their differences began to be articulated in terms of 'race'. The number of 'races' declined with the growing polarisation between centre and periphery. In the end, the difference between 'white' and 'non-white' is the one which remained central. In short, 'race' is the expression and the consequence of the geographical concentration of the horizontal division of labour. Wallerstein's example for this is the decision of the South African state to label the Japanese businessmen 'whites by honour'.

Almost always, the creation of a nation was preceded by a state which then created a nation and a people because 'national feelings' enable the stability, the interior cohesion of the nation state. It is the nation state that allows for a unified administration which facilitates the effect of political measures. It also allows for groups to claim their interests against other groups either outside of or within the nation state (foreigners). The concept of a unified nation is also necessary in order to claim rights or higher ranking within the hierarchical structure of the international system of states. Without being a nation state there is no claim to any international position.

Finally, ethnic groups are minorities, but not necessarily numerical minorities. The position of being a minority is dependent on its social power (examples are: women and blacks during South Africa's apartheid system). Minorities are tied to the borders of nation states and are defined in relation to a national majority.

According to Wallerstein, the capitalist system is based not only on the antagonism between capital and labour, but also on a complicated hierarchical system within the labour sector. Some sectors get a payment that lies beneath the normal price for the reproduction of the workforce. Wherever we find these underpaid households within nation states, we find that there is always a high correlation between them and what is called an 'ethnic group'. These groups are defined by certain rules of behaviour and systems of norms according to which they educate their children. These assumed or existing differences in relation to the national majority serve to solve the contradiction between theoretical equality and practical inequality in capitalist systems. If the state educated different groups in different ways it could be challenged, but if ethnic minorities do this 'themselves' it is welcomed (to a certain degree).

The ever changing nature of 'ethnic groups', their coming and going, serves the capitalist system quite well, says Wallerstein. As it is constantly changing and economic processes are constantly being shaped and reshaped, the attitudes of dependent workers must change as well. The formation, disappearance and emergence of ethnic groups is a valuable instrument to smooth the running of the economic machinery.

One could take as an example for this the present (2000) proposals in several European nation states, (e.g., Germany, France, Spain) in favour of a new immigration. As the economies grow and the native populations age, the discourse about immigration changes. Instead of fearing the waves of migrations, states are now scared that they may not attract enough migrants.This position has little to do with humanitarian considerations. In Germany, for instance, demands for a greencard system for computer specialists from India are linked to demands for abolishing the right to asylum altogether.

Racism and Modernity

Bauman (1989) has analysed a connection between modernity and racism – or proteophobia, as he calls it. (A detailed historical account of the connection between racism and modern culture has been presented by Goldberg, 1993. Gilman has analysed racist and sexist stereotypes in western cultures extensively, for example, 1992, 1985, 1993).

The 'state of mind' of modernity is characterised by the search for an ideal society, for perfection. An ideal society is one in which everything is controlled. Modernity's counter-culture, socialism, does not exist outside of this general frame. Its ideal is also the perfect society, although not one controlled by the state, but constructed by 'men the people themselves'.

Bauman compares the activities of the modern state with the activities of the gardener who, in order to produce the perfect garden, has to destroy 'the weeds'. In its strife for control and perfection it is the stranger who is neither friend nor foe that arouses the anxieties and the animosity of the state and its institutions. In modernity, ambiguity is a threat, and therefore, those who are not normalised and cannot be categorised are the targets of either exclusionary or assimilationist practices.

According to Bauman, one of the features of modernity, which made the holocaust possible, was the transformation of the individual's pre-social ethical concern into a concern to obey those in power and the rules imposed by them. Bureaucratic organisations suspended moral reservations for the duties they asked their members to fulfil. Members of such organisations are trained to obey orders and to fulfil their tasks meticulously. They learn to judge their deeds by the degree to which they have accomplished their task without asking questions about the morality of the task itself. Bauman calls this 'adiaphorisation' (1989). This made it possible for individuals during fascism to take part in the genocide, without feeling morally responsible. One remembers the excuses of those accused: 'We only followed the commands'.

The theories presented here explain the structural basis for racisms, but there is no automatic relationship between the necessities and interests of nation states or the international world economy and the way in which individuals think and act in everyday life. The question is then, how does racism become a motivating force in the everyday lives of individuals?

Everyday Cultures of Racism, or the Racism Of Individuals?

Racism as Xenophobia

Some theories explain the relations between the structural or societal forms of racism and the attitudes and beliefs of individuals in a reductionist way: because the state and the media disseminate racist ideas we find them in the everyday thinking of individuals. One way of proving this is to show that what we read in the press and what we find in conversation with people is the same or similar. However, we also find things in the media and in politician's speeches that people do not believe, for instance: that politicians are honest, and are doing the best for their country. Many people do not believe that.

Taking an example from our subject, the German state tried to convince its population that 'ethnic Germans' were Germans and should be treated as such. Yet, until today, they are generally seen as Russians and Poles, and their German identity is perceived as something they invented, in order to be able to come to the rich West.

The question then arises: why is it that people are likely to believe negative things about migrants and minorities (if that is the case) while they do not believe other things they are told? Moreover, there is also much talk in the media about the 'multicultural society'; the advantages of having 'foreigners' in the country to fill in the gaps of the labour market, and to enhance the national culture with their folklore. Why is it that these are not the dominant beliefs of people in everyday lives? To understand this, we have to look at the ways in which individuals become part of society, their societalisation or socialisation.

Some theories explain the 'fear of the stranger' (xenophobia) as a result of socialisation. (Erdheim 1992, similar: Gilman 1992). When the child is able to perceive that its mother leaves, it experiences this as negative, says Erdheim. Thus, it learns that its mother is not wholly good. To protect the image of the good mother it projects all her negative aspects onto the stranger. Equally, Erdheim argues, the child's perception that there is a difference between itself and the world results in a division of the self and the world into good and bad. Good is the Self, bad is the other, the stranger.

Such theorising raises some questions:

1. Why should the child want to suppress the negative sides of her/his mother and of itself? Is this a primordial feature of all humans or is it related to specific social conditions and if so, what kind of conditions are these? Are there gender differences within these processes? Feminists have criticised the idea that the child only resents being separated from its mother. It may be afraid to, but at the same time also want to separate itself from its mother and become independent.
2. There is an inherent contradiction in the notion of the stranger as a projection-site of the negative self: an individual or group thus constructed is not a stranger in the sense of the unknown. If we look at the targets of racism in daily life we often find that they live side by side with the majorities that reject them for decades or centuries. The problem is not that 'they' are strangers, but that they are supposedly 'well known', that is, constructed as having specific, always recognisable, threatening features. As Balibar points out (1988b): racism is never about the Arab, the Turk, etc. as such, but about the Fundamentalist, the Criminal, the Drug dealer, etc.

Contextualising Everyday Racisms

Phil Cohen's analysis (1988, 1992, 1993) of racism takes both elements into account: the individual's creation and appropriation of identity and the social context within which identities are created. He asks for a close analysis of racism in its specific contexts: the people to whom those that articulate racism speak; the situation they live in; the political conjuncture and the different rhetoric used towards different people (1992).

In asking these questions, Cohen can identify how racism serves individuals to 'make sense' of their lives. For instance, he analyses how neighbourhood cultures of working class people establish their ways of living as counter-cultures not against, but beside the state. As a result, they experience the arrival of blacks as a way in which the state intervenes into their neighbourhood (1988).

Racism as Rebellious Self-Subordination

I have tried to analyse everyday racism by connecting these individual behaviours to the construction of the nation state. (1994, 1997) The general idea is based on perceiving the state as an institution which has taken over the individual's ability to control and manage her/his production and reproduction. One can also formulate this as individuals handing over their abilities and capacities for self-organisation to the state. This is an ongoing process whereby the state uses coercion and organises consent, while individuals resist but also subordinate themselves. Racism is one of the means that individuals use to imaginarily solve this conflict. Some examples may clarify this.

Scapegoating or the Externalisation of Internal Conflicts

It is a well known strategy of politicians, and sometimes of trade unionists, to make 'foreign labour' responsible for a growth in unemployment. Anti-racists have analysed these strategies as 'scapegoating'. This is a religious term. It indicates a ritual where all the sins of the community are loaded onto a goat and this goat is then sent into the desert. The community will be liberated from its sins as those sins will die, with the goat, in the desert.

This picture has a double meaning. On the one hand, one is liberated from sins as they are taken over and away by 'someone' else. On the other hand, loading the goat and sending it into the desert is an act of self-liberation. Instead of being a victim one transforms oneself into a conscious social actor. I think this transformation is one of the reasons for the success of what I call the externalisation of internal conflicts.

In our western (post)modern societies, a majority of us believes in the self-regulating powers of the market. The notion of control is a negative one when applied to those processes. While it seems illegitimate to control production, the flow of goods and the allocation of capital, it seems perfectly correct to control people. It is acceptable to control the access of people to the labour markets, to the school system, to control the unification of families – as long as the people thus controlled are defined as not belonging to the nation state which executes such controls. This acceptance can be explained by the way in which control of the Other enables the majority to feel in control of their own fate: internal conflicts like unemployment, housing problems, cultural conflicts, etc., can be externalised, that is, projected on 'outsiders' and thus made the object of political and economic measures and convey the idea that things are under control.

It is important to stress though, that this 'externalisation of internal conflicts' is not a conscious process. There is a largely unconscious mechanism at play. Therefore, it cannot be tackled by rational explanations, for example, by tables showing how jobs held by migrants are not the ones that natives are looking for. Such enlightening does not have the same liberating effect as for instance scapegoating.

The Possibility of Another Life – the Rreturn of the Repressed

Racism can serve to transform subordination into autonomy. An example of this can be discovered in a letter to an editor we found in a newspaper (Kalpaka/Räthzel 1994): 'Look how the Turks sit on the grass in our parks. They use the space no German was allowed to enter'. This simple sentence shows a complex relationship between autonomy and subordination. First, the Turks are accused of inappropriately using something that belongs to 'us': the park. However, in the next sentence, the owner presents himself as a subordinated citizen who is forbidden to use what is his. That the Turks dare to ignore a command which the writer himself has obeyed is what causes his anger. His desire for the park has been transformed into a desire for order. Now the transgression demonstrates that this self-transformation was perhaps not necessary, that another way of life might have been possible. The only way to regain a sense of autonomy is to make sure that everybody else complies to the same rules. The appropriation of space happens through acting as if he was the state to which he is in reality subordinated. By demanding the subordination of others he can live his own life as one of autonomy. One could reformulate the notion of the 'return of the repressed' without a recourse to childhood. What is repressed and constantly returning here is a desire for self-determination.

The Obsession with Borders in the Age of Globalisation

If the theories summarised above are right, and racisms are connected to the construction and maintenance of nation states in modernity, what are we to expect in the course of neoliberal globalisation? Globalisation as neoliberalism leads to contradictory processes: On the one hand the economy is flourishing, on the other, the gap between the poor and the rich is increasing worldwide, including within the more wealthy countries. Jobless growth puts the traditional welfare systems under threat. Goods, productive capital and especially money are flowing ever more easily across borders. Some experts claim that the nation state has lost its capacity for regulating national economies. Others suggest that the recourse to 'globalisation' serves nation states and multinational corporations as an excuse for deregulating national economies, cutting down the welfare state and limiting the rights of workers. Whatever the reasons, deregulation occurs in the West and is forced on nonwestern states by the World Bank and the IMF, which is why some prefer to call globalisation neoliberalism.

One powerful means for organising identification with the nation state has been the social security it can provide to those entitled to it. It is precisely this power to secure access to at least some resources for individuals, which is withering away, or given up. Thus, the state's authority and ability to produce consent fades. In my view, European states are trying to reconfirm their power and reorganise consent through an obsession with borders.

These are some of the policies recently developed against refugees and migrants:

1. In all European countries, states are trying to deprive refugees of their right to social welfare payment. Either by refusing to allow them to register (Belgium), by reducing their payment, or by giving it in kind.
2. In all European countries, states are gathering data on non-nationals, collecting them in central databanks and passing them on to the police, to the inland revenue, the secret service, the criminal investigation agency, etc. In some countries the legislation had to be changed in order to allow for such an intervention into the individual rights of people.
3. While, on the one hand, we have the Schengen treaty, which has led to the reduction of border controls between the countries who have signed the treaty, and a shift of border- controls to the countries of the Schengen periphery, on the other hand, border-controls have been moved into these countries. Many of the Schengen signatories now have legislation demanding that people without the nationality of the country they are in have to carry an identity card with them. Every underground station, bus stop, or street corner can become a border where identities are checked. People who do not

look the way those belonging to the given nation state are supposed to look, can be stopped and asked to verify their identity anywhere. The stop and search policy that black people have been subjected to in different European nation states for decades is in the process of being generalised.

This proliferation of borders and the tightening of border controls, including the ever more sophisticated technology for this task is what I call the obsession with borders. It is this obsession itself which produces the illegal person, the treacherous immigrant, who then legitimates even more control. This is an old mechanism of racism: first, Jews were not allowed to do anything else than to lend money, then they were blamed as money lenders. International economic relations of exploitation, for which the West bears the main responsibility, produce poverty, wars and uproot people. When they seek refuge by fleeing into those countries that praise themselves for their wealth, democracy and universal human rights, they are made illegal by stricter rules of entry and blamed for wanting to live off 'our wealth' – a wealth which, seen in a more comprehensive and historical perspective, largely belongs to 'them' anyway.

Constant preoccupation with refugees and so-called 'illegal immigrants' is one of the few ways through which the nation state can still reproduce itself as a social agent and prove to a less consenting population that it has things 'under control' and is willing and able to protect its population – not from social hardships but from a threatening alien force.

New Ways of Constructing the Other

We are living not only in the age of neoliberalism but also in the age of hybridity, of cultural mix and cut. We have the 'exotic cuisine' (Hall 1991) everywhere and, despite the tightening of border controls, increasing numbers of people are not living in the places where they were born. Even if they are, they keep travelling all over the world.

Zygmunt Bauman (1995) claims that societies are disintegrating into groups – tribes – flexible entities which keep forming and falling apart. People identify through religious beliefs, cultural fashions, sections of the labour market and are identified as the homeless, the outcasts, the dying species of the working class.

How are images of the Other constructed against this background? The patriarchal attitude of civilising the natives (and, if they become dangerous, to teach them a lesson) is becoming replaced by a defensive attitude towards the threatening intruders. They are not so much pictured as being closer to nature (although these images still coexist) but rather are depicted as understanding modern society so well that they can take advantage of its institutions.

The notion of multiculturalism is accompanied by a multiplication of racist images and practices. For every social conflict there is a group of people who can be made responsible for it. To name just a few examples: The Russian Mafia, the Polish car stealer, the African and Kurdish drug dealer, the English construction worker dumping good German wages, the Rumanian gangster, the East European women-trafficker. These are expressions used by the police and the media when reporting on crimes.

In our study of young people in Hamburg, those of native origin confronted us with a whole range of different images assigned to young people of migrant origin. While some thought Turks where okay and Kurds the problem, others thought of Russians as the worst group. Images also differed according to gender: migrant girls could be okay, migrant boys were seen as a threat. Different neighbourhoods cultivated different images of each other and the threatening aliens or racists that were to be found there.

One could argue that the mechanisms producing racisms are gaining more momentum instead of disappearing. For instance, the necessity to organise consent, while denying people substantial influence over their living conditions through the construction of suprasates, opens a bigger gap between people's interest to control and their powerlessness. The possibilities for democratic interventions are decreasing. This makes it necessary to manufacture consent through processes of identification as a national or supranational group. The degree to which Europe and the Europeans have been constructed as a homogeneous cultural group in official documents of the EU has recently been analysed (Hansen 2000).

Resistance against globalisation and, more specifically, the building of the EU, can take the form of fascist and racist movements as can be observed in richer regions like Austria, Northern Italy, Flemish Belgium and Norway. This may indicate how racism is not so much about economic deprivation, but about losing control.

The politics of the European Union are quite contradictory in a number of respects: Borders are tightened, but at the same time there are discussions about the need of migrants to close gaps in the labour market in the face of what is portrayed as the 'demographic crisis'. The consistency between these seemingly contradictory politics lies in the priority of economic interests. The aim is to reduce the numbers of those who are 'not useful' while trying to import 'useful labour'. For instance, farm labourers doing what natives do not want to do and software specialists doing what the natives are not qualified to do.

However, while the first group is mainly held to be illegal and forced to leave immediately after their labour is done, the second group is offered green cards – although only for a restricted time (see the *Guardian* October 30 and 31, 2000).

A comparable contradiction occurs concerning racism. While the treatment of asylum seekers as criminals produces racism, programs are financed to reduce racism. These programs are oriented towards the attitudes of individuals – mostly extremist right-wing youth. State policies are not considered as contributory factors in racism.

Where in the past, it was the opposition of Judaism and Christianity which provided the Christians with a notion of what they were, today there is much talk of the Judeo-Christian culture which is contrasted with the Islamic world or, in more secular terms, the western world of universal values as against the world of fundamentalist particularism.

In the construction of an Islamic enemy, difference itself becomes a homogenising factor. What the (so-called) Muslim fundamentalists are blamed for, is their homogeneity, their resistance to the globalisation and praise of differences. Here, the Other is seen as backward because of promoting a homogeneous culture. Again, one main argument of antiracism, the emphasis on difference and ever-changing identities, is turned against it: Flexibility is embraced in an exclusionary way as a characteristic of the modern and progressive West – a static culture and a homogeneous self is assigned to the nonwestern Other. These constructions serve to legitimate the obsession with borders. The *racisme differentialiste* praised differences but saw them as static. Today, it is the internal diversity that is praised and opposed to notions of the internal homogeneity of a dangerous Other, which is, in fact, the poor. Maybe we are now facing a racism of the postmodern against an irreconcilable modern essentialist – the racism of hybridity or a hybrid racism.

Perspectives

Such shifts show that racism cannot be tackled by merely refuting its rationally posed assumptions. It will always be able to switch to a new 'theory' once the old one is worn out.

If we understand racisms as ways in which those who are defined as belonging to the nation state can experience themselves as masters/mistresses of their fate through the mechanisms of externalisation of interior conflicts and the transformation of subordination into autonomy, then antiracism cannot consist in producing nicer images of the Other, in telling 'the truth' about how the Other really is. Especially as telling the truth, even if it was to be a positive one, is just one more way of imprisoning the Other in definitions. Antiracism, in my view, must consist in addressing the social conflicts and contradictions that create the fertile ground for racisms head-on.

Concerning the racism of the everyday, one has to bear in mind that in spite of all its hatred and contempt, racism, as Stuart Hall has stated, is also nurtured by a desire. There is the desire for the imagined superior sexuality of black men, which Fanon has analysed, but there is also the desire for the imagined freedom and independence of the Other. That migrants are seen as able to cross borders easily, using the social systems and leaving whenever they like means that they are seen to be what the majority is not: masters/mistresses of their fate.

Therefore, any effort to combat racism should be based on supporting individuals and/or groups to articulate their hardships and to find ways of tackling them. To say it in a short and hopefully provocative way: resistance against subordination is the best way of overcoming racism.[2] However – as feminism and other liberation movements have shown – there are never any guarantees.

Notes

1. Naturalisation in this context means to present social processes as due to natural laws.
2. I do not mean to say that legislation against discrimination and racism, equal opportunities policy and other measures are wrong. However, I would say that they tackle only one side of the problem. They are necessary means for a direct intervention agains racist practices. Yet, in order to deal with racism at its origins, these measures do not suffice.

Bibliography

Amos, V., and Parmar, P. 1984. 'Challenging Imperial Feminism'. *Feminist Review*, 17: 3–19.
Anthias, F., and Yuval-Davis, N. 1992. *Racialised Boundaries*. London: Routledge.
Back, L. 1996. *New Ethnicities and Urban Culture*. London: UCL.
Balibar, É. 1984. 'Sujets ou citoyens?', *Les Temps Modernes*. 452–4: 1726–53.
———. 1988a. `Y a-t-il un neo-racisme?' In *Race, Nation, Classe*. E. Balibar, and I. Wallerstein, eds. Paris: La Decouverte.
Balibar, É., and Wallerstein, I. 1988b. 'Racisme et nationalisme'. In *Race, Nation, Classe*. E. Balibar, and I. Wallerstein, eds. Paris : La Decouverte.
Balibar, É., and Wallerstein, I. 1988c. *La forme nation: histoire et idéologies*. In *Race, Nation, Classe*. E. Balibar, and I. Wallerstein, eds. Paris : La Decouverte.
Barker, M. 1981. *The New Racism*. London: Junction Books.
Bauman, Z. 1989. *Modernity and the Holocaust*. Oxford: Oxford University Press.

———. 1995. *Life in Fragments*. Oxford and Cambridge: Blackwell.
Benoist, A. de. 1981. 'Philosophie'. In: *Das unvergängliche Erbe*. Pierre Krebs, ed.Tübingen: Grabert.
Carby, H.V. 1982. 'White Women listen! Black feminism and the boundaries of sisterhood'. In: *Centre for Contemporary Cultural Studies: The Empire Strikes Back*. London: Hutchinson.
Carmichael, S., and C.V. Hamilton. 1968. *Black Power, The Politics of Liberation in America*. London: Jonathan Cape.
Cavalli-Sforza, L.L. 1999. 'A Panoramic Synthesis of My Research'. In *The International Balzan Foundation*. www.balzan.it/cavalli/paper.htm.
Cohen, P. 1992. 'It's racism what dunnit: hidden narratives in theories of racism'. In *'Race', Culture and Difference*. J. Donald, and A. Rattansi, eds. London: Sage.
———. 1993. *Gefährliche Spiele. Theorie und Praxis antirassistischer Erziehung*. Hamburg/Berlin: Argument.
Cohen, P., and H.S. Bains. 1988. 'The Perversions of Inheritance'. In *Multi-Racist Britain*. P. Cole and H.S. Bains, eds. Hampshire: Macmillan.
Collins, P.H. 1990. *Black Feminist Thought. Knowledge, Consciousness and Empowerment*. Cambridge: Unwin and Hyman.
Cox, O.C. 1976. *Race Relations*. Detroit, Wayne State: University Press.
Davis, A. 1983. *Women, Race and Class*. New York: Random House, Vintage Books.
Erdheim, M. 1992. 'Heimat, Geborgenheit und Unbewußtheit'. In: *Neue Heimaten – Neue Fremden*. Wolfgang Müller-Funk, ed. Wien: Picus.
Fanon, F. 1952. *Peau noire, masques blancs*. Paris: Editions du Seuil. English edition 1986. *Black Skin, White Masks*. London: Pluto Press.
Finkielkraut, A. 1987. *La défaite de la pensée*. Paris: Gallimard.
Frankenberg, R. 1993. *White Women, Race matters*. London: Routledge.
Gilman, S.L. 1985. *Difference and Pathology: Stereotypes of Sexuality, Race, and Madness*. Ithaca: Cornell University Press.
———. 1992. *Rasse, Sexualität und Seuche*. Reinbeck bei Hamburg: Rowohlt.
———. 1993. *Freud, Race and Gender*. Princeton, New Jersey: Princeton University Press.
Gilroy, P. 1993. *The Black Atlantic*. London: Verso.
Goldberg, D.T. 1993. *Racist Culture*. Oxford and Cambridge: Blackwell.
Guillaumin, C. 1972. *L'idéologie raciste. Genèse et language actuel*. Paris-La Haye: Mouton.
Hall, S. 1997. 'The spectacle of the ‚Other'. In *Representation. Cultural Representations and Signifying Practices*. S. Hall, ed. London: Sage.
———. 1991. 'The Local and the Global. Globalisation and Ethnicity'. In *Culture, Globalisation and the World-System*. A.D. King, ed. London: Routledge.
———. 1996. 'New Ethnicities'. In: *Stuart Hall – Critical Dialogues in Cultural Studies*. D. Morley, and K.-H. Chen, eds. London: Routledge.
Hansen, P. 2000. 'Europeans Only? Essays on identity politics and the European Union'. Umeå: University of Umeå, Department of Political Science.

Haraway, D. 1990. A Manifesto for Cyborgs. 'Science, Technology, and Socialist Feminism in the 1980's'. In: *Feminism/Postmodernism*. L.J. Nicholson, ed. New York and London: Routledge.

Hirschfeld, M. 1938. *Racism*. London: Victor Gollancz.

Hooks, B. 1981. *Ain't I a Woman? Black Women and Feminism*. Boston: South End Press.

Hull, G.T., P. Bell Scott, and B. Smith. 1982. *But Some of Us are Brave*. New York: The Feminist Press.

Kalpaka, A., and N. Räthzel. 1994. *Die Schwierigkeit, nicht rassistisch zu sein*. Köln: Dreisam Verlag.

King, D. 1988. 'Multiple Jeopardy, Multiple Consciousness'. *Signs* 14/1: 42–72.

Koonz, C. 1986. *Mothers in the Fatherland*. New York: St. Martin's Press.

Lange, A.1993. *Was die Rechten lesen. Fuenfzig rechtsextreme Zeitschriften. Ziele, Inhalte, Taktik*. Muenchen: C. H. Beck Verlag.

Memmi, A. 1982. *Le racisme. Descriptions, définition, traitement*. Paris: Editions Gallimard. (Engl. Edition. 2000. *Racism*. Minnesota: University of Minnesota Press).

Miles, R. 1989. *Racism*. London: Routledge.

———. 1993. *Racism after race relations*. London: Routledge.

Rommelspacher, B. 1994. 'Frauen in der Dominanzkultur'. In: *Frauen zwischen Grenzen. Rassismus und Nationalismus in der feministischen Diskussion*. O. Uremovic, and O. Gundula, eds. Frankfurt: Campus.

Räthzel, N. 1994. 'Harmonious *Heimat* and Disturbing *Ausländer*'. In: *Shifting Identities, Shifting Racisms*. Kum-Kum Bhavnani and A. Phoenix, eds. London: Sage.

———. 1997. *Gegenbilder. Nationale Identitäten durch Konstruktionen von Anderen*. Opladen: Leske und Budrich.

Silverman, M. 1992. *Deconstructing the Nation. Immigration, Racism and Citizenship in modern France*. London and New York: Routledge.

Silverman, M, and N. Yuval-Davis. 1999. 'Jews, Arabs and the Theorization of Racism in Britain and France'. In *Thinking Identities: Ethnicity, Racism and Culture*. A. Brah, M. Hickman, and M. Mac, eds. London: Macmillan.

Smith, B. (ed.). 1983. *Home Girls: A Black Feminist Anthology*. New York: Kitchen Table Press.

Taguieff, P.-A. 1987. *La force du préjugé*. Paris: La Decouverte.

Venner, M. 1994. *Nationale Identität. Die Neue Rechte und die Grauzone zwischen Konservatismus und Rechtsextremismus*. Koeln.

Wallerstein, I. 1988. *The politics of the world-economy: the states, the movements and the civilizations*. Cambridge: Cambridge University Press.

Wallerstein, I., and Balibar, E. 1988. *La construction des peuples*. In *Race, Nation, Classe*. E. Balibar, and I. Wallerstein, eds. Paris: La Decouverte.

Ware, V. 1992. *Beyond the Pale*. London: Verso.

Wodak, R., and T.A. van Dijk., eds. 2000. *Racism at the top. Parliamentary Discourses on Ethnic Issues in Six European States*. Klagenfurt: Drava Verlag.

Zack, N., ed. 1997. *Race/Sex. Their sameness, difference, and interplay*. London: Routledge.

UNDERSTANDING INSTITUTIONAL RACISM

Marc Verlot

Introduction

Since the 1980s, various national and regional governments within the European Union have converted to the development and implementation of minority policy. This policy has been taken to task by radical antiracists as being insufficient and even counterproductive. Rather than the inequalities between ethnic minorities and the dominant majorities being eradicated, it would appear that the discrepancies between the various population groups are actually on the increase. Examples of such analyses are to be found in Belgium in research carried out by Deslé (1993) or Blommaert and Verschueren (1998).[1] They analyse the discourse of policy and examine the processes of categorising, which are evidenced in the use of written and spoken language. Their conclusion points to the marginalisation of minority groups by means of the very policies that were intended to give them a place in mainstream society. It is the emphasis on cultural differences on the one hand, and the push towards a homogeneous society on the other hand, that has led to a discourse on tolerance being based on the same principles as that of intolerance. The very promotion of a homogeneous society on the part of government institutions is, according to these authors, the basis of institutional racism. Institutional racism is understood, then, as racism produced by the functioning of institutions. A synonymous phrase for institutional racism, which is often found in the literature, is structural racism.

Institutional or structural racism is a far more complex phenomenon than discourse analysis would lead us to suspect, however. Discourse analysis tends to place the different levels of policy on a single level, thereby oversimplifying the institutional and structural networks that lie behind policy. As a consequence, the tensions and contradictions within policy-making are often blurred (Verlot 1999). Stating that a certain policy is institutionally or structurally racist only labels that policy. It neither offers any insight into how this type of racist policy comes about, nor suggests what modifications can be made to counteract or prevent such policies. In the end, labelling policies often prevents a thorough and theoretically more complex analysis of policy and its relation to politics. The necessity of such an insight becomes apparent when one realises that every policy and its underlying ideological legitimisation contains elements that could not only reduce racism but also promote it. I agree with Herzfeld when he states that: 'Any ideology, no matter how consistent its formal expression, may produce racially divergent applications and interpretations' (1992:14). In order to examine how racist policy is developed, it is imperative to use an approach that does not automatically reduce social reality to a priori ideological categories, but rather takes the complexity of policy making and implementation into account.[2]

Let us take, for example, the case of convicted immigrants in France. On top of their conviction, the state is empowered to impose on the convicts an administrative sanction and send them out of the country. This looks like a clear case of institutional/structural racism, the policy here being the administrative act of imposing an extra sentence. Nevertheless, it is possible to find many (French) politicians and judges with an outspoken antiracist orientation who will defend this type of policy. At best they will recognise that this policy is discriminatory, but policy, even under French republican egalitarianism, is in itself always discriminating, as it differentiates between individuals and groups in society. The underlying question is whether this discrimination can be morally justified or if it is driven by racist intentions or has racist effects, be they explicit or implicit. This last question is often tackled from a moral or a broader philosophical point of view. Although legitimate, such an approach only clarifies points of view and rarely leads to a change in policy.

To overcome this type of unproductive polarising of views, I argue that an anthropological approach to policy can provide a more in-depth insight by looking more closely and rigorously to policy, whilst taking the cultural sensitivities of the dominant group and its institutions into account. Ethnographic research of institutions needs to be carried out within a comparative framework in order to facilitate a better understanding of the complex nature of institutional and structural racism, which research will, in its turn, allow us to combat that racism more effectively. More precisely, I propose to begin by researching the influence of 'basic cultural intuitions' on (minority) policies. This will bring me to two core notions that form the basis of potential institutional and structural racism. Finally, I propose to confront the outcomes of these ethnographical case studies to facilitate a broader, international view. This international comparison is intended to gain a more substantial insight into the universals of institutional and structural racism.

Are We Talking About the Same Thing?

Before tackling the issue of researching institutional/structural racism, it seems necessary to clarify the meaning of these terms. Within the literature one finds that terms like racism, discrimination and segregation are closely connected. Social scientists, historians and philosophers do not agree on the relation between discrimination, racism and segregation. Miles (1989:41 in Bulmer and Solomos 1999:344) describes the diverging points of view:

> First, for those who define the concept as referring to a particular instance of ideology, there is a disagreement about the form and content that ideology must possess to warrant categorisation as racism. Second some writers have claimed practices and/or unintended processes or consequences. There has been, therefore, a process of conceptual inflation whereby the concept has been redefined to refer to a wider range of phenomena.

A broadening of the scope of racism as a social phenomenon rather than an ideological stance has led to very different perceptions of the term. Social psychologists, for instance, refer most of the time to processes of discrimination. Racism is then seen as a racially intended specific form of discrimination (Pincus 1994, 1996). Social geographers, conversely, while concentrating their research on segregation, often emphasise outcomes rather than intentions in defining a policy as racist.

This emphasis on outcomes enlarges the concept of racism considerably. Banton and Miles (in Cashmore 1994:308–309) indicate that: 'In the 1960s the word was used in an expanded sense to incorporate practices and attitudes as well as beliefs'. They declare that 'in this sense racism denotes the whole complex of factors which produce racial discrimination, and sometimes, more loosely, designates also those which produce racial disadvantage'.[v] Stressing intentions as well as outcomes, racism is more and more seen in sociology, anthropology, history and philosophy, as a form *sui generis*, that is to be distinguished from, but linked with, discrimination and segregation. Referring to Wieviorka (1994), I believe that, as long as research has not falsified the nature of racism and its links with discrimination and segregation, we cannot dispense with racism as a separate and independent category, because to do so would diminish the problematic character of racism and its effects on society.

Accepting, although reluctantly because of its vagueness, that racism is a distinguishable category in its own right that can not be reduced to a simple consequence of discrimination, does not, however, imply that all is racism, nor that all types of racism are the same. Researching racism as a social phenomenon, therefore, calls for a more analytical and theoretical approach; a more complex approach. This implies a more meticulous use of terminology in order to make explicit the different levels they refer to and the way in which those levels are interconnected. For the sake of clarity I propose for the moment to distinguish three levels on which social phenomena can be analysed: everyday, institutional and structural forms (Pincus 1996). This brings me to the following scheme.

Table 1

	Discrimination	Racism	Segregation
Every day			
Institutional			
Structural			

The only claim this scheme makes is that it helps in a better definition of the notions, which should allow for a more analytical approach. The goal is to formulate hypotheses on the way institutions create or sustain racism.

The Levels of Racism

In 1984, the philosopher Philomena Essed published an essay on everyday racism. Although contested, the term has been used by many since then.[4] Essed defines everyday racism: 'In terms of categories and social relationships that play a role in everyday life and in terms of the characteristic properties of everyday life' (1991:58). Put more simply:

> Everyday racism is the racism of the grey areas, the ordinary automatic preference for the white [Dutch], the ordinary automatic assumption that

renders the black [Dutch] a less attractive prospect. In the work force, in policy-making circles and in many situations in between people make choices on the basis of these automatic assumptions which have consequences for the position and opportunities of both white and black [Dutch] (1991:10).

In this sense, everyday racism can be seen as a synonym for ethnocentrism.

As distinct from everyday racism there is structural racism. I define structural racism for the moment as 'referring to policy that has negative effects on minorities'. An example of this in Belgium is the general rule that political parties are subsidised by the state, which produces the result that racist parties like the *Vlaams Blok* can organise themselves better.

Often, structural racism is used synonymously with institutional racism. This too general use of the term institutional racism has often been criticised. Cashmore, in his dictionary of race and ethnic relations, quotes Jenny Williams who calls institutional racism: 'A bridging concept, linking and blurring the distinction between the material and the ideological'. The consequence is that institutional racism is to be seen as a component of structural racism as well as of everyday racism. It specifically refers to racism that exists, is developed or is legitimised through the workings of institutions. In other words, institutional racism: 'refers to the manner in which institutions generate or sustain racism, whether through the daily handling of people (everyday level) or through the mechanics of the society (structural level)'. This is also the sense in which the term is used by the black activists Stokely Carmichael and Charles V. Hamilton, which they introduced in *Black Power: the politics of liberations in America*: 'Racism permeates society on both the individual and institutional level, covertly and openly' (Cashmore 1994:170).

Discrimination and Segregation

Racism as a social phenomenon is linked with discrimination and segregation. For the sake of convenience, the link may be hypothetically described as discrimination being the motor or the potential cause, and segregation the result or the effect, of racism.[5]

Discrimination is often described as: 'the active or behavioural expression of racism or sexism and is aimed at denying members of certain groups equal access to scarce and valued resources' (Troyna & Cashmore in Cashmore 1994:305). This *sensu stricto* definition is problematic, because it stresses an a priori racist intention and excludes all types of nonracist intended behaviour of differential treatment. As I am looking for a more analytical use of terms, I prefer to understand discrimination as: 'any process that deliberately differentiates between people, be it positive or negative'. This type of behaviour can lead to racism, but is not necessarily in itself racist. With this conception of discrimination in mind it becomes clear what I mean by everyday, structural and institutional discrimination. Everyday discrimination is: 'The day by day differential treatment of people on certain subjective or objective criteria'. Structural discrimination refers to: 'Policy like affirmative action or positive discrimination'. It is intended to differentiate between groups or individuals to make up for existing social inequalities. Institutional discrimination then refers to: 'The way institutions differentiate between groups or individuals in a systematic way'.

Segregation refers to the literal setting apart of people. Segregation is related to racism when it is imposed or guided in a direct or indirect way.[6] I perceive imposed or guided segregation as a process that is the result of discrimination and that in its turn strengthens racism. 'Segregation-by-law' can be understood as structural segregation and 'de facto segregation' refers to everyday segregation. Institutional segregation is the result of institutional practices and to be observed in various social sectors such as housing, labour market and education.

Policy and its Relation to Structural Racism/Discrimination

Having at least hypothetically clarified the different terms on three levels, I now want to focus on policy in relation to the above-described phenomena.

Policy refers to: 'The manner in which politicians and administrators give shape to the management of society by way of regulations and practices'. Minority or integration policies refer to: 'The manner in which these political actors manage social and cultural diversity in regulations and administrative practice'. It implies the structural level (parliament and government) and the institutional level (administration). Policy, in the sense of political decision making, is closely linked with the structural processes. In my opinion, structural processes are not an aggregation of processes, but are analogous with that which Sahlins (1999) describes as structures, being those processes that create a framework within which everyday and institutional processes are to be found. Policy as a result of politics is the point from which structural processes are generated or directed. The question here is how policy relates to racism.

The traditional view on this matter is that racism is rooted in a differential policy approach and can be countered by a more egalitarian policy. This point of view has, since the 1960's, been brought to the fore by minorities themselves, most especially black activists in the United States who demanded to be treated 'equally but different'. This shift constituted the start of the development of multicultural and antiracist policies in postindustrial democratic societies. With this shift, a shift in theory appeared. It is not simply differential policy that was now said to generate and legitimise racism, but specifically, differential policy that is inspired by nationalism.

Although this insight seems to be probable at first sight, in fact it obscures a better understanding of the complexity of racism as it focuses too much on the underlying ideologies and in doing so denies the impact of institutions. To illustrate this, I come back to the example of the double conviction of immigrants in France. Abdelmalek Sayad (1996) addresses the topic of the double conviction (*double peine*) on a conceptual level. His central statement is that the immigrant is twice guilty, first as a convicted offender and secondly, on a more semantic level, as an immigrant. 'La double peine existe objectivement dans notre façon de penser, avant même qu'on la fasse exister sous une forme objectivée, la forme de la sanction d'un tribunal judiciaire ou d'une décision administrative'(1996:17).[7] The reason for this double conviction lies with the concept of the immigrant and his relation to the nation state: 'Pourquoi? ... l'immigration constitue comme la limite de ce qu'est l'Etat national, comme une limite qui donne à voir ce qu'il est intrinsèquement ... qui pour exister, s'est donné à lui-même des frontières ... nationales' (1996:13).[8] The result is that everyone who crosses that limit (border) challenges the established order, symbolised by the State. The idea of the challenging immigrant is not an overt action of 'nationals' but a natural process of thinking:

> Ainsi, sans qu'on a eu la possibilité d'en parler, ou avant même que l'on puisse parler de racisme ou de xénophobie, la notion de double peine est contenue dans tous nos jugements pris sur l'immigré (et non seulement les jugements des juges des tribunaux). Elle fait partie de la sorte d'anthropologie sur laquelle se formulent tous nos jugement sociaux, base que nous avons appelée 'pensée d'Etat'.(1996:17)[9]

This 'state thinking' by citizens seems, at first sight, to confirm the link between racism and nationalistic thinking. Sayad, however, pushes the analysis further and shows that state thinking is embedded in the mind of every 'national' and goes much deeper than can be explained by nationalistic ideology: 'Car on n'existe que sous cette forme et dans ce cadre, le cadre et la forme de la nation' (1996:15).[10] Those citizens who are aware of the nature of nationalism and who may even have a critical view on it, are also influenced by the mental representations that the state embodies. This explains the acceptance of the *double peine* as a justifiable discrimination. Because the State always discriminates: 'Il est comme dans la nature même de l'Etat de discriminer et, pour cela, de se doter préalablement de tous les critères de pertinence possibles pour procéder à cette discrimination sans laquelle il n'y a pas d'Etat national' (1996:13).[11]

At this point we might conclude that, as everybody is profoundly influenced by the state, everybody thinks in nationalistic terms. The final conclusion is that everybody is a potential racist and that racism is unavoidable. Although this associative line of thinking might contain some semantic truth in itself, it leads us nowhere. Racism thus becomes an all-inclusive generic category that seems unavoidable. In terms of research it loses all analytical value. The alternative to this deterministic thinking is to define racism as a specific category, to be distinguished from discrimination and segregation. This is precisely what Fredrickson does, when he defines racism as: 'An ethnic group's assertion or maintenance of a privileged and protected status vis à vis members of another group or groups who are thought, because of their defective ancestry, to possess a set of socially relevant characteristics that disqualify them from full membership in a community or citizenship in a nation-state' (1997:85). Applying Fredricksons definition of racism to the case of the double conviction of the immigrant in France, it becomes apparent that this is not necessarily a case of structural racism. Immigrants in France can, under certain conditions, become nationals and receive the same rights as any other national despite their ethnic belonging. This nuance indicates that the *double peine* is to be interpreted as structural discrimination, more precisely discrimination by the functioning of the state when it willingly differentiates between nationals and non-nationals. At the same time, it is clear that the difference between structural discrimination and structural racism is very small. The moment that the conditions of naturalisation become more strict, with the consequence that less immigrants become citizens, this *double peine* becomes a racist policy.

Sayad, in his analysis of this policy, aimed to go beyond ideological categorisation in terms of nationalism and looked for the underlying cultural features of the French State that influence the mental framework of its citizens. This *pensée d'Etat* is an example of what I call basic intuitions (Verlot 1999). These are ingrained cultural attitudes that take the form of natural features (as defined by Bourdieu) under the influence of laws, institutions and policy practices. Comparative ethnographic research into minority policy over a ten-year period in the French speaking and Dutch speaking part of Belgium shows that minority policies differ considerably in the two parts of the country. These differences become understandable by looking at the basic intuitions, which are put into practice in policy making by the political elite of a given society. The conclusion that we are to draw from this analysis is that policy on a structural level is strongly influenced by basic intuitions. To gain an in-depth insight into the processes of structural racism and discrimination, one has to take the basic intuitions on which policies are built into account. A characterisation on the basis of ideological assumptions of policy and politics alone is not sufficient, because it categorises, but fails to explain in itself why and how racist or discriminatory policy comes about. Such an analysis must at least be supplemented by an anthropological enquiry into the actual functioning of policy that takes into account its cultural presuppositions and the daily practice of political decision making.

Institutional Racism and Administrative Praxis

An analysis of the structural features of policy only gives a partial view of what is going on. The example of the *double peine* is again enlightening. It is not the judge who, compelled by law, passes the double sentence of deportation. Deportation is decided upon by the administration, which has the power to convert the judge's conviction into a double conviction. Where the administration would systematically apply this possibility on xenophobic, ethnocentric or racist criteria, the structural discrimination is complemented by an institutional racist practice. In the end a discriminatory rule thus becomes a racist practice. To examine this shift, research into the functioning of administrations is needed. This type of research should focus on the influence of basic intuitions on the patterns of collective functioning of administrations. Herzfeld, in his study of Greek administration, proposes a similar approach: 'Theoretical arguments about the way national bureaucracies work, have not paid sufficient attention to the common ground on which bureaucratic practices and popular attitudes rest' (1992:15).

The case of the *double peine* illustrates that the relationship between basic intuitions and the institutional order is still not very clear. One thing is certain, and that is that they reinforce each other. The linkage seems to come about through symbols. Herzfeld indicates that administrations 'draw on resources that are common to the symbolism of the Western nation-states and to that of long-established forms of social, cultural, and racial exclusion in everyday life' (ibid. 1992:13). As basic intuitions some symbols prove to be extremely durable. 'As a consequence, it is often assumed that their meanings are constant' (ibid.

1992: 11). In order to be able to explain these symbols and processes, and the way they produce institutional discrimination, racism or segregation, there is a need for what Abeles (1995) has called institutional anthropology. This type of anthropology starts with the ethnographic study of administrative patterns.[12] Herzfeld proposes:

> ... To treat nation-state bureaucracy as directly analogous to the ritual system of a religion. Both are founded on the principle of identity: The elect as an exclusive community, whose members' individual sins cannot undermine the ultimate perfection of the ideal they all share ... The labour itself is highly ritualistic: forms symbols, texts, sanctions, and obeisance. (1992:10)

The goal of such research is to clarify the cultural rationale of administrative thinking and acting. This kind of analysis takes the researcher to a more thorough exposure of the concepts of modernity and related concepts of rationality, effectiveness, efficiency and the linear perception of time.

My research into Belgian government bodies demonstrates the value of such an approach in relation to the issue of institutional racism. A striking example is the decision process in 1994/95 with regard to the yearly inspection of Muslim teachers by the Belgian State security. Muslim teachers have been working in schools since 1978. Because of the shortage of Belgian born and trained teachers, most of the Muslim teachers come from abroad and have, since the very beginning, not met language and nationality demands. Normally speaking, state security should provide a report on every new teacher before he or she begins in a school. From 1995, in the French speaking Community, the number of sacked Muslim teachers appeared to be on the rise. The reason for this was to be found in the negative reports being provided by the state security, which were increased from the one-off approach of an annual inspection. The reason for this stepping up of inspection could be traced back, not to the state security, but to a junior official in the French Community's Ministry of Education. After searching for several months, I learned that the state security had been systematically late in providing reports and teachers were already working in the schools. Faced with a negative report about a Muslim teacher, who was already in service, the junior official in question decided to cover himself in the future by sending the teachers' files to state security every year. Once this routine was started, it appeared that neither more senior officials, nor even the Minister, dared to stop this practice.

This example illustrates how the administrative management of diversity is a source of institutional racism, both explicitly and implicitly. The explicit level is visible in the issuing of instructions. Such instructions are discriminating in the neutral sense of the word, as the religious teachers were treated differently to the Belgian teachers. However, the instruction is not racist because all kinds of religious teachers who do not come from the European Union are subject to this control. This measure only became racist when the fear of Islam grew to such proportions that when a junior official applied this rule only to teachers of Islam, neither his superiors nor the Minister dared to change the systematic administrative practice.

In this example, the conjunction of particular official practice (exaggerated and continuous control) and basic intuitions that generate an islamophobic climate, turned a structural discrimination into a racist practice. The result is a racist policy.

Although little ethnographic fieldwork in administrations has been done, the literature provides us with some valuable insights.[13] I summarise here the conclusions of various researches that seem to me relevant to the development of institutional discrimination and racism. I mainly use the work by Herzfeld because of its quality, and, through his work, the work of Britan (1981).[14]

Administrative cultures are founded on two core concepts, which are, to a large extent, relevant to the understanding of the phenomena of institutional discrimination and racism. The first is the concept of professionalism. Professionalism in administrations is built on a 'culture of accountability': 'Both bureaucracy and the stereotypical complaints about it are parts of a larger universe that we might call, quite simply, the ideology and practice of accountability' (Herzfeld 1992:3). This accountability gives rise to a number of very recognisable processes of interaction. Citizens blame lower officials, who in turn blame higher officials. These latter blame 'the system' (the laws, the politicians, the budget, ...). This phenomenon is known as the umbrella technique, and is an indicator of the first vertical structural characteristic: hierarchy. The second characteristic of administrative structure is horizontal and is indicative of the compartmentalisation of services. It is the splitting up of services, in virtue of which the citizen is sent from pillar to post; passed from desk to desk. The less secure people feel with the local customs (not knowing which papers they should have, which services they should call, how to ask questions, what they may expect), the more powerless they are in the face of the negative effects of bureaucratic management. This is where the basis of institutional discrimination is to be situated.

The second core concept of administrative cultures consists of the dichotomy of indifference/sense of differentiation. The egalitarian ethos of administrations (i.e., that every citizen is the same before the law) establishes the norm, which is that the rules come first. As

Herzfeld notes: 'Indifference to the plight of individuals and groups often coexists with democratic and egalitarian ideals' (1992:1). This deferment to the authority of rules is often used with minorities as an excuse for not taking their specific situation or needs into account. The primacy of the value of 'the rules' legitimises these inequalities. Eventually, this leads to 'the rejection of common humanity' (Herzfeld 1992:1). Exaggerated norm-based egalitarian behaviour also lies at the root of institutional racism. It is the not wanting to/being able to/being allowed to take the differences in need between people into account that makes institutional discrimination (which can, in itself, provide a sense of differentiation enabling citizens to be treated according to need) move over into institutional racism. Here I want to quote Herzfeld (1992:184) again: 'Unless we can allow difference to oppose a productive discomfort to the certainties of bureaucratic classification, indifference must eventually, to cite the official cosmology that informs and maintains it, become the unblinking destiny of all'.

Over the last two decades, politicians have started to introduce modern management techniques to administrations in order to meet the changing needs of the more conscientious citizen. Modern management techniques in relation to the optimisation of the government bodies are based on the principle that razing the hierarchy and developing a client-oriented organisation with a system of open counters will have a positive effect on the behaviour of the official to the citizen. Taking into account all that I have said above on the way administrations are influenced by basic intuitions, it should be clear that this is no more than an assumption on the part of policy makers. Neither do we know what effect this modernisation of the official bodies will have on the relationship between officials and minority groups. It is therefore entirely possible that the modernisation of administrations through the levelling of hierarchies and the development of client-oriented services will potentially or actually increase institutional discrimination or racism rather than prevent it. The final conclusion is that there is a clear need for more and better understanding of the working of institutions to prevent institutional racism. Thus, the relationship between professionalism and indifference (or its counterpart, i.e; a sense for differentiation) remains unclear.

A Plea for International Comparative Research

Insight into the basic intuitions of policy and the order of administrative practice is necessary to understand and make tangible the complex processes of institutional and structural racism. This requires a closer and more culturally sensitive analysis of policy development and praxis, as an addition to the current exposure-based discursive research. Ethnographies of policy-making and institutions are instructive in gaining insight into national and regional practices. However, in order to understand better and reach a broader theoretical framing, the comparative element is essential. After all: 'Thinking without comparison is unthinkable. And in the absence of comparison, so is all thought and scientific research' (Swanson 1971:145).[15] This is all the more necessary if we wish to understand the sensitive, indirect processes that we describe with the vague notions of culture and cultural differentiation.

International comparative research into the issues of institutional and structural racism implies that research needs to move into a more rigorous and methodological ethnography of policy on the one hand, and of the ethnography of institutions on the other hand.

Ethnographic policy research, in my view, should focus on the way basic intuitions of political elites in different countries or regions influence the management of diversity as comes about in, for example, identity or minority policies.[16] Rather than looking at traditional immigrant countries like the United States, Canada or Australia, I would focus in the first instance on the European countries that have a strong national tradition and, until recently, regarded immigration as a temporary phenomenon. Most of the countries in the European Union have started to implement so-called integration policies. At the same time they are adapting their immigration policies in the framework of an evolving European Union. Comparing the cultural premisses of these policies will lead to a more thorough insight into the differences and similarities underlying these policies. In a second movement, a comparison between traditional immigrant countries and the European countries can broaden the perspective.

This type of comparative policy research needs to be complemented with ethnographic research on administrative practices in national and regional administrations. Such research can be linked to the ongoing process of administrative optimisation by looking at the cultural components and processes of professionalism/indifference.

In the end, combining the research on policy and administrative cultures should enable different political actors like politicians, administrators, unions, the media and nongovernmental organisations to elaborate strategies that take into account and anticipate the cultural sensitivities of majorities as expressed by their politicians and administrators. These more culture-sensitive strategies will, in my view, allow us to counter and prevent institutional racism more effectively than the exposure based discursive research has done so far.[17]

Notes

1. Desle, E. 1993. In: Desle, Lesthaeghe, R., Witte, E. (eds) *Denken over migranten in Europa*. Brussel, Balans, VUBpress; Blommaert, J. & Verschueren, J. 1998. *Debating diversity. Analysing the discourse of tolerance*. London, Routledge.
2. A similar need is expressed by the historian G.M. Fredrickson (1997:77) 'But comparative historians need sharper tools and stronger conceptualisations; otherwise they are likely to find implicit, attitudinal racism in most times and places – a given of any situation that appears to involve 'races' – or an explicit ideological racism in only a few places and for limited periods'.
3. Banton and Miles indicate a third, more academic meaning: 'Racism as a historical complex in which black labour is treated as a commodity'. They also point out that: 'There is no reason why the word racism should not be used in different senses for different purposes' (Cashmore 1994:308).
4. E.g., Eliaspoh, N. 1999.
5. Solomos and Back (1996) point out that the links between racism, discrimination and segregation are complex because the phenomena evolve all the time.
6. Segregation can also be voluntary. Research shows, for example, that immigrants of the first generation often tend to group together to recreate their home environment. Except for particular religious groups, voluntary segregation rarely continues more than one generation.
7. Although this text has been published in a later version (Sayad, A. 1999. 393–413) as a posthumous tribute to the author, I use the earlier, more elaborated version, published as a paper in 1996.
8. Why ? immigration constitutes the limit of the nation state, a limit that makes clear what it really is, ... to be able to exist has given itself national borders.
9. As such, without having had the possibility to speak about it, or even before one could speak about racism or xenophobia, the notion of the double sentence is included in all our judgements on the immigrant (and not only the rulings of the judges). This notion is part of that kind of anthropology on which our social judgements are formulated, which we named 'state thinking'.
10. Because one only exists in that form and in that framework, the framework and the form of the nation.
11. It is in the nature of the State to discriminate and for that reason to give itself all the possible and pertinent criteria to procede towards discrimination, without which there is no national State.
12. Concerning the field of institutional ethnography: Grahame, P. 1998. O'Neill, B.J. 1998. Townsend, E. 1996.
13. The reason for the scarcity of institutional ethnography has different reasons. The first is the high inaccessibility of administrations, the second is the complexity of administrations, and the third is that ethnographers have rarely seen administrations as an object of study.
14. Britan, G.M. 1981.
15. Swanson, G. 1971.
16. Verlot, M., and Dietz, G. 2000. 'Comparing subnational and transnational identity processes in Belgium and Spain'. Paper delivered at the sixth Biennial Conference of the European Association of Social Anthropologists - Krakow, Jagiellonian University, 26–29th July (workshop 13).
17. For an example in the field of educational politics, see: Verlot, M. 2000.

Bibliography

Abeles, M. 1995. 'Pour une antropologie des institutions'. *Homme*, 135, 35: 65–85.
Blommaert, J., and Verschueren, J. 1998. *Debating diversity. Analysing the discourse of tolerance*. In *Denken over migranten in Europa*. E. Desle, R. Lesthaeghe, E. Witte, eds. Brussel, Balans, VUBpress. London, Routledge.
Britan, G.M. 1981. Bureaucracy and innovation: an ethnography of policy change. Beverly Hills: Sage.
Bulmer, M., and Solomos, J. 1999. 'General Introduction'. In: Bulmer M. and Solomos, J. (eds.). *Racism*. Oxford readers, Oxford, Oxford University Press: 3–17.
Cashmore, E., et al. 1994. *Dictionary of race and ethnic relations*. London and New York: Routledge.
Eliaspoh, N. 1999. 'Everyday racism' in a culture of political avoidance: civil society, speech and taboo. In *Social problems* (4) 46: 479–502.
Essed, P. 1991. *Inzicht in alledaags racisme*. Utrecht, het Spectrum, Aulaboeken. Simultaneously published in English: *Understanding every day racism*. Sage.
Fredrickson, G.M. 1997. 'Understanding racism. Reflections of a comparative historian'. In: *The comparative imagination. On the history of racism, nationalism and social movements*. Berkeley/Los Angeles/London, University of California Press, chapter 5: 77–97.
Grahame, P. 1998. Ethnography, institutions and the problematic of the everyday world. In: *Human studies*. (4) 21: 347–360.
Herzfeld, M. 1992. *The social production of indifference. Exploring the symbolic roots of western bureaucracy*. Chicago-London, University of Chicago Press.
O'Neill, B.J. 1998. 'Institutional ethnography: studying institutions from the margins'. In: *Journal of sociology and social welfare*. (4) 25: 127–144;
Pincus, F. 1994. 'From individual to structural discrimination' In *Race and ethnic conflict: contrasting views on prejudice, discrimination and ethnocentrism*. F.L. Pincus and J. Eherlich, eds. Boulder: West Press: 82–87.
———. 1996. 'Discrimination comes in many forms: Individual, institutional and structural'. *American Behavioral Scientist*, 2, 40: 186–194.
Pinxten, R. 1997. *When the day breaks. Essays in anthropology and philosophy*. Frankfurt-am-Main: Berlin.
Sahlins, M. 1999. 'Two or three things that I know about culture'. *Journal of the Royal Anthropological Institute*, 5: 399–421.
Sayad, A. 1996.'L'immigration et la pensée d'Etat. Réflexions sur la double peine'. In *Délit d'immigration/Immigrant delinquency. La construction sociale de la déviance et de la criminalité parmi les immigrés en Europe/Social construction of deviant behaviour and criminality of immigrants in Europe*. S., Palidda, ed. Bruxelles/Brussels, Communauté Européenne/European Community: COST A2 Migration/Migration (EUR 17472 FR/EN): 11–29.

Shore, C. 2000. *Building Europe. The Cultural Politics of European Integration*. London- New York: Routledge.

Shore, C, and Wright, S. 1997. 'Policy: a new field of anthropology'. In *Anthropology of policy. Critical perspectives on governance and power.* Ibidem, eds. London/New York, Routledge, European Association of Social Anthropologists: 3–42.

Solomos, J., and Back, L. 1996. *Racism and society.* Hampshire and London, Macmillan press.

Swanson, G. 1971. 'Framework for comparative research: structural anthropology and the theory of action'. In *Comparative methods in sociology: essays on trends and applications.* L. Valier, ed. Berkeley: University of California press.

Townsend, E.. 1996. 'Institutional ethnography: a method for showing how the context shapes practice'. In *Occupational therapy journal of research.* (3)16: 179–199.

Verlot, M. 1999. 'Allochtonen in het onderwijs. Een politiek-antropologisch onderzoek naar het integratie- en onderwijsbeleid in de Vlaamse en Franse Gemeenschap van België (1988–1998)'. Ph.D. diss., Universiteit Gent.

———. 2000. 'Implementing integration through strategic education policy development'. In *Council of Europe, Strategies for implementing integration policies. Proceedings.* Prague 4–6 may 1999 (CDMG (2000)8, pp. 35–43.

Verlot, M, and Dietz, G. 2001. 'Dual tracking in identity politics. Interrogating 'territorialization' through the case of Belgium/Flanders and Spain/Andalusia (forthcoming)'.

Wieviorka, M. 1994. *Racisme et modernité.* Paris: La découverte.

HATE SPEECH, VIOLENCE AND CONTEMPORARY RACISMS

John Solomos and Liza Schuster

Introduction

In thinking about the issues we are addressing in this paper and the conference as a whole, we had two statements in mind. First, the statement by W.E.B. Du Bois to the effect that 'the problem of the twentieth century will be the problem of the colour line' (Du Bois, 1903). This is a phrase that has, in many ways, shaped much of the discussion about race and racism over the past century or so. Second, we were reminded of a more recent statement by the British sociologist Stuart Hall that, 'the key problem of the twenty-first century will be the issue of how we can live with difference' (Hall, 1993).

This is perhaps not surprising, since it seems clear as we stand at the beginning of the twenty-first century that we need to reflect deeply about the reasons for the continuing significance of racism as a social and political phenomenon in contemporary Europe and other parts of the globe (Hainsworth, 2000; Holmes, 2000). The prognostications of both Du Bois and Hall can be seen as tied in to concerns that were dominant at the beginning and then at the end of the twentieth century. However, they seem to us to remain pertinent to an understanding of the politics of contemporary racisms as they evolve and change at the beginning of the twenty-first century. The pertinence of Du Bois' prognosis for the twentieth century can be seen from the fact that there can be little doubt that, for many countries across the globe, one of the key questions that confronted them throughout much of the century was the issue of the 'colour line'. Manifestations of racial and ethnic conflict remained a key issue for much of the past century. In the European context we saw the emergence of fascist and extreme nationalist movements in the early part of the century and a variety of racist and anti-immigrant groups in the second half of the century (Mosse 1985; Goldberg 1993). All of these mobilisations played an important role in shaping social and political change, often with deadly consequences when such ideas have been interlinked with state power (Wieviorka 1995; Solomos and Back 1996).

At the same time, at the beginning of the twenty-first century we see around us a proliferation of movements and political organisations that espouse racist, anti-immigrant and neofascist politics. The role and impact of such mobilisations became a particular source of public concern throughout the 1990s, particularly in the aftermath of public manifestations of racial violence and expressions of hatred against groups such as migrants and refugees. These developments raise important dilemmas for those concerned with how to respond to the political and social threats that they pose. Recent research has highlighted the complex ways in which we still live in an environment in which racial, ethnic and national minorities are the target of everyday violence and exclusionary practices (Wrench and Solomos 1993; Pettigrew 1998; Pred 2000).

It is against this background that we shall attempt to explore the role and impact of two contemporary manifestations of racism, namely hate speech and violence. Drawing on conceptual and empirical research in Europe and the United States we want to analyse the background and contemporary expressions of racism and the connections between specific political cultures and racist violence. This paper will explore some of the issues arising from the research we are currently carrying out on the changing forms of racism and anti-Semitism. The paper will focus particularly on the processes through which questions about hate speech and racist violence came to the fore, and the impact of hate speech and violence on minorities within everyday life and political situations. In addition, we shall reflect on the question of what effective means of action can be taken to control hate speech and violence, and the implications of trends and developments at the beginning of the twenty-first century.

An underlying concern of the paper will be to situate manifestations such as hate speech and racist violence in the context of the complex social and cultural environments to be found in specific national situations. Racist movements are by no means uniform, and it is clear from the experience of the twentieth century that they can take a wide range of ideological forms and be aimed at a wide range of target groups. Ethnocentric forms of racism seem to be targeted at particular minority groups depending on the specific national context and their specific histories of migration and racialisation and nationalism (Billig 1995; Back, Keith and Solomos 1996; Kaplan and Bjørgo 1998; Cohen 1999). In addition, however, the paper will attempt to outline some possible commonalities and linkages between the variety of manifestations of racism in contemporary Europe.

Contemporary Forms of Racism

In recent times, the resurgence of racism in contemporary European societies has become an important feature of political debates and mobilisations. There has been a similar trend beyond the European political and social environment, particularly in the USA (Ezekiel 1995; Kincheloe, Steniberg, Rodriguez and Chennault 1998; Lamont 1999). It is now widely acknowledged that we have seen a growth in new forms of racist politics, violent attacks on minorities and a rapid expansion in the use of cultural symbols associated with racist and neofascist movements. All of these trends have been the subject of much journalistic attention and research over the past few years (Bjørgo and Witte 1994; Wrench and Solomos 1993; Baumgartl and Favell 1995; Cheles, Ferguson and Vaughan 1995). There has been a wide ranging discussion in the press among researchers and policy makers about both the origins of this renewed racist activity and its impact in specific environments. The spectre of racist violence and other forms of attack on minorities has hung over these debates, particularly as a result of increased evidence that sections of the extreme right have become involved in attempts to organise these forms of action. A good example of this was the experience of Germany during the early 1990s, when we saw a proliferation of neo-fascist groups and a growth in racist attacks and violence aimed at "immigrants" and "foreigners". (Bjørgo 1995).

The everyday experience of racism necessarily forms the backdrop against which any rounded analysis of contemporary racial ideologies and movements needs to be placed. What is clear, however, is that relatively little attention has been focused on the new cultural and technological devices that are being used to express racial bigotry and to mobilise support for racist movements in a variety of national and crossnational contexts. One particular issue that we want to explore in the course of this paper, and which has been raised by a number of writers in recent years, is the manner in which the manifest growth of far right movements across Europe and other parts of the globe has drawn on international networks whilst simultaneously reinforcing virulently nationalist patterns of racism and antiracism (Kushner 1994; Koopmans and Statham 2000). This has occurred through the appropriation of modes of communication that transcend national boundaries, such as the internet and related electronic forms of communication (Kohn 1995).

The growth of new forms of racism and the resurgence of cultural forms and expressions associated with racist movements is a noticeable feature of the present conjuncture. This development has caused widespread concern among those who are concerned with fighting the growth of racism and ensuring that racist ideologies do not become a dominant political force.

The relevance of the issues we are addressing needs to be evaluated in view of the rise in neofascist activity in Europe and the growing intensity of popular racism. If these movements are to be effectively countered, it is essential to develop a sophisticated appraisal of the changing nature of racist cultures and their networks of circulation. George Mosse, an eminent scholar of fascist culture, has commented that a key part of the power of racism is the way in which it helps to account for specific social relations in a simple manner. He argued, with reference to racial ideologies over the past two centuries, 'Racist myths not only explained the past and brought hope for the future, but through their emphasis on stereotypes rendered the abstract concrete' (Mosse 1985: 233).

This process of rendering the abstract concrete is part of the work of all ideologies. What is important in relation to the morphology of racist ideas is that they intrinsically involve a visual ideology in which particular categories of people are classified on the basis of stereotypes, and are attributed specific social and cultural characteristics: 'Racism was a visual ideology based upon stereotypes. That was one of its main strengths. Racism classified men and women: this gave it the clarity and simplicity essential to its success' (Mosse 1985: xii).

Despite these incisive points, which have been developed by Mosse and others in their work, the literature on racism has paid relatively little attention to the visual power of racist symbols.

Recent theoretical work has emphasised that racism needs to be conceptualised through a sensitivity to the historical context in which it is expressed and its changing character (Solomos and Back 1996; Kaplan and Bjørgo 1998). In short, one must speak of racisms in the plural (Gilroy 1987). David Goldberg, in his incisive account of racist culture, comments that the theoretical analysis of racism:

> Entails not only that there is no single characteristic form of racism, but also that the various racisms have differing effects and implications.

Racisms assume their particular characters, they are exacerbated. and they have different entailments and ramifications in relation to specific considerations of class constitution, gender, national identity, region, and political structure. But the character and implicature of each racism are also set in terms of its own historical legacy and the related conception of race (Goldberg 1993: 91).

However, as Goldberg goes on to rightly point out, the impulse to specify racisms spatially and historically may overlook the consideration of what processes tie different racisms together (Ibid: 96). Images of hate and otherness are an intrinsic element of racist discourses.

The contemporary cultures of the ultra-right pose real difficulties with regard to definition and classification. A wide range of terms are currenttly used to describe these groups, including neo-Nazi, white supremacist, fascist and racist. These labels are used to describe a complex range of ideologies, movements and groups. For the sake of conceptual clarity we shall be deploying the notion of neofascism to classify the movements with which we are concerned.

While these movements are diverse, they exhibit the following common features:

1. A rhetoric of racial and/or national uniqueness and common destiny.
2. Ideas of racial supremacy and superiority.
3. Conceptions of racial Otherness.
4. A utopian revolutionary world view that seeks to overthrow the existing order.

Contemporary racist movements possess a 'family of resemblances', but there is no necessary reason why specific groups should hold to all of the social features outlined above. Our concern is to explore the ways in which contemporary forms of expression are articulating new variants of racism and anti-Semitism and how these, in turn, relate to notions of race and culture.

For some conventional scholars of the far-right, the current interest in the relationship between xenophobia, popular culture and new technologies is little more than a fashionable intellectual chimera. They caution that the 'real issue' is what is happening in terms of the ballot box and the macroeconomic and political trends that underpin political mobilisations. This warning has a point, but we would argue that such a view misses the point. In order to understand racism, either in its generic or contemporary forms, it is crucial to develop a sensitivity to the relationship between politics, culture and the mass media.

Hate Speech, Violence and Forms of Racism

The spectre of racist violence and other forms of attack on minorities haunts contemporary debates about racism in European societies. This is largely because, during the 1990s and the first decade of the twenty-first century, we have witnessed a resurgence of racism and anti-Semitism in Europe and North America on a scale that has resulted in intense academic and political debate. There has been a wide ranging discussion in the press, and among researchers and policy makers, about both the origins of this renewed racist activity and its impact in specific environments (Bjørgo and Witte 1994; Wrench and Solomos 1993). The spectre of racist violence and other forms of attack on minorities has hung over these debates, particularly as a result of increased evidence that sections of the extreme right have become involved in attempts to organise these forms of action. The experience of Germany since the early 1990s provides a poignant reminder of the real and symbolic impact of racial violence on the popular imagination.

It is worth remembering, however, that there are no easy explanations for this phenomenon. After all, one of the recurrent themes in recent scholarship about racism is the argument that we have to see it as a plural and complex phenomenon. A good example of the importance of this argument can be found in the changing forms of racist expression in contemporary Europe, particularly in relation to the targets of race hate and violence. During the 1990s and the early part of the twenty-first century the focus of extreme right wing groups is no longer just on 'blacks' or 'immigrants', but on 'asylum seekers', 'refugees', 'gypsies'.

In historical terms this is not surprising. Racism has been expressed over the past two centuries through the construction of impassable symbolic boundaries between racially constituted, or racialised, categories. Its typical binary system of representation constantly marks and attempts to fix and naturalise the difference between belongingness and otherness. A principal means of accomplishing this is to perceive the self as carried in the genes rather than transmitted via culture; as distilled through what appears to us as most 'natural' and immediate: the body. Corporeal properties, and most fetishistically, skin colour, thus come to furnish an 'epidermal schema', not only for anchoring difference, but for distinguishing the pure from the impure, the included from the excluded. To the extent that the body comes to signify difference, so too does it become a site and target for strategies of normalisation and discipline, a site for an obsessive imperative that aims to expunge any kind of syncretism which destroyed the authenticity of the 'truth propositions' about these embodied polar identities of 'black' and 'white'. We see this in the protective rules of interaction of Victorian and Edwardian society, indeed even today, that policed sexual relationships between constructed categories of black and white people. It is here that the marriage of information and myth-making was to reach its apogee: 'inter-race-ial' sex was presented as an act of bestiality, miscegenation as a curse against civilisation, and both perceived as the product of folly and physical immorality (Mosse 1985; Ferber 1997).

Race and ethnicity, then, are not 'natural', even though both concepts are often represented as if they were. Their boundaries are not fixed, nor is their membership uncontested. Race and ethnic groups, like nations, are imagined communities. They are ideological entities, made and changed in struggle. They are discursive formations, signalling a language through which differences are accorded social significance and may be named and explained. What is of importance for us as social researchers studying race and ethnicity is that such ideas also carry with them material consequences for those who are included within, or excluded from, them.

The everyday reality of brutal racist aggression and anti-Semitism should be the starting point for any rigorous analysis of the changing role of racial ideologies and movements in the contemporary environment. Equally, the question of racial attacks is not merely confined to actions on persons because the language and rhetoric of violence is carried over into cultural and technically mediated forms of racist and fascist expression, be it a computer game or urban graffiti (Back, Keith and Solomos 1999; Kaplan and Bjørgo 1998; Kaplan 2000). It is against this wider historical background that we have to see contemporary expressions of racist violence and racial hatred (Matsuda et al. 1993; Whillock and Slayden 1995).

Racist violence or expressions of racial hatred are not new phenomena in themselves. The experience of the past two decades has highlighted the importance of locating any analysis of expressions of racism in specific social and political environments and the need to understand the varieties of issues that are covered by generic categories such as 'racist violence' (Bjørgo and Witte 1993; Panayi 1996; Witte 1996; Bowling 1999) or 'racial hatred' (Gates 1994 and 1996; Butler 1997; ADL 1998).

The role of racial violence and harassment in contemporary European societies involves a complex range of processes including:

1. The history of race and racism, including the development of ideologies of racial domination and exclusion.
2. The role of neofascist and extreme right-wing ethnoracial forms of political mobilisation in contemporary Europe.

3. The history of the construction of racial violence as a social issue and the management of political responses to it.
4. Forms of terrorist violence aimed at racial and ethnic minority communities.

It is precisely because expressions of racist violence and hatred are the product of a complex range of processes that we need to see racism as a constantly evolving phenomenon. Recent developments in western and Eastern European societies are a case in point. The rise of extreme right wing and neofascist movements and parties has resulted in the development of new forms of racist politics and in the articulation of popular racism and violence against migrant communities. At the same time, we have seen a noticeable rise in anti-Semitism in both western and Eastern Europe, evident in both physical and symbolic threats to Jewish communities. In this environment it is perhaps not surprising that questions about immigration and race have assumed a new importance, both politically and socially, helping to construct an environment in which the future of both settled migrant communities and new groups of migrants and refugees is very much at the heart of public debate.

Developments such as these show why it is impossible in the present political and social environment to ignore the impact of race and ethnicity on the social and political institutions of most advanced industrial societies. Whereas, until the 1980s, it was still relatively common to treat questions about racism, ethnicity and nationalism as relatively marginal to the agenda of both social scientists and policy makers, it is perhaps no exaggeration to say that in many ways these issues have moved right to the core of public debate. Almost every aspect of contemporary social and political relations is deeply inflected with a racial or ethnic dimension. In this context, it is vital that we develop a grounded and historically based view of the role that racialised social relations play in contemporary societies and are likely to play in the future.

There is a clear need for more rigorous and empirically based accounts of various forms of racialised situations, particularly at a time when the terms of both official and popular discourses about race and racism are in a constant state of flux. The recent changes we have seen in European societies are perhaps the most clear example of this volatility, represented both by the development of new racist political movements and by intense official debate about what kinds of policies should be pursued to deal with issues such as immigration and the political and social rights of migrants (Pettigrew 1998).

There is by now a wealth of historical research which shows that the social and political impact of ideas about race needs to be seen in the context of the experience of modernity and postmodernity which has shaped our societies over the past two centuries. However, if modern racism has its foundations in the period since the late eighteenth century, there is little doubt that it has had a major impact on the course of historical development during the twentieth century and seems destined to continue to do so in the twenty-first. It seems clear as we move further into the twenty-first century that racist ideas and movements are continuing to have an impact on a range of contemporary societies in a variety of ways. What is more, in recent years we have seen the growth and genocidal impact of new forms of racial and ethnically based ideologies. This phenomenon is evident in many parts of the globe, including, most notably, West and East Europe and parts of Africa. It is almost impossible to read a newspaper or watch television news coverage without seeing the contemporary expressions of racist ideas and practices, whether in terms of the rise of neofascist movements in some societies or the implementation of policies of genocide and what is euphemistically called 'ethnic cleansing'.

An interesting example of the changing forms of racist expression in the contemporary environment can be seen in the presence of far right groups on the Internet in the period since the mid-1990s. The history of the use of computer networks by racist and neofascist groups is by its nature relatively recent. Evidence first appeared in the early 1990s that racist and neofascist groups were using the Internet and other computer networks on a noticeable scale. Part of the attraction of these technologies was that they were virtually inaccessible to law enforcement agencies and potentially provided neo-fascist groups with an international communication network free of surveillance. Racist and fascist materials could thus be circulated through these means regardless of the laws which prohibit them in individual nation states. For example, although in Germany the use of Nazi symbols is banned, these international networks effectively allow neofascist pop music, printed matter and information to be imported from the United Kingdom, Switzerland and the United States. In addition to the relative openness of cyberspace and the lack of effective means of control, from the perspective of racist and neofascist groups, virtual means of communication had other advantages. The most significant of these was the ability to use them as a means of mobilisation and communication between groups and individuals both within particular nation-states and globally.

Since the early 1990s, the pace of change in this field has been staggering and there has been a proliferation of Internet sites, Email groups, chat lines, newsgroups and other forms of activity associated with racist and neofascist groups. There has been an ongoing discussion throughout this period about how best to control and regulate the use of cyberspace for the dissemination of racist, anti-Semitic and related 'hate' material, but this has done little to hold back the rapid expansion of new racist subcultures in cyberspace. If anything, recent reports have highlighted the increasing complexity, quantity and sophistication of the ultra-right-wing's usage of electronic means of communication.

Responding to Hate Speech and Violence

The trends and developments outlined above raise important questions about what can be done to respond effectively to the threats posed by racist violence and hate speech. This has become an important political and social issue in a number of European countries at the present time, particularly in the aftermath of growing racism and forms of violence directed at minorities (Bjørgo 1997; Iganski 1999; Hamm 1993 and 1994). In the Britain, for example, the case of Stephen Lawrence, a young black man who was killed in a racist attack, has become a symbol of the changing politics of race and ethnicity in British society (Home Office 1997; Cathcart 1999; Perekh 2000). Yet, even after a decade of intense debate and public reflection on the need for concerted action against racist violence, there remains much confusion about the kinds of initiatives that need to be taken. Part of the reason for this seems to be linked to (1) the weakness of legislation and policy intervention against racist violence or expressions of racial hatred, and (2) the lack of coherent political strategies at the local, national or European level for tackling racist movements and political parties (Solomos and Back 1996; Virdee 1997; Pred 2000).

The history of public responses to racist violence over the past two decades reflects both of these weaknesses. Research in a number of countries has highlighted both the failure to prioritise racist violence as a key issue for state action and the limitations of state policies. As a result, it is only recently that the police have shown a clear awareness of the need to treat racial violence as a serious issue (Bowling 1999). In this environment, initiatives to tackle violence and hate speech have been both limited and largely have only emerged in response to specific events or crises. A case in point is the Metropolitan Police Racial and Violent Crime Task Force in London. This body was set up in the aftermath of cases such as the killing of Stephen Lawrence, and has helped to change everyday practices within the police in relation to cases of racial violence and terrorism. It seems clear that the Task Force has had some notable successes in the few years it has been in operation, though the belated nature of the police response to racist violence remains a point of contention.

The situation in relation to expressions of racial hatred is even more complex. In this field it has become clear that racist activists and movements have become adept at finding ways around attempts by nation states to control their activities. The example of how they have managed to use the internet and related technologies to facilitate transnational networks and disseminate their ideas has helped to highlight some of the difficulties that are faced in legislating against 'hate speech' and 'hate material' and the weakness of possible controls on mechanisms of expression such as the internet.

It seems important to remember that legislation against racist violence and hate speech will not be enough on its own to tackle the root causes of racist inequality and forms of exclusion. In his critique of contemporary American debates about hate speech Henry Louis Gates Jr points out that: 'Alas, even if hate speech did disappear, aggregative patterns of segregation and segmentation in housing would not. Conversely, in the absence of this material and economic gap, no one would much care about racist speech' (Gates Jr. 1996: 156).

From this perspective, there is a need to analyse contemporary racisms in a context where we link the analysis of race hate and violence to the analysis of new forms of racial inequality, cultural racism, political racism. This raises a number of questions. First, what kind of policies could tackle racism more effectively? Second, what kind of positive social policy agenda can be developed to counter both racist violence and expressions of racial hatred? All of these questions are at the heart of contemporary debates and have given rise to quite divergent policy prescriptions. It is quite clear that in the present political environment it is unlikely that any sort of agreement about how to develop new policy regimes in this field will be easy to achieve. On the contrary, it seems likely that this will remain an area full of controversy and conflict for some time to come.

Acknowledgements

An earlier version of this paper was presented at the Conference on 'New Manifestations of Racism in 'the twenty-first century' Europe: Threats and Responses', Ghent, 10–12 April 2000. We are grateful to a number of colleagues who gave us useful suggestions in the process of working on this paper, in particular Les Back, Chetan Bhatt, Clive Harris and Michael Keith.

Bibliography

Anti-Defamation League. 1998. *1999 Hate Crime Laws*. New York: Anti-Defamation League.
Back, L., Keith, M. and Solomos, J. 1999. 'Reading the Writing on the Wall: Graffiti and the Racialized City.' In D. Slayden, and R.K. Whillock, eds. *Soundbite Culture: The Death of Discourse in a Wired World*. Thousand Oaks: Sage.
(1996) 'Technology, Race and Neo-Fascism in a Digital Age: The New Modalities of Racist Culture' *Patterns of Prejudice* 30, 2: 3–27.
Baumgartl, B., and Favell, A., eds. 1995. *New Xenophobia in Europe*. London: Kluwer Law International.
Billig, M. 1995. *Banal Nationalism*. London: Sage.
Bjørgo, T. 1997. *Racist and Right-Wing Violence in Scandinavia: Patterns, Perpetrators, and Responses*. Tano Aschehoug.
Bjørgo, T, ed. 1995. *Terror from the Extreme Right*. London: Frank Cass.
Bjørgo, T, and Witte, R., eds. 1993. *Racist Violence in Europe*. Basingstoke: Macmillan.
Bowling, B. 1999. 'Violent Racism: Victimisation, Policing and Social Context'. Revised Edition Oxford: Oxford University Press.
Butler, J. 1997. *Excitable Speech: A Politics of the Performative*. New York: Routledge.
Cathcart, B. 1999. *The Case of Stephen Lawrence*. London: Viking.
Cheles, L., Ferguson, R., and Vaughan, M., eds. 1995. *The Far Right in Western & Eastern Europe*. London: Longman.
Cohen, P., ed. 1999. *New Ethnicities, Old Racisms?* London: Zed Books.
Du Bois W. E. B. [1903] 1996. *The Souls of Black Folk*. New York: Penguin.
Ezekiel, R. 1995. *The Racist Mind*. New York: Viking.
Ferber, A. L. 1997. 'Of Mongrels and Jews: The Deconstruction of Racialised Identities in White Supremacist Discourse.' *Social Identities* 2, 2: 193–208.
Gates Jr, H. L. 1996. 'Critical Race Theory and Freedom of Speech.' In *The Future of Academic Freedom*. L. Menand, ed. Chicago: University of Chicago Press.
Gates Jr, H. L., et al. (eds.). 1994. *Speaking of Race, Speaking of Sex: Hate Speech, Civil Rights, and Civil Liberties*. New York: New York University Press.
Gilroy, P. 1987. *There Ain't No Black in the Union Jack*. London: Hutchinson.
Goldberg, D. T. 1993. *Racist Culture*. Oxford: Blackwell.
Hainsworth, P. (ed.). 2000. *The Politics of the Extreme Right: From the Margins to the Mainstream*. London: Pinter.
Hall, S. 1993. 'Culture, community, nation' *Cultural Studies* 7, 3: 349–63.
Hamm, M. S. 1993. *American Skinheads: The Criminology and Control of Hate Crimes*. Westport, Conn.: Praeger.
Hamm, M. S. (ed.). 1994. *Hate Crime: International Perspectives on Causes and Control*. Cincinnati, OH: Anderson Publishing.
Holmes, D. R. 2000. *Integral Europe: Fast-Capitalism, Multiculturalism, Neofascism*. Princeton: Princeton University Press.
Home Office. 1997. *Racial Violence and Harassment: A Consultation Document*. London: Home Office.

Iganski, P. 1999. 'Legislating against hate: outlawing racism and antisemitism in Britain' *Critical Social Policy* 19, 1: 129–41.
Kaplan, J. (ed.). 2000. *Encyclopedia of White Power* Walnut Creek CA: AltaMira Press.
Kaplan, J, and Bjørgo, T. (eds.). 1998. *Nation and Race: The Developing Euro-American Racist Subculture*. Boston: Northeastern University Press.
Kincheloe, J. L., Steniberg, S. R., Rodriguez, N. M., and Chennault, R. E. (eds.). 1998. *White Reign: Deploying Whiteness in America*. Basingstoke: Macmillan.
Kohn, M. 1995. *The Race Gallery: The Return of Racial Science*. London: Jonathan Cape.
Koopmans, R., and Statham, P. (eds.). 2000. *Challenging Immigration and Ethnic Relations Politics: Comparative European Perspectives*. Oxford: Oxford University Press.
Kushner, T. 1994. 'The Fascist 'Other'? Racism and Neo-Racism in Contemporary Britain'. *Patterns of Prejudice* 28, 1: 27–45.
Lamont, M. (ed.). 1999. *The Cultural Territories of Race: Black and White Boundaries*. Chicago: University of Chicago Press.
Matsuda, M. J., Lawrence, C. R., Delgado, R., and Crenshaw, K. W. (eds.). 1993. *Words that Wound: Critical Race Theory, Assaultive Speech, and the First Amendment*. Boulder: Westview Press.
Mosse, G. L. 1985. *Toward the Final Solution: A History of European Racism*. Madison: University of Wisconsin Press.
Panayi, P. (ed.). 1996. *Racial Violence in Britain in the Nineteenth and Twentieth Centuries*. Revised Edition London: Leicester University Press.
Parekh, B. 2000. *The Future of Multi-Ethnic Britain*. London: Profile Books.
Pettigrew, T. F. 1998. 'Reactions toward the new minorities of Western Europe.' *Annual Review of Sociology* 24, 1: 77–104.
Pred, A. 2000. *Even in Sweden: Racisms, Racialized Spaces, and the Popular Geographical Imagination*. Berkeley: University of California Press.
Solomos, J., and Back, L. 1996. *Racism and Society*. Basingstoke: Macmillan.
Virdee, S. 1997. 'Racial Harassment.' In *Ethnic Minorities in Britain: Diversity and Disadvantage*. T. Modood, et al., eds. London: Policy Studies Institute.
Whillock, R., and Slayden, D. (eds.). 1995. *Hate Speech*. Thousand Oaks: Sage.
Wieviorka, M. 1995. *The Arena of Racism*. London: Sage.
Witte, R. 1996. *Racist Violence and the State*. London: Longman.
Wrench, J., and Solomos, J. (eds.) 1993 *Racism and Migration in Western Europe*. Oxford: Berg.

THE ROLE OF INTERNATIONAL LAW

Natan Lerner

This article is based on a paper submitted to the 'Inter-University Conference on New Manifestations of Racism in twenty-first century Europe: Threats and Responses' that took place in April 2000. The subject of the conference is strongly relevant to today's international life, not only in Europe. Governmental and nongovernmental responsible sources have been stressing, for several years, the threat involved in the evident rise of intolerance and violence against minorities and foreigners in several countries. The special dangers that xenophobia, racism and anti-Semitism imply have prompted the establishment, only a few days before the aforementioned Conference, of a European Monitoring Center on Racism and Xenophobia.[1] Already in 1993, the first Summit of Heads of State and Government of the Council of Europe's member states had already expressed its alarm at 'the present resurgence of racism, xenophobia and anti-Semitism, the development of a climate of intolerance, the increase in acts of violence, notably against migrants and people of immigrant origin, and the degrading treatment and discriminatory practices accompanying them'.[2]

Since then, no improvement can be registered in this area. In October 2000, the member States of the Council of Europe held a special conference on the European contribution to the World Conference Against Racism, Racial Discrimination, Xenophobia and Related Intolerance, to take place in 2001.[3] The European Conference, convened under the heading 'All different, all equal: from principle to practice', adopted a Political Declaration and a series of General Conclusions.[4] The Political Declaration, after expressing alarm at the 'continued and violent occurrence of racism, racial discrimination, xenophobia, anti-Semitism and related intolerance, including contemporary forms of slavery', that target, 'notably on grounds related to language, religion or national or ethnic origin, persons such as migrants, asylum-seekers, refugees, displaced persons, non-nationals, indigenous peoples', or persons belonging to minorities, urged member states to take legal, policy and educational and training measures to prevent and eliminate the mentioned evils. The proposed legal measures are of particular relevance to the role of international law.

They include:

1. A full and effective implementation at the national level of the relevant human rights instruments.
2. The adoption and implementation of national legislation and administrative measures 'that expressly and specifically counter racism and prohibit racial discrimination'.
3. Bringing to justice those responsible for racist acts and violence, 'ensuring the prohibition of racial discrimination in the enjoyment of the right to freedom of expression'.
4. Combating all forms of expression which incite racial hatred and taking action against the dissemination of such material.

The suggested policy measures call for special attention to vulnerable groups and creating conditions for the promotion and protection of the ethnic, cultural, linguistic and religious identity of persons belonging to national minorities.[5]

The Conference also approved a set of General Conclusions urging all states to reject ethnic and religious cleansing and genocide and never to forget the Holocaust. The document recognises the persistence, for targeted persons, of problems such as: discrimination in employment, housing, education and services; the occurrence of contemporary problems of slavery; incitement and discrimination against immigrants and refugees and violence against them; the manifestations of racial violence and incitement to hatred and intolerance; the proliferation of extremist groups exacerbating such phenomena; a rise in religious intolerance; violence against Jewish communities and dissemination of anti-Semitic material; prejudice and discrimination against Roma/Gypsies, and the use of mass communication by racists.[6]

In order to combat such developments and provide legal protection to the targeted persons and groups, all states are called to ratify the International Convention on the Elimination of All Forms of Racial Discrimination (ICERD) – dealt with below – and accept the optional right to individual petition foreseen by its Article 14, as well as to withdraw reservations to the Convention and comply with the reporting procedure. The Conference recommends that the national legislative frameworks in criminal, civil and administrative law should 'expressly and specifically' prohibit discrimination on grounds of race, ethnicity, national origin, religion and belief, and provide effective remedies, including adequate reparation or satisfaction.[7] As will be seen, the extent to which the Convention involves a positive duty for states to outlaw discrimination is one of the major issues that engendered controversy during and after its adoption.

Not less controversial were the problems with regard to criminal law. The Conference decided that high priority should be given to the prosecution of offences of a racist or xenophobic nature, taking into consideration the racist motives. Efficient measures to combat racist organisations should be taken; the offence of Holocaust-denial should be made punishable; prosecution should be ex officio, and legal protection and support for persons belonging to the targeted groups should be ensured. States should establish mechanisms for examining the conformity of their legislation with principles of nondiscrimination on the basis of race, ethnic or national origin, religion or belief. Public authorities should promote equality and prevent and correct situations of inequality.[8] Matters related to religion and belief and specific situations such as anti-Semitism, discrimination against Roma, Gypsies, Sinti and Travelers are also dealt with, as well as the role of education and the media.

The preoccupation shown by the European states underlines the gravity of the growth of racist trends, but the problem is certainly not only a European one, and other areas of the world have been affected by similar developments. The academic discussion of these developments is, of course, not a sufficient response to the alarming trend and the threats involved. It is, however, a necessary, complementary and preparatory activity in order to stimulate an adequate approach on the part of the organised international community. The obvious strengthening and, in some cases, electoral achievements of political groups that not only propagate racist and religious hatred but also translate their ideology in deeds and legislation, cannot be ignored. The Secretary General of the United Nations has recently stressed the need to attach a meaningful content to the notion of sovereignty and to clarify the right of intervention of the international community when human rights are brutally violated, ethnic and religious hatred erupts in violence and warfare, and conventional responses developed during centuries are insufficient to cope with the new situations.[9]

My task is to describe the role of international law in combating the threats and allowing a proper response based on mandatory law accepted as such by a large part of the world community and involving clear-cut obligations to act against manifestations of racism.[10] I shall not separate regional responses from the general, global scene. Racism is a universal plague. The reaction to it should have the same reach.

The Legal Meaning of Racism

A generally accepted legal definition of the notion of 'racism' – wider than 'racial discrimination'– does not exist. The terms of appointment of a Special Rapporteur of the Commission of Human Rights may help to describe some of the implications of the word.[11] The Rapporteur has to deal with 'contemporary forms of racism, racial discrimination, xenophobia and related intolerance, including activities against blacks, Arabs and Muslims, xenophobia, Negrophobia, and anti-Semitism'. The only legally clear element in this listing is racial discrimination, prohibited by a well established and widely ratified treaty, the 1965 Convention on the Elimination of All Forms of Racial Discrimination.[12] Xenophobia means hatred against the stranger, the foreigner, the different one, in loose terms, and is not, at this stage, a legal concept properly defined. Anti-Semitism is a term describing hatred for and persecutions against the Jews.[13] As to 'activities' against some specific groups, it is, from a legal viewpoint, too vague a term, and the singled-out groups do not exhaust the sad, and long, list of victims of racism. What about Gypsies in Europe, mentioned specifically in the European texts, Hispanics and blacks in the United States, Indians in Latin America, and Aborigines in Australia or New Zealand, among others?

A UNESCO Declaration on Race and Prejudice, of 1978,[14] states that any theory which involves the claim that racial or ethnic groups are inherently superior or inferior has no scientific foundation and is contrary to the moral and ethical principles of humanity. The Declaration lists, in its Article 2 – leaving to Article 3 the description of what racial discrimination means – the ingredients of racism. It includes:

> Racist ideologies, prejudiced attitudes, discriminatory behavior, structural arrangements and institutionalized practices resulting in racial inequality, as well as the fallacious notion that discriminatory relations between groups are morally and scientifically justifiable; it is reflected in discriminatory provisions in legislation or regulations and discriminatory practices as well as in antisocial beliefs and acts.

This is, adds the Declaration, 'contrary to the fundamental principles of international law'. This may not be a technically precise definition, and the Declaration is not a legally binding document, but it enumerates the different components of racism.

Succinct Article 20(2) of the 1966 International Covenant on Civil and Political Rights[15] contains the concept of 'hatred': 'Any advocacy of national, racial or religious hatred that constitutes incitement to discrimination, hostility or violence shall be prohibited by law'. 'Hatred' is a feeling or sentiment, a difficult concept that can hardly be defined without the help of psychology. According to the Covenant, the law should prohibit 'advocacy' of hatred, when it is addressed to three categories – national, racial or religious groups – and when it involves 'incitement' to three evils: discrimination, hostility or violence.

The approach of the Covenant seems to be limited: what about homosexuals, new immigrants not belonging to one single defined group, linguistic minorities, new religions not yet consolidated, and similar groups not included in the three traditional categories? The basic rule should be that advocacy of, or incitement to, hatred against 'any' clear-cut group conscious of its collective character, and recognised as such by the surrounding society, should be outlawed. By clearcut group I have in mind every group which is permanent, or relatively permanent, and membership in which is, in general, beyond the will of individuals. I am aware, of course, of the fact that, in some cases, membership in a group may be avoided or discontinued – as in the cases of religion, language or culture, and, to a far lesser degree, in the cases of race or color – but a broad approach seems to be needed.[16] The term 'racism' should include 'all' manifestations of hatred, bigotry, persecutions, or other illegal ways of behavior, motivated by race, ethnicity, color, religion, basic or fundamental beliefs, culture, language, and other features that determine the existence of a permanent and coherent group, as indicated. People are victims of such manifestations because of what they are, seldom because of what they do.

The most far-reaching provision on racism in positive international law is Article 4 of the UN Convention on the Elimination of All Forms of Racial Discrimination,[17] ratified, at the time of this writing, by 155 states.

With due regard to the principles embodied in the Universal Declaration of Human Rights – a provision to protect freedom of expression and association – states party to the Convention shall:

1. Declare an offence punishable by law all dissemination of ideas based on racial superiority or hatred, incitement to racial discrimination, as well as acts of violence or incitement to such acts against any race or group of persons of another color or ethnic origin, and also the provision of any assistance to racist activities, including the financing thereof.
2. Declare illegal and prohibit organisations, and also organised and all other propaganda activities, which promote and incite racial dis-

crimination. States shall recognise participation in such organisations or activities as an offence punishable by law.

This article was a compromise. Its text is not entirely satisfactory and it involves difficulties that should not be underestimated and were expressed in formal reservations. The introduction of a saving clause invoking the Universal Declaration of Human Rights made the compromise possible. On the whole, Article 4 is an ambitious provision, although it does not provide a precise definition of racism. It does, however, clarify the meaning of the term and proclaims that when there is a clash between provisions of the Convention and other rights, such as freedom of speech and freedom of association, the prohibition of racism should prevail. The Article avoids referring to religious groups, which is understandable in the light of the decision, pointed out below, to separate the racist issue from the religious one. It seems, however, reasonable and legitimate to extend its provisions, by analogy, to religious discrimination or hatred. The mandatory character of Article 4 is today accepted, despite the reservations entered by several countries. Together with Article 20 of the Covenant on Civil and Political Rights, it constitutes a clear affirmation of the prevalence of the prohibition of racism in the UN work. Such work should now be reviewed.

The Role of the United Nations

Except for the protection of minorities, ethnic, religious and linguistic, under the League of Nations,[18] international law did not deal with racism until the creation of the United Nations. The minorities system failed because of political reasons, but granted ethnic and religious minorities some protection against bigotry, including implementation measures and individual petitions, that could reach the Council of the League.[19] The Permanent Court of International Justice also contributed some interesting jurisprudence.[20]

After World War II and the establishment of the United Nations, a first, very significant, although not effective, step, inspired by the horrible lessons of the war, particularly the Holocaust, was the adoption of the 1948 Convention on the Prevention and Punishment of the Crime of Genocide, a crime the essence of which is the intent to destroy a national, ethnic, racial or religious group, as such. Genocide is, of course, the ultimate and most criminal expression of racism, but the Convention did not incorporate measures of implementation or a monitoring system.[21] While these lines were written, public opinion showed strong interest in the trial promoted by David Irving against

Deborah Lipstedt. The British Court rejected Irving's claims and restated the facts about the Holocaust, denied by Irving.

Since 1948, and until the early 1960's, no measures were adopted to protect racial or ethnic (or religious) groups from discrimination, intolerance, persecution, and/or hatred. The UN Charter, the Universal Declaration of Human Rights, the regional treaties on human rights and other antidiscrimination instruments, condemned or prohibited manifestations of racism, particularly racist discrimination. However, specific international legislation only followed the 1959–1960 anti-Semitic outbursts that took place mainly in Europe. On 12 December 1960, the General Assembly, after condemning all manifestations and practices of racial, religious and national hatred in the political, economic, social, educational and cultural spheres of the life of society, was asked to prepare declarations and conventions against racial discrimination and prejudice and against religious intolerance. For political reasons, it was decided to separate the spheres of racism and religious intolerance.[22]

The result was the adoption of the United Nations Declaration on the Elimination of All Forms of Racial Discrimination in 1963;[23] the International Convention on the Elimination of All Forms of Racial Discrimination in 1965, and the Declaration on the Elimination of All Forms of Intolerance and of Discrimination Based on Religion or Belief in 1981.[24] No convention on religious rights is in sight, but, in the meantime, the 1966 International Covenant on Civil and Political Rights was adopted. It includes the highly relevant Article 20.[25]

The 1965 Convention is a comprehensive and far-reaching treaty. It was influential on domestic law and many States adopted legislation, inclusive penal legislation, in accordance with the Convention's provisions. As pointed out above, recent European documents show the influence of the Convention. It is being reasonably well implemented by a Committee (CERD), composed of independent experts that have been performing monitoring work. CERD examines the reports of the states, is entitled to request supplementary information, which it does frequently, issues interpretative comments, and has already produced a very significant body of authoritative views on the subject of racial discrimination, in a broad sense.[26] As indicated, one of the crucial articles of the Convention is Article 4, that has been criticised, and even prompted reservations on the part of some states. It has also been praised as the 'key article' of the Convention, in the words of a Special Rapporteur designated by CERD.[27]

The implementation system established by the ICERD includes an optional right of individual complaints. The relevant Article 14 requests a declaration by the states willing to permit individual communications concerning them. Only a minority of states have made such a declaration.

Article 20 of the 1966 Covenant on Civil and Political Rights was already cited and was the object of a General Comment on the part of the implementation organ, the Human Rights Committee, ratifying its aims.[28]

Other United Nations instruments, particularly the 1981 Declaration on Discrimination and Intolerance Based on Religion or Belief and the 1992 Declaration on the Rights of Persons Belonging to National, or Ethnic, Religious and Linguistic Minorities,[29] contain condemnation of racist practices. Treaties adopted by United Nations-related bodies, such as UNESCO and the ILO, also carry provisions prohibiting racial manifestations.

At the regional level, in Europe, the Summit of Heads of State and Government of the member States of the Council of Europe established, in 1993, the European Commission against Racism and Intolerance (ECRI), with the task 'to combat racism, xenophobia, anti-Semitism, and intolerance' in greater Europe, to review member states' legislation, to formulate general policy recommendations and to study international legal instruments applicable. ECRI's program comprises a country-by-country approach, and work on general themes.[30] The European Human Rights Court's jurisprudence dealt with the issue of racism, interpreting antiracist provisions in the European Convention for the Protection of Human Rights and Fundamental Freedoms.[31] Reference has already been made to the recent instruments on racism adopted by the Council of Europe at its conference on the European contribution to the 2001 World Conference. Mention should also be made of the adoption by the Council of Europe of Protocol No.12 to the European Convention on Human Rights. Its Article 1 includes a general prohibition of discrimination:

> The enjoyment of any right set forth by law shall be secured without discrimination on any ground such as sex, race, colour, language, religion, political or other opinion, national or social origin, association with a national minority, property, birth or other status.[32]

Also relevant are the 1975 Final Act of the Helsinki Conference on Security and Cooperation in Europe (Principle VII); the Concluding Document of the Vienna Meeting in 1989 (particularly Principles 16 and 17); the 1990 Document of the Copenhagen Meeting of the CSCE Conference on the Human Dimension, and the 1990 Paris Charter for a New Europe.[33]

In America, the Inter-American Commission on Human Rights and the Human Rights Court had no opportunities to deal with the issue of racism, since they mainly concentrated on subjects related to personal freedom and security. On the other hand, and this is already not international but domestic law, several states on the American Continent have adopted antiracist legislation.[34]

The tragic events in former Yugoslavia and the horrors of 'ethnic cleansing' had the effect of intensifying the efforts to develop international criminal law by curbing extreme expressions of racist violence and illegality. The statutes of the ad hoc international tribunals for the crimes of 'ethnic cleansing' in Yugoslavia and in Rwanda, as well as the proposed statute of the general International Criminal Court to be established according to the decision of the 1998 Rome Conference convened by the United Nations, contain antiracist clauses.[35]

How to use International Law

Education at all levels is, needless to say, the basic way to combat racism. It means formal instruction at school, as well as extracurricular education, taking full advantage of modern technology in the area of communications. Parallel to the use of education, law, international and domestic, is an indispensable instrument to deal with manifestations of bigotry, whatever their source. In practice, the differences between the various motivations for group hatred – race, religion, culture, ethnicity, residential seniority, the mere fact of being different – are flexible and, in effect, not decisive, at least with regard to their consequences. A Roma, or Gypsy, who is being discriminated or persecuted in the Balkans, or a Kurd being submitted to discriminatory treatment in western Europe, or a new immigrant threatened by aggressive spokesmen of the old and new Right, or indigenous people in many places, or Jews, or blacks, or Arabs, or Hispanics, could not care more about the deep causes of their being defamed, persecuted or attacked. They do care about the consequences of such behavior.

In many cases, however, there is reluctance to use law, particularly criminal law, to prohibit, prevent and suppress manifestations – meaning 'fighting' words and acts of racism – except, naturally, when they clearly involve violence or a present and immediate danger of violence. By law, I have in mind international treaties, domestic legislation and, also, litigation, either by individuals or nongovernmental organisations, in order to obtain judicial remedies.

The 1965 Convention on Racial Discrimination and the 1966 Covenant on Civil and Political Rights open avenues for individual complaints, although on an optional basis. States may or not take the risk of being exposed to complaints from persons or NGO's. They are free to ratify the global instruments containing antiracist provisions without submitting themselves to the possibility of being accused by their own citizens of violating their rights. This explains why so few communications have been addressed to the implementation bodies. The situation is different at the regional level, in the cases where implementation organs, including judicial resources, exist, and are mandatory for the states adhering to the antiracist treaties. Europe is, in this respect, outstanding. NGO's and individuals should take maximum advantage of the possibilities involved in the individual complaints arrangements.

Clash with Other Freedoms

The argument that the use of law – preventive or repressive – may endanger essential basic rights, mainly freedom of expression and of association, has been frequently invoked to advise caution and self-restraint. This was particularly the case in connection with Article 4 of the Convention on Racial Discrimination and Article 20 of the Covenant on Civil and Political Rights. In both cases, authoritative interpretations of the respective texts are in favor of the mandatory character of the limitations imposed by those instruments on racist activities. The Committee on the Elimination of Racial Discrimination (CERD) adopted General Recommendation XV (42) in 1993, following previous Recommendations, affirming that Article 4 is of a mandatory character.[36] The same year, referring to a report from the United Kingdom, the Committee considered that, in the light of the increase in manifestation of racist ideas and of racially motivated attacks, the restrictive interpretation of Article 4 violated the purpose and objective of the Convention and was incompatible with the general recommendation XV of the Committee. This was also the view forcefully advanced by Special Rapporteur Jose Ingles, in his study on Article 4.

The Committee stated:

> The prohibition of the dissemination of all ideas based upon racial superiority or hatred is compatible with the right to freedom of opinion and expression ... The citizen's exercise of this right carries special duties and responsibilities ... among which the obligation not to disseminate racist ideas is of particular importance. The Committee wishes furthermore to draw to the attention of States parties Article 20 of the International Covenant on Civil and Political Rights, according to which any advocacy of national, racial or religious hatred that constitutes incitement to discrimination, hostility or violence, shall be prohibited by law[37]

CERD 'is of the opinion that article 4(b) places a greater burden upon ... states to be vigilant in proceeding against (racist) organisations at the earliest possible moment. Organisations, as well as organised and other propaganda activities, have to be declared illegal and prohibited. Participation in these organisations is of itself to be punished.'[38]

The European Court of Human Rights decided in 1994, by a vote of 12 to 7, that Article 10 of the European Convention on Human Rights, limiting the right to freedom of expression for the 'protection of the rights and reputation of others', was necessary in a democratic society.[39] There is, thus, consistency between the global and the European approaches to this issue.

A distinguished member of CERD, Professor Michael Banton,[40] wrote not long ago that the conflicts in and between the States of the former Yugoslavia, and in Rwanda, 'have demonstrated once again that prevention is much better than cure', although 'political considerations frequently govern the use that is made of law'. This explains why, despite the fact that a state's accession to a treaty gives others powers to make that state keep its promises, 'states may be loath to use their powers if they fear that they themselves are open to criticism for not keeping all their own promises'. This remark may not be essentially of a juridical character, but it illuminates the way in which international law is conducted and the weakness of the monitoring systems established by international norms.

Conclusions

Summing up my former remarks, I would describe the present situation in the following terms:

1. International law provides today, at the global as well as at the regional level, reasonable basic norms to fight racism. (Needless to say, there is also abundant domestic legislation, but this is beyond the scope of my article.)
2. In the term 'racism' it is necessary to include all manifestations of discrimination, persecution, hatred, or violence, motivated by membership in a group of a racial, ethnic, religious, or cultural character.
3. While substantive measures are in general reasonable and clear, there is an evident problem related to implementation, either because of weakness of the respective bodies, or of states' reluctance to act unless directly involved, or by political reasons or considerations related to global affairs, or by the use of violence which makes legal measures insufficient or inadequate.
4. Educational steps to combat racism and intolerance should be combined with an energetic use of the law, preventive and repressive.

Both ways of action are complementary. Developments in the area of international criminal law in recent years are relevant.
5. There is no incompatibility between the use of law, including criminal law, to fight racism, on the one hand, and promote freedom of expression and association, on the other. Safeguarding the principles of the Universal Declaration on Human Rights and coinciding treaties, there is no legal reason, and certainly no moral reason, to tolerate racist activities out of fear of limiting some other rights. There are no absolute rights.
6. There is an obvious relationship between the antiracist struggle and world peace and security, and this justifies international intervention when it is necessary to stop mass-murder and generalised violence.
7. While several countries have already outlawed the denial of the Holocaust and its magnitude as a way of inciting racist hatred, international law still has to address this attempt to distort history and engender racism.

In 2001, a worldwide conference convened by the UN will discuss the present state of the struggle against racism. It will be called upon to adopt decisions intended to curb the affront to human dignity and the rule of law involved in racial hatred and discrimination. To that effect, it should elaborate a generally accepted international minimum standard concerning racist abuse, discrimination and violence against all population sectors exposed to such practices.

Notes

1. On the situation in Europe in this respect see ECRI (European Commission Against Racism and Intolerance), Annual Report for 1998, Strasbourg, 23 March 1999, and Activities of the Council of Europe with Relevance to Combating Racism and Intolerance, Strasbourg, September 1999.
2. Ibid., p. 7.
3. Similar regional conferences have been taking place in different regions of the world, with the purpose of preparing the respective contributions to the world conference.
4. See, respectively, EUROCONF documents (2000)1 and (2000) 7 Rev.
5. EUROCONF (2000), 1, p. 5.
6. See, EUROCONF (2000) 7 Rev., 3–4.
7. Ibid., 5.
8. Ibid., 7.
9. See, Kofi Annan, 'Two concepts of sovereignty', the *Economist*, September 18, 1999.
10. I have dealt with the subject in my *The UN Convention on the Elimination of All Forms of Racial Discrimination*, Sijthoff & Noordhoff (Alphen aan den Rijn, 1980) and *Group Rights and Discrimination in International Law*, Nijhoff (Dordrecht, 1991). In my recent *Religion, Beliefs, and International Human Rights*, part of the

Religion and Human Rights Series published for the Law and Religion Program of Emory University by Orbis Books, (Maryknoll, New York, 2000) I have reviewed the relationship between racism and religious intolerance. The new European texts on racism acknowledge such a relationship.
11. See UN Doc. E/CN.4/1994/661).
12. For its text, United Nations, Human Rights: a Compilation of International Instruments (1988) (hereinafter, Human Rights) 56–69. See, also, supra, note 10.
13. On recent manifestations of anti-Semitism, see Tel Aviv University, Stephen Roth Institute for the Study of Contemporary Anti-Semitism and Racism, Anti-Semitism Worldwide 1998/9 (2000).
14. See its text in Lerner, The UN Convention ..., supra, note 10.
15. For its text, Human Rights, 8.
16. I have discussed the issue of which groups are of the interest of international law in my *Group Rights and Discrimination in International Law*, supra note 10.
17. See, in this respect, Natan Lerner, 'Incitement in the Racial Convention: Reach and Shortcomings of article 4', *Israel Yearbook on Human Rights* 22 (1992) 1–15; Jose D. Ingles, *Study on the Implementation of article 4 of the Convention on the Elimination of All Forms of Racial Discrimination*, UN Sales No. E.85.XIV.2 (1986).
18. There is an enormous literature on the minorities system under the League of Nations. For an authoritative interpretation of the system, Jacob Robinson et al., *Were the Minorities Treaties a Failure* (1943); Patrick Thornberry, *International Law and the Rights of Minorities* (1991); Yoram Dinstein and Mala Tabory, eds., *The Protection of Minorities and Human Rights* (1992); Catherine Brolman et al., eds., *Peoples and Minorities in International Law* (1993); Lerner, *Group Rights*, supra, note 10.
19. See, for instance, the well known Bernheim case. Cfr., P.G.Lauren, *The Evolution of International Human Rights* (Philadelphia: University of Pennsylvania Press, 1998) 131 ff.
20. See, i.a., the 1925 case of the Rights of Minorities in Upper Silesia (Minority Schools), PCIJ, Ser.A, No. 15, and the Advisory Opinion concerning Minority Schools in Albania (1935), PCIJ, Ser.A/B, No. 64.
21. For the text of the Convention, Human Rights, 669. For an authoritative commentary, Nehemiah Robinson, *The Genocide Convention*, Institute of Jewish Affairs (New York, 1969).
22. For the history and political implications of the drafting process of the respective instruments, see Lerner, *The UN Convention*, supra note 10.
23. General Assembly Resolution 1904 (XVIII). For the full text of the Declaration, see Human Rights, supra, note 12, 52–56.
24. For an analysis of the 1981 Declaration, Lerner, *Religion*, supra, note 10, 20 ff. For its text, Human Rights, supra, note 12, 125–129.
25. For the Covenants, generally, Louis Henkin, ed., *The International Bill of Rights*, Columbia U.P., (New York, 1981); Philip Alston, ed., *The United Nations and Human Rights* (1992); see also the reports of the Human Rights Committee, published as Official Records of the General Assembly (GAOR), Supp. No. 40.
26. For the CERD reports, see GAOR, Supplements No. 18, which constitute a useful source of information and authoritative quasi-judicial decisions.
27. See, Lerner, supra, notes 10 and 17.
28. See, Report of the Committee, UN GAOR 38th Sess., Supp. No. 40, Annex VI, at 110.
29. See its full text in Natan Lerner, 'The 1992 UN Declaration on Minorities', 23 *Israel Yearbook on Human Rights* (1994), 111–128.
30. Cfr., supra, note 1.
31. 213 U.N.T.S. 211.

32. For the full text of the Protocole, see press.coe.int/ECHR50, 14/11/00.
33. For the CSCE (now OSCE) documents, see *Council of Europe, Human Rights in International Law Basic Texts* (Strasbourg, 1992).
34. On human rights in America, see, generally, Thomas Buergenthal et al., *Protecting Human Rights in the Americas* (1995); Scott Davidson, *The Inter-American Human Rights System* (1997).
35. On ethnic cleansing and the development of international criminal law, see Lerner, *Religion*, supra, note 10, at 68.
36. See, Report of CERD, GAOR, Supp. No. 18 (A/48/18), at 115.
37. Ibid.
38. Ibid.
39. Jersild v. Denmark, 36/1993/431/510.
40. See, also, Prof. Banton's book *International Action Against Racial Discrimination* (Oxford, 1996).

RACISM AND POVERTY IN A HUMAN RIGHTS PERSPECTIVE

Bas de Gaay Fortman

Introduction

After the British colony of Northern Rhodesia had acquired its independence in 1964, the new state of Zambia was proclaimed as being based on 'the nonracial society'. In the light of all those years of racial discrimination – not less humiliating than in South Africa and Southern Rhodesia (later Zimbabwe) – this meant a step of revolutionary significance. Typically, in those days there was little doubt that a new constitution and a new political regime would serve to wipe out racism just like that; we still lived in a time of faith in the 'engineerability' of society.

It was a few years after independence that I was personally challenged to rethink the nonracial society in some of its aspects. Waking up in Kasama Inn, a government lodge in the outlying North of the country, I saw a gentleman standing at my bed. He introduced himself as Mr Mulenga, Chief Enumerator for the region. His duty was to count me and to ask me some questions in regard to the new Census. 'Sir', he went on, 'are you an African, an Asian or a European?' 'But Mr Mulenga', I protested, 'this is a racial question and we are living here in the nonracial society!' 'No Sir', the Chief Enumerator replied, 'in South Africa you would not be asked the question. There it is the authorities that classify people. Here people can say for themselves with which group they identify. And that information is important for government. For example, if inequalities correspond to racial categories as identified by people themselves, we know there is a problem'.

I was taught two important lessons here. Firstly, race is not a fixed objective reality that can be determined by direct observation. Secondly, neither is race a mere chimera, an issue that can just be ignored. In the nonracial society, in other words, deeply rooted patterns of socialisation of people in terms of superiority and inferiority are not likely to be eliminated by one word or one stroke of the pen.[1]

Figures on Brazil are illustrative. In effect, the category 'black' there implies association with significantly higher infant mortality rates; entering school later and leaving it earlier than either 'brown' or 'white'; entering the labour market at the lower end of the occupational hierarchy, and being confronted with strong negative wage differences. Lovell and Wood conclude that the persistence of such relative disparities 'cannot be reduced to differences in human capital endowments alone'.[2] Not surprisingly, then, people have little inclination to identify themselves with a marginalised, excluded category. Consequently, in a period of thirty years (from the 1950s to the 1980s), racial self-identification resulted in a considerable reduction of the part of the population that called itself 'black'.[3]

Obviously then, while racial categories cannot in any way denote scientific realities, racism remains a reality determined by disqualification and discrimination of people regarded as different in the sense of inferior. Indeed, racism constitutes one specific type of 'us/them' divide. It manifests itself in three distinct ways: racial prejudice, racial discrimination (exclusion of people belonging to racially defined groups) and structural racial inequalities. While each of these is likely to result in individual cases of violation of human dignity, racism, in essence, remains a 'collective' phenomenon. This is the focus we intend to take in this chapter, while analysing racism particularly with regard to its collective socio-economic aspects.

Facts such as those following from the figures on Brazil represent a general picture. Thus, in the United Kingdom too, the black population is overrepresented in low paid and insecure jobs and in jobs with antisocial working hours and unhealthy working environments. Juvenile unemployment also hits the black population disproportionately.[4] In the United States, a country in which racism constitutes a daily reality for millions of people, the economic dimension is reflected in evident figures on poverty: with nine percent of the total population living below the poverty line, the figure for Afro-Americans is thirty percent.[5] Racial prejudice is reflected in differential treatment in housing, the mortgage market and the labour market, to mention just a few areas of discrimination.

The problematic of racialised inequalities is the major focus of this chapter. Remedies will be sought in human rights. First we shall go into the meaning of human rights. The international project for the realisation of human rights will then be confronted with racism in general. Next, we shall concentrate on the specific problem area of racism and poverty. Then it will be time to look at human rights as possible weapons in the fight against 'racialised' poverty.

The Meaning of Human Rights

Human rights are based on the necessity of protecting each and every human being against violation of basic human dignity. At their roots lies the conviction that human dignity has to be respected and that no individual is worth more than any other: 'All human beings are born free and equal in dignity and rights': Article 1 of the Universal Declaration of Human Rights. The founding principle of 'equality' is further reflected in Article 2: 'Everyone is entitled to all the rights and freedoms set forth in this Declaration, without distinction of any kind, such as race, colour, sex, language, religion, political or other opinion, national or social origin, property, birth or other status'. The term *everyone* is crucial. There are, in other words, 'no nobodies'.[6]

The way in which human rights constitute an attempt to protect people against discrimination and other forms of violating basic human dignity is, primarily, through 'law'.[7] Notably, rights are interests protected by law. An essential element in the term 'law' is enforcement. Hence, as 'rights', human rights denote what ought to be 'enforced' in the relations among people. Claims based on such rights should, generally, be accepted. Yet, when this does not happen in daily practice, actual enforcement depends on some other factors also: awareness on the part of the rights-holders, possibilities of clearly identifying duty-bearers, and the way in which existing legal systems function (rule of law, accessibility of the judicial system, etc.). Litigation or contentious action is not always the most effective strategy towards enforcement. From an abstract acknowledgement of claims towards daily implementation tends to be a complicated process, also depending on counterforces and on the means to overcome these.

Although formulated as 'subjective rights', human rights can also be approached from an 'objective' angle. The interests behind them are of a strongly normative character: the fundamental freedoms and needs directly related to basic human dignity. In this sense, human rights embody standards of what is right – and hence ought to be enforced – whenever power is being exercised. Human rights bind all use of power, in other words, and as such they are general standards of what is right, or 'principles of legitimacy'. The subjective implication of legitimacy is that the rule of the rulers must be acceptable to the ruled. From an objective perspective, legitimacy means that the execution of power must be constitutional and in conformity with rules of due process and principles of good government.[8] Strategically, this may mean a shift in emphasis from human rights as legal resources towards human rights as political instruments. In the struggle against racism, as we shall see, this is a point of great relevance.

Racism and Human Rights

Although racist acts often result in disputes between identifiable individuals, their background lies, as was pointed out, in collective prejudice; collective discrimination and collectively structured inequalities. Thus, racism violates human dignity primarily in its communal aspects. Individual cases, in other words, find their ideological roots not so much in 'Me/You' but rather in 'Us/Them' divides: 'they are different ... ',[9] 'we should not allow them ... ', 'they should be kept in their place ... ', etc. Consequently, in the struggle against racism, juridical universalism – rules or standards that are to be applied equally to individual cases of an equal nature – has its limitations.

Notably, neither in texts issued in preparation for the European Year against Racism in 1997, nor in the documents pertaining to the establishment of a European Monitoring Centre for Racism and Xenophobia, is any reference made to United Nations standards and mechanisms to combat racism. Theo van Boven, himself a former member of the UN Committee for the Elimination of all Forms of Racial Discrimination (CERD), wonders how such neglect is possible.[10] With three consecutive 'Decades to Combat Racism and Racial Discrimination', a major International Convention for the Elimination of All Forms of Racial Discrimination (ICERD) with its own supervisory Committee, and a Special Rapporteur on contemporary forms of racism, racial discrimination, xenophobia and related intolerance falling under the Commission on Human Rights, one would have expected at least some connection with United Nations efforts in the struggle. Van Boven gives four reasons, all relating to weaknesses and complexities in UN antiracism strategies: European prejudice against the UN as an organisation dominated by forces insensitive to European thinking, European self-satisfaction, timidity in the UN itself when confronted with state interests and the sensitivities of governments, and finally, the diversity of sometimes conflicting interests in UN circles as reflected in the mandate of the UN Commission on Human Rights' Special Rapporteur 'to examine according to his mandate incidents of contemporary forms of racism, racial discrimination, any form of discrimination against blacks, Arabs and Muslims, xenophobia, negrophobia, anti-Semitism, and related intolerance'.[11] 'This complex formula', Van Boven feels, 'proves that divergent forces are at work in the United Nations, which by their nature tend to corrode a common platform of struggle against racism and racial discrimination'.[12] While he certainly has a point here, I see a more significant cause of neglect in the 'juridical' nature of UN mechanisms.

Evidently, legal systems do not provide much of an instrument to deal with collective 'prejudice'. What law has to offer in efforts to rectify structural racial inequalities, will be discussed below. In regard to individual rights, its use lies primarily in the struggle against racial discrimination. In a society with a strong juridical culture such as the United States, law played an obvious part in getting rid of much systemic discrimination. However, when the laws are not observed, universalist legal systems can only deal with disputes if cases come from recognised legal personalities, or, in practice, 'individuals'. In regard to such individual cases of discrimination, domestic law may provide certain remedies, although the collection of evidence is usually not very easy, particularly when the 'presumption of innocence' lays the burden of proof completely on the victims of racial discrimination.[13]

In the international setting, direct remedies are lacking. So, with all due respect to the Committee on the Elimination of Racial Discrimination (CERD), which receives occasional individual complaints and scrutinises state reports while making useful comments and policy recommendations, the lack of effective mechanisms for direct enforcement tends to reduce its role to checking the effectiveness of national institutions. Where national instruments are lacking completely because specific forms of discrimination have not been established as human rights violations – such as castism and discrimination against certain (unrecognised) minorities – CERD may still play its part in bringing issues to the fore and mobilising shame. Yet, we should not underestimate the role the Universal Declaration of Human Rights and the major human rights covenants play in stimulating the enactment of domestic law against racism and racial discrimination. A global civil society is emerging that uses the international legal order in the fight against racism and racial discrimination in regional and national contexts. The interest taken in the World Conference on Racism in South Africa (2001) by groups that are victim to systemic discrimination, is a case in point.

Racism and Poverty

Racism and poverty tend to be linked in two distinct ways. Firstly, poverty 'breeds' racism. I am referring here to the socio-economic background of the spreading of collective prejudice and racist ideologies. Nazism is a notorious example of racist hatred that could be aroused in a context of economic insecurity, hyperinflation and mass unemployment. There are, however, more recent instances. In Europe and elsewhere it is particularly in the poorer countries, and within these in the poorer regions, cities and suburbs, that racist sentiment appears to have its chance. It is apparently connected in this respect with the search for scapegoats.[14] SecondlyMoreover, poverty tends to be racial in the sense that people from certain racially defined categories are likely to be overrepresented among the poor. It is on this latter aspect that the present paper is focused.

Facts indicating the racialisation of poverty were already presented in the introduction to this paper. The figures on the United States are most striking. RemarkablyNotably, with the so-called new economy and a GDP growth rate of about 4 percent for 1997/1998, low inflation and a fall of unemployment to 4 percent, poverty is still on the increase. Thirty million Americans cannot afford three meals a day. Since 1992, the demand for charity food aid has increased by 18 percent and the demand for emergency shelter by 12 percent.[15] Impoverishment is closely related to enrichment. Notably, 1 percent of all Americans own 40 percent of all private wealth while 20 percent own 80 percent. On average Afro- and Hispano-Americans own less than 7 percent of the median wealth of white citizens. Nine percent of the whites live below the poverty line as against 30 percent of black families and 26.5 percent of Hispanic families. Cole summarises the effects of racial poverty as follows:

> The consequences of the country's race and class divisions are felt in every aspect of American life, from infant mortality and unemployment, where black rates are double white rates; to public education, where the proportion of black children educated in segregated schools is increasing; to housing, where racial segregation is the norm, integration the rare exception. Racial inequality, which Alexis de Tocqueville long ago recognised as 'the most formidable evil threatening the future of the United States', remains today the most formidable of our social problems.[16]

Not surprisingly, structural racial inequalities tend to be reflected in the statistics on crime and the criminal justice system, too. For blacks, the incarceration rate is seven times higher than for whites. Strikingly, while 12 percent of the total population is African-American, more than half of the prisoners belong to that category. One in four young black males is likely to get into prison during his lifetime, and, shockingly, 'for every one black man who graduates from college, 100 are arrested'.[17] This is not just a matter of poverty breeding crime, but rather of systems of criminal justice themselves producing their own clientèle.[18] In his impressive 'No Equal Justice' David Cole shows how methods of criminal investigation based on collective prejudice and using an intolerable degree of discretion – police sweeping through poor communities and stopping and searching at random – have resulted in a total lack of trust in the ruling system of criminal justice on the part of the black population. In effect, it is not only the black communities themselves that suffer, but the whole public/political community has to pay a high price for that lack of trust in criminal justice. For one thing, people who know there is 'no equal justice' tend to obstruct law enforcement, thus undermining the rule of justice.[19]

Apparently, a racialised 'underclass' and increased racial violence go together with the institutionalisation of new forms of discrimination and exclusion. western Europe is also faced with increasing problems of 'racialised' unemployment and 'racialised' criminality; one need only look at the situation of the Moroccan youth. Hence, there are lessons to be learned. Solomos and Back conclude:

> The crisis of race and racialised class inequalities in the United States is a timely reminder that the Civil Rights Movement and other movements have had at best a partial impact on established patterns of racial inequality and have not stopped the development of new patterns of exclusion and segregation.[20]

With this background we shall now examine possible remedies, particularly from a human rights perspective.

Remedies

The primary response to racism is the constitutionally guaranteed equality of all before the law. However, in regard to substantial inequalities that are structurally rooted, it does not help very much to group all people together. In this respect, Anatole France's ironical observation on the equality of all before the law, which prohibits the rich and the poor alike to sleep under bridges and to beg on the streets, is enlightening. The roots of structural inequalities lie in double standards and falsely used discretion; these ought to be eliminated or at least reduced in order to restore legitimacy. In other words, the problematic should be acknowledged in its real (structural) dimensions.[21]

What is needed, then, is 'special and concrete measures' to address the 'structural' inequalities behind systemic discrimination. We may think here of, firstly, policies for 'employment equity' that aim at securing equal opportunities by removing discriminatory barriers. Secondly, remedies are sought in 'affirmative action', 'that attempts to achieve a more level playing field – for example in the jobs market – by facilitating education, training and work experience'.[22] 'Reverse discrimination' is particularly controversial: the application of 'racialised' quota systems in, for example, education, housing or employment. Such preferential treatment leads to the exclusion of others who otherwise would have qualified. Here lies a basic dilemma, as such measures should be taken for the 'advancement of certain racial or ethnic groups' as the ICERD calls it, and hence such groups should be well defined. The way out adopted in the International Convention is to prescribe, 'that such measures do not, as a consequence, lead to the maintenance of separate rights for different racial groups and that they shall not be continued after the objectives for which they were taken have been achieved' (Art. 1.4; see also 2.2). Yet, there remains an inherent paradox: racial categorisation of people in order to find remedies against racialised patterns of socialisation. While devised to repudiate racial categories, these may, in effect, be precisely reproduced.[23] Thus, people tend to be reduced to their 'racial' categories, implying that all those categorised as being from a 'racial' underclass can benefit from affirmative action policies, including individuals with a privileged personal background. The problem has been pointedly typified by Cole: 'to what extent can a solution that expressly takes race into account be a valid remedy for a wrong that consists in taking race into account'.[24] Notably, behind racialised patterns of socialisation are power relations, and these are likely to be rooted in the entitlement systems upon which people's access to resources is based.[25] Not rarely, reverse discrimination leads to unintended indirect effects as expressed in a term such as 'racial backlash'. However, the 'conscientising' effects of 'scheduling' – as it is called in the Indian context of castism – should not be underestimated. Political efforts to abolish quota systems run the risk of being interpreted as a sign of the complete abandonment of the struggle against structural 'racial' inequalities.

Another major issue here is how far legal rules can be used to enhance substantive equality in its three aspects of equality of opportunity, equality of treatment and equality of outcome. It is particularly in regard to the latter that race-based treatment is regarded as a necessary remedy.

In terms of instruments four regulatory approaches are proposed:[26]

1. Agency regulation 'designed to create pressures for organisations to implement a group justice approach'. For example, permits may be withheld if certain prescriptions on allocation of jobs or admission of students are not followed.
2. The use of 'incentives to encourage organisations to change their practices.'
3. For example, subsidies are made available in rato with acceptance of students from underprivileged backgrounds.
4. The use of 'the state's power of *dominium*, in particular through attaching equality requirements to government contracts'. For example, government accepts tenders only from companies which employ workers of underprivileged categories in proportions corresponding to the national or regional figures.

Naturally, the problem with all such rules is that they are not automatically followed. In actual practice, rules can be abused, circumvented and evaded. Indeed, regulators should have an open eye to the phenomenon of 'side-law', i.e. in the sense of rules which do have effects, but not those that were intended. Hence, there is good reason to take a critical view of legal 'instrumentalism' in the sense of a generally optimistic belief that law will change society as intended.[27] In regard to the anti-discrimination challenge, Griffith has pointed at an alternative approach: the 'social working of the law'.[28] This implies a focus on, first of all: 'What will the (wo)man on the shop floor do?' Applying this methodology to the struggle against racism and its manifestations in structural inequalities Griffith concludes that rules that are based upon individual rights approaches, in the sense of individuals having to mobilise legal institutions, are not generally the most effective: 'Rules that do not require people to initiate a legal process in order to secure a new 'right' are often likely to be more effective than those that do. And rules aimed at large organisations are more likely to be effective than rules aimed at individuals'. He considers those approaches that could fall under the heading of 'indirect positive discrimination' as the most hopeful: 'that is measures designed indirectly to improve the position of the disadvantaged group'. One might think here, for instance, of reducing educational requirements for certain jobs and hence opening these positions up for individuals belonging to educationally underprivileged groups; in other words, the removal of indirect barriers,. The effectiveness of such measures also depend on the activities of voluntary associations in awareness-building and on actual pressure on institutions to seriously attempt employing people from disadvantaged backgrounds.

Structural racial inequalities are often rooted in a long past of discrimination, exploitation and oppression. In this light, the real challenge is enormous. John Coetzee's incredible novel *Disgrace*(1999) in which it becomes immediately apparent that the legal and political liquidation of apartheid does not mean the end of structural racial inequalities, illustrates this. Actually, this important step just means a beginning as it now raises expectations of social justice. The struggle ahead is not a positive-sum game (or 'win-win' situation) as idealists might believe. South Africa remains a country with extreme pressure on resources. After having been robbed of his car and seriously manhandled, Coetzee's principal character, the white 'disgraced' professor David Lugard, counts himself lucky to have escaped with his life:

> A risk to own anything: a car, a pair of shoes, a packet of cigarettes. Not enough to go around, not enough cars, shoes, cigarettes. Too many people, too few things. What there is must go into circulation, so that everyone can have a chance to be happy for a day. That is the theory, hold to the theory and to the comfort of the theory. Not human evil, just a vast circulatory system, to whose workings pity and terror are irrelevant. That is how one must see life in this country: in its schematic aspect ... .[29]

Of course, a major force behind apartheid was the desire to keep the wealth of whites out of such circulation. The legal and political dismantling of that system is no more than the start of a new period. Lugard's daughter Lucy realises this when she tells her father she is not leaving:

> Go to Petrus (her black neighbour) and tell him ... I give up the land. Tell him that he can have it, title deed and all ... Perhaps that is what I must learn to accept. To start at ground level. With nothing. Not with nothing but. With nothing. No cards, no weapons, no property, no rights, no dignity.[30]

Notably, however, 'racial justice' cannot be built upon personal acceptance of the necessity of transferring wealth and income from the 'racial' haves to the have-nots. There is a need for deliberate policies to attack 'racial poverty'. Not even in the wealthiest parts of Europe have such policies been impressive in their effects. In respect of the United Kingdom, for example, Solomos and Back conclude: 'In the past policy initiatives have at best been ad hoc and piece-meal'.[31] These initiatives have consisted mainly of antidiscriminatory legislation, antiracist programmes in the spheres of housing, unemployment, education and social services, and attempts to address certain specific issues. The problem lies in the incidental character of such policies. Since racism is an institutional phenomenon, the real effort is to effectuate an institutionalisation of antiracist policies.[32]

New policies begin with the realisation that the existing structural racial inequalities undermine public/political 'legitimacy'. The significance of human rights as 'principles of legitimacy' in this connection has already been underlined. Let us now go a little deeper into this key notion of good government.

Legitimacy, which has both objective and subjective aspects, transforms power into authority. Subjectively, legitimacy is based on people's conviction that the way power is exercised over them and the way they are being ruled are 'right', and hence that they are morally bound to obey. Objectively, the use of power is bound to certain norms or principles. While some of these may have been laid down in the national constitution as well as in other domestic legislation of a fundamental nature, others have been enshrined primarily in international treaties and documents such as the Universal Declaration of Human Rights (UDHR).

Legitimacy, then, relates to the 'principles', 'means' and 'outcome' of the use of power. It should be seen not so much as a fact but as a process. Central to this process is the 'public interest' or 'common good', in the sense of all that keeps the public/political community together. The public interest is not to be interpreted as the highest common factor of all private interests. (While many thieves might concede that punishment of theft is in the public interest, few would consider that their own punishment would be in their own private interest). The notion of the public interest is rooted in the idea of society as a living community.

Dworkin (who uses the term 'integrity') specifies what this means:

1. 'Fairness', 'the right structures for the political system, the structure that distributes influence over political decisions in the right way'.
2. 'Due process', 'the right procedures for enforcing rules and regulations the system has produced'.
3. 'Justice', the right outcome of the socio-economic and political order: 'the right distribution of goods, opportunities and other resources'.[33]

In all three major aspects of legitimacy human rights as based on the fundamental dignity and equality of human beings play a crucial part:

1. 'The right institutions' imply systems of education, health, criminal justice, employment, etc. conducive to structural equality among people from different 'racial' categories.
2. 'The right procedures' imply non-discriminatory practices in all aspects of life.
3. 'The right outcome' implies employment, education, medical care and a decent living standard for everyone, including people belonging to disadvantaged groups.

Obviously, to effectuate 'racial' legitimacy is an ongoing struggle. Its starting point lies in efforts to bring the injustices out into the open. This implies disaggregating data by racial or ethnic groups. Indeed, statistics can be most revealing. Significantly, the South African apartheid regime stopped collecting data on the kwashiorkor disease after its statistics had revealed that the incidence of this disease was 300 times as high among blacks as among whites.[34] More recently, the World Bank was severely criticised for its neglect of race in its World Development Report 2000/2001 on Poverty.[35] Officials of the Inter-American Development Bank complain of lack of data on excluded 'racial' groups. This is regarded as a major impediment towards spending more on the advancement of these people.

Once the facts are known, processes of change begin with dissent in regard to a status quo that does not meet fundamental standards of legitimacy. A conventional follow-up is 'benchmarking': declaring general objectives such as the reduction of 'allochthonous' unemployment to a certain percentage at a specified time. This is unlikely to be effective without accompanying steps that challenge the status quo through protest, opposition, and collective action aimed at reform. Here, although often not so much directed towards immediate remedies, the role of legal resources (litigation, contentious action) should not be underestimated. One might think, for example, of public interest litigation in India and class action suits in the United States. By drawing attention to the public interest that is at stake, such action may also contribute to awareness-building. The challenge to power is crucial in all its aspects: formation, process and actual use. This will always require inventive strategies, combining legal resources with political instruments. It is precisely this combination which typifies the significance of human rights.

Notes

1. See, for example, Howard Winant. 1998.
2. P.A. Lovell and C.H. Wood. 1998.
3. Ibid.
4. John Solomos and Les Back. 1996.
5. David Cole. 1999: 4.
6. Cf. Bas de Gaay Fortman. 1996: 117–21. Illustrative, too, is the following story from the Hasidic tradition. Rabbi Shmuel comes to an inn, where the innkeeper, not aware of the identity of his guest, treats him harshly and disrespectfully. On Sabbath, in the synagogue, the innkeeper observes the high esteem in which the guest he treated so rudely is held. Approaching Rabbi Shmuel, he apologises, pleading his ignorance as to the rabbi's identity. The latter replies: 'When you harassed me, I thought you knew who I am and that I deserved your behaviour.

Now that you inform me of the contrary, I am astonished that you could treat a human being unknown to you in such manner'.
7. See Berma Klein Goldewijk and Bas de Gaay Fortman. 1999: 5.
8. The term *government* is used here in the wider sense of all use of office, whether in public or in private spheres.
9. 'Hulle is net bobbiane' ('they are just like monkeys'), one could hear 'white' Afrikaners say about black people in general. Indeed, it is typically their dignity as human beings that the others are being denied. Such categorization then serves as a justification of all forms of dehumanisation and humiliation.
10. Theo van Boven. 1999.
11. Commission on Human Rights, *Resolution 1994/64*, para. 4.
12. Theo van Boven. 1999.
13. See Nasser Negrouche. 2000. On the unsuitability of French law on discrimination. However, the law enacted by the European Union tends to offer more effective remedies.
14. On the relative importance of this factor there is scholarly dispute, not only in the case of Nazism but also in regard to the civil wars in the former Yugoslavia, for example. Of course the economic factor is to be seen as part of a context rather than a 'cause' in itself.
15. See some recent reports quoted in *Trouw*, 8 February 2000, p. 11.
16. Cole, 1999: p. 4.
17. Ibid., p5.
18. This is not a new insight. See Edgar Z. Friedenberg's convincing chapter on 'the conscript clientèle' in his *The Disposal of Liberty and Other Industrial Wastes*, New York 1975.
19. Cole, 1999: chapter 6: The costs of inequality.
20. Cole, 1999: p. 218.
21. Cf. Cole, 1999: pp 184ff.
22. Martin MacEwen. 1999: 431.
23. Cf. H. Winant, 1998.
24. Cole, 1999: p. 182.
25. For an analysis of entitlement systems in connection with distribution of income and wealth, see my 1999: 29–74.
26. Christopher McCrudden. 1999.
27. See John Griffith. 1978: 339–374.
28. John Griffith. 1999.
29. J.M. Coetzee. 1999: 98.
30. Ibid., p. 205.
31. John Solomos and Les Back. 1996: p. 73.
32. Ibid., pp 77–78.
33. Ronald Dworkin. 1986: 404.
34. See the United Nations Development Programme's *Human Development Report 2000*, New York: UNDP, p. 94.
35. *Terraviva*, the European Edition of the IPS Daily Journal, Vol. 2, No. 227, Monday, October 30, 2000, pp 3–4.

Bibliography

Coetzee, J.M. 1999. *Disgrace*. London: Secker and Warburg.
Cole, D. 1999. *No Equal Justice*. New York: The New Press.

Dworkin, R. 1986. *Law's Empire*. London: Fontana.
Fortman, B. 1996. 'No Nobodies'. In *Towards Global Human Rights*. P. Morales, ed., Tilburg, International Centre for Human and Public Affairs.
———. 1999. 'Beyond Income Distribution: An Entitlement Systems Approach to the Acquirement Problem'. In *The Economics of Income Distribution: Heterodox Approaches*. J. van der Linden, et al., eds. Cheltenham: Edward Elgar.
Friedenberg, E.Z. 1975. Convincing chapter on 'the conscript clientèle'. In *The Disposal of Liberty and Other Industrial Wastes*. New York.
Goldewijk, B.K., and Fortman, B. 1999. *Where Needs Meet Rights. Economic, social and Cultural Rights in a New Perspective*. Geneva: World Council of Churches Publications.
Griffith, J. 1978. 'Is Law Important'. In *New York: University Law Review*.
———. 1999. 'The Social Working of Anti-Discrimination Law'. In Van Loenen and Rodrigues, *New York: University Law Review*.
Lovell, P.A., and Wood, C.H. 1998. Skin Color, Racial Identity and Life Chances in Brazil. *Latin American Perspectives*, Vol. 25, No. 3, Issue 98, January 1998, p. 106.
MacEwen, M. 1999. 'Comparative Non-Discrimination Law: an Overview'. In *Non-Discrimination Law: Comparative Persepctives*. T. Van Loenen and Peter R. Rodrigues, eds. The Hague: Kluwer International.
McCrudden, C. 1999. 'Regulating Discrimination: Advice to a Legislator on Problems Regarding the Enforcement of Anti-Discrimination Law and Strategies to Overcome them" In Van Loenen and Rodrigues, *Non-Discrimination Law: Comparative Persepctives*. The Hague: Kluwer International.
Negrouche, N. 2000. 'Discrimination raciale à la française' *Le Monde Diplomatique*, Mars 2000, p. 7.
Solomos, J., and Back, L. 1996. *Racism and Society*. London: Macmillan, 1996, pp 69–70.
van Boven, T. 1999. United Nations Strategies to Combat Racism and Racial Discrimination; A Sobering but not Hopeless Balance-Sheet. In *The Role of the Nation-State in the 21st Century. Human Rights, International Organisations and Foreign Policy. Essays in Honour of Peter Baehr.* Monique Castermans-Holleman et al., eds. The Hague: Kluwer International, 1999, pp 251–264.
Winant, Howard. 1998. Racism today: continuity and change in the post-civil rights era. *Ethnic and Racial Studies* 1998 II, Vol. 21, pp 755–766.

DOES A SUPRANATIONAL EUROPE STIMULATE AND/OR COMBAT RACISM?

Robert Maier

Introduction

Europe is a very complex and unfinished entity. Geographically, Europe is an edge of the Eurasian landmass without any clear demarcation with respect to eastern territories or with respect to the Mediterranian space. Politically, Europe is not properly speaking a nation state, but its constitution has some state-like characteristics (see for example Wiener, 1998). Moreover, the constitution of Europe is in a process of dynamic transformation in two respects. Firstly, there is a project to integrate in the near future a great number of nation states which are at present not member of the European Union. Secondly, the constitutional framework, fixed in treaties and agreements is continuously rearranged and transformed.

The analysis of the problem of the position and attitude of Europe towards racism is rather complicated. I have chosen to attack this problem in the following ways: in the first part, I will examine the various explicit measures Europe has undertaken concerning racism, and the answer will be quite straightforward. Europe attempts in several ways to combat manifestations of racism. In the second part, I will enquire whether Europe, in its factual functioning, is stimulating, either directly or indirectly forms of racism. In order to execute such an examination it is necessary to refer to theoretical insights concerning factors stimulating racism. The answer will be less straightforward, because Europe in its actual functioning is indeed stimulating racism in several ways.

Before starting the examination of these two points, I would like to offer in this introduction some remarks on racism on the one hand, and on the occurence of racism in Europe on the other. A few words should be sufficient in order to indicate how the concept of racism is used in this article. Racism concerns beliefs and behaviour. The beliefs concerning individuals and groups and the behaviour towards individuals or groups are racist when based on and justified by the characteristics (mental, emotional, etc.) attributed to a set of people because of their biology or ethnicity. Such a general definition covers 'old' and 'new' forms of racism. (Barker 1981; Cole 1997; Taguieff 1988; Wieviorka 1998). Usually, the following distinctions are made between (1) Racist beliefs (opinions, jokes, ideas, theories, discourses) which can contribute to create a climate of racist harassment, (2) the various forms of racist discrimination (unequal treatment, for example on the labour market, or by the police, etc) and finally (3) aggressive racist actions, ranging from personal attacks to genocide.

Concerning racism, including anti-Semitism and xenophobia in Europe, a few indications should be sufficient in order to show the existence of racism and the importance and urgency of a serious examination of this phenomenon.

The results of the Eurobarometer Opinion Poll (Nr. 47.1; 12/1997) from 1997 offer the following data:

Table 2   EUROBAROMETER OPINION POLL NO 47.1 (12/1997)

	European average
very racist	9 %
quite racist	24 %
Our country has reached its limits concerning incorporation of minority groups	65 %

Table 3   The results for the countries with the highest scores and for the Netherlands:

Country	Belgium	France	Austria	Netherlands
Very racist	22%	16%	14%	5%
Quite racist	33%	32%	28%	26%

If, on average, 33 percent of the citizens of the European Union consider themselves as very or quite racist, one must recognise that there is at least a problem, even if the precise meaning of such surveys is questionable. As another set of data, I present the percentage of votes that more or less racist, or at least xenophobic, parties have obtained in recent general elections in several European countries.

Table 4 NEW POPULIST PARTIES (with at least some xenophobic characteristics)

Austria	1999	FPÖ	26.9%
Belgium	1999	Vlaams Blok	10%
Denmark	1998	Two different parties	16.8%
Italy	1996	Northern Ligue	10.1%
Norway	1997	Party of Progress	15.3%
Switzerland	1999	UDC	23%

These results of the Eurobarometer Poll and of recent election results point to the fact that racism is a real problem in Europe. It is extremely difficult to know whether the seriousness of the problem has increased in recent years. As far as election results are concerned, there is an overall increase in support of nationalist parties, but with a large degree of variation between different countries. With regard to discrimination there are almost no serious overall data for European countries. When considering racist attacks, it is clear that these forms of violence do exist and that there appears to have been little change over the last ten years (See for example the study of the Commission Nationale Consultative des Droits de l'Homme of 1998 in France).

How does Europe Combat Racism?

In this part I will examine the specific measures that the European Union and its organs such as the Commission or the European Parliament have taken in order to combat racism. As already announced in the introduction, on this point we can find a relatively clear picture. There seems to be a definite will to combat racism in its different manifestations, and, as a precondition for doing this, the European Union has founded an independent organ with the task to register the various manifestations of racism in the member states of the European Union.

In the last twenty years there have been many clear declarations against racism and xenophobia by the European Parliament and the

Commission. In 1986, the European Parliament, the Commission and the Council adopted a common declaration against racism and xenophobia. In the European year against racism, 1997, the study on racism cited in the introduction was conducted by Eurobarometer. This study offered comparative data for all the member countries of the EU for the first time. More recently, the European Monitoring Centre on Racism and Xenophobia has been established. This Centre was officially opened in Vienna (on April 7, 2000).

It is extremely important to have reliable comparative data concerning manifestations of racism for all the member states. The quality of the data will depend on the independence and autonomy of the bodies collecting and publishing the data; the Eurobarometer and the Monitoring Centre fulfil these qualifications. The Monitoring Centre, with its headquarters in Vienna must enjoy maximum autonomy according to the Council Regulation which established this Centre (Council Regulation (EC) No 1035/97). The task of this Centre is defined in this regulation in Article 2:

> The prime objective of the Centre shall be to provide the Community and its member states with objective, reliable and comparable data at European level on the phenomena of racism, xenophobia and anti-Semitism in order to help them when they take measures or formulate courses of action within their respective spheres of competence.

In order to execute this task, the Centre will not only coordinate existing sources, but also initiate new surveys and forms of research.

In 1997, during the European year against racism, another important initiative consisted in introducing Article 13 of the Treaty of Amsterdam, which provides the Community with specific powers to take action to combat discrimination based on gender, racial or ethnic origin, religion or belief, disability, age and sexual orientation.

The introduction of Article 13 has been justified in the following way. The European Union is founded on the principles of liberty, democracy, respect for human rights and fundamental freedoms and the rule of law, principles which are common to the member states. The right to equality before the law and the protection of all persons against discrimination constitutes a fundamental right and is essential to the proper functioning of democratic societies.

Article 13 expressed a clear will, but did not offer an actionable instrument for citizens of the EU to, for example, undertake legal action when being discriminated against. However, Article 13 has been taken up by the Community, and two directives have been elaborated by the Commission, discussed by the European Parliament and submitted to the Council for a decision. The first directive, concerning the right of equal treatment of persons whatever their race or ethnic origin will have consequences in the fields of work, schooling, social protection and social services. This directive is limited to forms of discrimination of persons because of their racial or ethnic origin. The second directive will be limited to the labour market, and will not only concern forms of discrimination based on race or ethnic origin, but also forms of discrimination on the grounds of gender, religion or belief, disability, age and sexual orientation. A decision on the first directive is expected in June 2000; in December 2000, a decision can be expected on the second directive.

These two directives will provide legal instruments which have to be adopted and applied in all the member states of the EU, with the intention of offering a minimum guarantee of protection against discrimination in all the member states. As the discussion about the precise formulation of these directives is not yet finished and also because there is not yet any final decision taken I will not discuss the exact content of these directives here. Instead I will limit myself to pointing out some definite limitations of these directives. For example, questions of nationality fall outside the scope of these directives, because nationality is not mentioned in Article 13.

The fact that such directives are being elaborated and discussed by the various instances of the Community shows that there is not only a general will to combat racism, but that there are also very concrete steps being taken in the fight against racism. These directives will have to be put into practice within two years by the member states, and will provide possibilities to combat racial forms of discrimination by legal means in all of the member states.

As a last point, I would like to mention the fact that the Community and its member states can also decide on specific measures concerning the fight against racism and xenophobia. For example, in the case of Austria, two such measures have been undertaken recently. At the beginning of 2000, a coalition government was formed in Austria by the Christian Democrats and the FPÖ. The FPÖ, with 26.7 percent of the vote in the general election of the autumn of 1999, is a party with clear xenophobic (and also racist according to many observers) characteristics. In order to express disapproval of such a government, the other 14 member states of the EU have reduced their diplomatic relations with Austria to a minimum. Furthermore, the European Commission has declared that it will follow what is going to happen in Austria under this coalition government with care, paying particular attention to possible instances of racial discrimination. Indeed, the European Commission has a responsibility to check whether the basic principles of the Treaty of the Union are applied and followed in the member states, and, in cases where these principles are not applied, the Commission can take action against a member state, and can ultimately exclude it. These specific measures directed against Austria, and in particular against the participation of the FPÖ in the government, show that there is a definite sensibility in Europe concerning racism and also a determination to act against manifestations of racism.

In summary we can see that Europe is very sensitive about racism, anti-Semitism and xenophobia. The European Community has put into place autonomous centres of registration of manifestations of racism, and shows a determined disposition to act against racism in specific areas.

Conditions Stimulating Racism

Before I can examine the question of whether Europe stimulates racism in some way, it is necessary to undertake a little excursion in the field of social theory of racism. It is one thing to agree to characterise an action as racist, such as a specific form of discrimination, and to let this be known and to combat it. It is certainly not always easy at all to reach an agreement about the racist character of the discrimination and to act on it, but as we have seen, Europe has reached such an agreement. It is another thing altogether, however, to understand the conditions which stimulate racism, and to act on the basis of such an understanding in order to influence the conditions in a way which might prevent manifestations of racism.

In the introduction, a short general definition of racism was suggested which covers 'old' and 'new' forms of racism. This definition is equivalent to the concept of racism which is used in international law and which forms the basis of the directives elaborated in Article 13 of the Treaty of Amsterdam. In short, there is a large consensus concerning the definition of racism.

Racism in its various 'old' and 'new' forms is nothing new. It is a very general strategy of domination and control. One can find manifestations of racism in almost all cultures and in all periods of social history. In other words, racism is not a mysterious phenomenon, but the question remains when, why and by what actors it is used as a strategy of domination, and what kind of conditions can stimulate this use.

The problem here is to understand which factors (economic, social, psychological, etc.) have a direct influence on the actual occurrence of racism. Let us consider a fictional example in order to clarify this problem. Let us suppose, for the sake of argument, that the following general law is verified: if the percentage of unemployment increases by 5 percent, manifestations of racism increase by 2 percent. In this case we would have knowledge of a specific factor which directly influences manifestations of racism, and the questions will be what can be done about this factor, or if anything can or should be done about it. Unfortunately there are no such general laws about direct relationships between social, economic or whatever factors and manifestations of racism.

When examining the literature on racism a much more complicated reality emerges. The following discussion is based on the work of Balibar 1991; Cole 1997; Miles 1989; Taguieff 1988, 1993 and Wieviorka 1998.

We may distinguish three families of conditions for manifestations of racism. Firstly, it is possible to indicate a number of socio-psychological, economic and political factors, which can stimulate racism, and the following three factors can be found in the work of many authors:

1. Rapid transformations of the social fabric which profoundly disturb the existing social cohesion.
2. A growing division of society between 'haves' and 'have-nots'; employed and unemployed; rich and poor.
3. A clear tendency of the political authority (in general considered at the level of the nation state) to fail to promote a just and equal society.

It should be noted that these three kinds of factors are not really independent of each other. For example, if the political authority loses the capacity to promote a just society it seems quite probable that social cohesion will decrease. If the relationships between these three factors are problematic, one thing is at least evident: they put the accent on different aspects of living conditions in society, the one centres more on political aspects, the other more on economic aspects. Wieviorka (1998) has attempted to specify the conditions of present day Europe in the following way.

1. There is a general difficulty of articulation between a concept of nation or of a supranational entity on the one hand and a project of modernity on the other hand, with the concomitant rise of nationalist or regional or other forms of identity.
2. In Europe, we can find what has been called the end of 'industrial society', described as a social-economic fracture, generally visible in social space.
3. In particular, Europe is experiencing a crisis of the social state; new forms of social intervention by the state no longer succeed in imposing universal principles of equality.

It should be made clear that each of these points is contested, and that each point can be interpreted in many different ways. It is also quite easy to find counterexamples in present day Europe. For example, in Belgium (and especially in the Flemish part of it) and in Austria, where the percentage of citizens declaring themselves as racist is high and where many vote for xenophobic and racist parties, there is almost no unemployment and the general economic conditions seem to be quite good. As the various authors are well aware of these difficulties, they are rather careful, and avoid adopting a straightforward determinist view. In other words, the various authors do not pretend that these factors offer a general causal explanation of the rise of racism.

A second family of conditions is of a very different order. This second family is concerned with the specific local, regional or national context and with the actors that manifest themselves in this context. The theoretical and empirical work realised around this family of conditions examines how the general factors enumerated in the first family appear within the specific context under examination. In these studies, the precise meaning of the various factors for the different actors involved will be analysed, with the aim of understanding why at any particular period some of the actors use racism in their struggle to influence the ongoing process and in order to acquire a more dominant position.

Two specific case studies, by Cole (1997) and Tribalat (1999) can serve as illustrations. Jeffrey Cole has conducted an extensive ethnographic study in a poor quarter of Palermo in Sicily in an attempt to understand the new forms of racism directed against African migrants in Sicily. In this study, the central focus was on the Sicilian underclass of the quarter, who live in very poor conditions and have a very precarious position in the labour market. Many of the group studied have experienced a personal history of migration, either to other European countries or to the north of Italy. Even in their precarious situation, these Italians will not consider taking on certain jobs which they perceive as low-status, for example, cleaning jobs. This kind of work is left to the African immigrants. Given their own history of migration, the Italians are rather tolerant towards the African immigrants, but when getting to know them better, Cole could detect some convictions which can be mobilised in a racist way. The Italians believe that they have contributed to a civilising task in their migration history by their work in Sicily and elsewhere, but they consider the African migrants to be unable to realise any civilising effect because of their nature. So, even if they are, in general, quite tolerant, they can be mobilised, for example, in actions protesting against legal protections offered to the African migrants, on the grounds that the situation of the Italians should be improved before concessions are made to the African migrants. In other words, the beliefs and convictions of the Italians constitute the basis manifestations of racism in which the Italians are opposed to the African migrants by actors attempting to profit from such a mobilisation.

Quite different is a study by Michèle Tribalat (1999), who has examined in detail the situation of Dreux, a small town where the 'Front National' has won the local elections, and formed the city government. In this study, she examines the history of the town, where, in the 1960s, North-African migrants had been invited in great numbers to work in the local industry. A large part of the industrial activity was closed down by the end of the 1970s, and many French professional workers left the town. The North-African migrants, who formed a majority in two quarters, remained in Dreux. This history, which I simplify here enormously, has produced an explosive situation which is real, but which has been exploited by the Front National in a specific way, exploiting forms of racist discriminations. The policy of this city government does not offer any perspective to transform the situation in a way which eliminates the evident divisions between local French inhabitants and North-African migrants.

These two examples seek to illustrate this second family of conditions concerning the emergence of racism. In these approaches, attention is given to the local actors, such as, for example, political parties, which use and transform the meaning of real social and economic problems in racist ways in order to gain powerful positions. As such, this second family offers a necessary complement to the studies belonging to the first family, because particular attention is given to the specific and situated actors and their use of the meaning of the interplay of the various social and economic factors.

Finally, there is a third family of conditions which can influence racist manifestations. According to the definition offered in the introduction, racism presupposes that a social actor (be it a person or a group) can identify members of another group, with characteristics which are attributed to the group because of their biology or ethnicity. In short, it is necessary that there exist categories which are well known and a practical knowledge to apply these categories in order to classify people. Racism presupposes that social and personal identities are constructed and used, and that this use appears as natural and justified.

The creation and transformation of social categorisations is realised by social actors. Therefore, this point belongs in fact to the second family of conditions discussed above. However, as this aspect is very important, and because it is increasingly studied in its own right in the name of identity politics or ethnic identity, I have chosen to present it in this third family of conditions.

The question is, who has the power to impose a general vision of the social world with specific divisions between groups, which defines the identity of the groups and informs a consensus concerning the meaning of this identity, a meaning which situates each group in a more or less powerful position.

During the recent history of the constitution of Europe, several new categorisations have been created. One example should be sufficient to illustrate this point. In 1960, Italian and Spanish workers in Germany or other Northern European countries were called 'guest workers', but in the 1990s, these workers, supposing they settled themselves in the guest country, were transformed into European co-citizens. In the following section, an example of a new categorisation which is indeed very problematic will be examined in more detail.

In conclusion, I would like to point out that recent research on racism has more and more integrated these three families of conditions which can stimulate manifestations of racism, and that there are good reasons, which I have offered, why such an integration is necessary.

How does Europe Stimulate Racism?

Does Europe in its actual functioning stimulate racism, in either a direct or indirect way? From the preceding discussion we have learned that any serious answer to this question should take into account the three families of conditions: general factors, context and actors and new categorisations.

It seems clear that, Europe does indeed, both directly and indirectly, stimulate racist manifestations, and in two interconnected ways. Firstly, Europe has introduced a new categorisation, the 'third-country residents' as a by-product of the introduction of a European form of identity and citizenship. This type of categorisation, both legal and social, entails direct effects of discrimination, and therefore stimulates racism. Secondly, Europe has in recent years transformed immigrants – or more precisely certain categories of immigrants – into a problematic category, which must be controlled and regulated in a very strict way because of all the difficulties which this category of people are perceived to cause in the various European countries. The elaboration of such a category of potentially dangerous and 'undesirable' people promotes, at least indirectly, racism.

European Identity and 'Third Country Residents'

During the last three decades, supporters of European integration defended the promotion of a European consciousness and the creation of a European identity as a crucial policy goal. When, in the early 1990s, the Single Market had actually come into effect, the promotion of European identity regained momentum. In order to encourage and foster a European identity several strategies have been used. Efforts have been made to discursively construct a common culturally defined European identity in a similar way to that in which national identities have been constructed. This goal was pursued through the use of historical myths referring to a common Christian heritage, to a common political and legal history going back to the Roman period and to the tradition of humanism. Moreover, ideologies (Europe as a peaceful and democratic project with modernising and civilising aspirations), the performance of secular rituals (European elections) and the use of a common Euro-symbolism (flag, anthem, format of passport, etc.) were used in promoting a common cultural identity. In addition, a broad scheme of cooperation programs in different European states was introduced at the levels of education, research and arts. One can summarise these efforts by stating that Europe appears as both the source and bearer of what is generally called 'western culture'.

Moreover, in the Treaty of Maastricht and in the Treaty of Amsterdam a new kind of supranational legal status has been introduced, the so-called European citizenship. Citizens the member states of the EU have acquired the right of free movement in the different countries of the EU along with several other rights, see Jacobs & Maier (1998) for a detailed analysis of the new European identity and citizenship. Legal residents in one of the member states coming originally from outside the EU are called 'third-country residents', and in many respects they have much more limited rights than European citizens, for example concerning free movement or settlement in other European countries; see Staples (1999) for details.

In short, the traditional differentiation between nationals and non-nationals has been shifting in the direction of new divisions between nationals, European co-citizens and foreigners, with an important distinction between foreigners coming originally from a country with a western culture on the one hand, and 'real' foreigners on the other hand. Legally, there are only three categories: nationals, European co-citizens and 'third-country residents', but this categorisation is elaborated further by using the dimension of 'western culture' as a further subdivision. According to Fuchs, Gerhard & Roller (1995), in countries such as Belgium, Denmark, France, Germany, Britain and the Netherlands the 'real' foreigner is most frequently thought of as being Turkish, Arab, Asian or African, although in reality most non-nationals are of European nationality. In addition, these non-European foreigners tend to be disliked more than European foreigners. Even if the identification with the European project remains problematic for many European citizens, the boundaries between 'them' and 'us' are more and more drawn between natives and immigrants from other European countries on the one hand, and immigrants from outside Europe – especially from 'non-white-countries' or 'non-western countries' – on the other hand.

This differentiation between groups of non-nationals is not merely a populist phenomenon or a purely accidental consequence of the official policy efforts to create a European identity and citizenship. The realisation of a European identity and citizenship was stimulated primarily by the aim of inclusion of European nationals in a common economic, cultural and political project. However, if in practice this inclusion entails the internal exclusion of foreign residents of non-European origin, then it is evident that such a project has discriminatory effects. Indeed, the introduction of the status of 'third-country-resident' as a product of the creation of a European citizenship has clear racist qualities when combined with the qualification of 'non-western culture' as a by-product of the strengthening of European identity characterised by western culture. That this combination has become to an important extent a socio-psychological and political reality in European countries can be seen in the results of the Eurobarometer Opinion Poll of 1997 on racism and xenophobia.

The Construction of Immigrants as a Problematic Category

During the last twenty years, Europe as an entity and as a set of nation states has transformed the status of immigrants, and particularly immigrants from (North-)African and Asian countries through a multitude of very complex legal, practical and discursive procedures.

The complexity of this transformation can only be understood in relation to the always contested nature of the construction and constitution of Europe. There have been, and there still are, quite different conceptions and projections of (a future) Europe, and the ongoing process of unification has to find compromises between these different conceptions.

In a very simplified way, one can distinguish between three different projections for Europe. The first one aims to 'restore' Europe as a world power. This projection favours Europe conceived as a single market and as a financial pool. Europe as a political and military entity is defined in this case as a functional accessory to an efficient economic world power able to compete with the United States and Japan for world markets and for developing important sectors of innovative technology. This would mean that Europe should once more become an important empire, not in the traditional sense, but as an actor defending and fighting for its spheres of influence in the new world order.

In partial opposition to this first projection, there is a competing projection for the future of Europe, also quite in evidence in the ongoing debate concerning the further construction of the European Union. This second projection stresses the social character of a future Europe. In this perspective, an important place is given to human rights and democracy, to combating racism and social inequality in Europe and, beyond that, throughout the world. The various formulations of this perspective integrate amore or less economic perspective, but never in the sense of conceiving Europe as an unscrupulous supranational actor engaged in ruthless competition with other economic powers. A stronger political unity of Europe is seen as a condition for the realisation of such a project.

There is, however, a third projection of the future of Europe, less ambitious and clearly in opposition to both aforementioned projections. This third projection sets out to defend the traditional system of nation states and would even prefer to strengthen them in the Europe of the twenty first century. This projection, defending to some extent the status quo, can be found in the programs of the new right-wing parties with a definite racist, xenophobic and nationalist character. However, there are also elements of the traditional left and right in favour of a status quo of a Europe of nation states. That this third perspective is quite important at present can be concluded from the percentage of votes the right has garnered, as cited in the introduction.

As Europe is not a nation state, decision-makers have to take into account all the various actors (such as political parties and associations with their own convictions and discourses). As only the actors putting forward the second perspective are resolutely antiracist, it is easy to understand the difficulties Europe has to confront with respect to racism.

The social, economic and political situation can be summarised in a schematic way. Europe, as a centre of economic development, had invited (particularly in the 1960s) many 'guest workers', not only from Southern European countries, but also from North-Africa and from Turkey and some other countries, for work in classic production sites. However, in the last twenty years, the modernisation of production – sometimes described as the passage to a postindustrial society – has, to a large extent, made this work force redundant. It was naively assumed that these workers would return to their countries of origin once the work ran out. As a consequence, no effort was undertaken, either by the former employers or by the political authorities, to undertake a serious effort to school and requalify these workers once they lost their jobs. Therefore, these workers had – and in many cases, still have – a clear disadvantage compared with the long-term resident population in terms of social and cultural capital: useful contacts, schooling, language and communication facilities, professional qualifications (See Wilson 1999, for a similar analysis with regard to the United States). Contrary to the naive expectations, a great number of these guest workers have settled permanently in their new European host countries. As all the studies on migration have shown, once there is a settlement of an ethnic, or religious or national group in some new country, it will always attract others members of that group, for a multiplicity of reasons.

Europe, as an economic centre, has been quite successful in the last few decades, and the growing inequalities concerning work, wealth and safety in the world contribute to making Europe an attractive place for many people trying to find safer living conditions and real social and economic opportunities. In other words, there is a real problem for Europe, which is manifest by the migration pressure in the form refugees or in the form of newcomers joining the already settled immigrant population. These populations – newcomers and former guest workers – are, in general, less well adapted to the demands of the labour market, because of the lack of social and cultural capital at their disposal. Therefore, these populations are increasingly perceived as a problematic group.

Three interlocking processes, which have a specifically European dimension, have contributed to stimulate racist forms of belief and behaviour: the first is quite straightforward; the existing nationalist and xenophobic parties have exploited, in a more or less successful way, the real problems European countries are confronted with. These parties and their spokespersons have introduced a further step which has a typically racist character in explaining why these migrant populations constitute a problem group. These groups are portrayed as problematic not because of the careless negligence with which they have been treated by former employers or by the state, but because of their origin, in other words their culture, which is depicted as 'non-western'. Their religion or their ethnic origin explains why they do not fit into the European social fabric. This discourse has enjoyed a large popular success, and has yet to be forcefully countered by democratic parties.

The second process, closely related to the first, which can be observed in all the European countries, results from the ambiguous reactions of the traditional democratic parties. These parties, in order to control and to regulate the perceived problematic character of the migrant population have continuously imposed more restrictions on the access of migrants. In doing so, these parties recognised, sometimes quite explicitly, the problematic character of these populations.

The third process is a direct result of the unification of Europe. Europe is attracting newcomers from unsafe and poor areas who present themselves as refugees, which is certainly quite often the case. As the EU has an inside and an outside, one can understand that any European country that is less strict than the others in recognising refugees, will attract a proportionally higher number of refugees. Therefore, the last decade we have witnessed a real competition between the different member states of the EU concerning the reduction of the number of refugees by adopting ever more strict criteria for the recognition of the status of refugees.

These three processes clearly interact with each other, and together they contribute to ethnicise and to racialise the real problems European countries confront with the old and new migrant populations. The effect at the moment is rather evident. In several European countries, new right wing populist parties with racist characteristics exploit this situation.

From this discussion it follows that Europe stimulates either directly (by introducing the discriminatory status of 'third-county resident') or indirectly (by transforming the migrant populations into problem groups which facilitates racist explanations) racism.

Concluding Remarks

One could say that Europe acts like the sorcerer's apprentice. Complex processes have been initiated, sometimes quite innocently and naively, sometimes with an intention of regulation, and these processes stimulate racism. At the moment, these processes seem to be completely out of control; it is as if they have acquired an autonomous dynamic. At the same time, Europe manifests a clear will to combat evident manifestations of racism. A very strange, and, at least at the moment, a rather tragic battle.

What can (and should) be done may be outlined quite simply in the light of these considerations. In the first place, the very problematic status of 'third-country residents' has to be changed by attributing rights comparable to European citizens to legal residents. For example, Staples (1999), among many others, has formulated clear propositions in this direction. However, to change this status is not a small affair, and will have profound consequences. It would mean that once a migrant has legal resident status in one of the member states, this status is also valid in, and recognised by, all of the other European states. In short, decisions in one member state concerning resident status will have consequences in every other member state, and this consequence is perceived as a serious threat of the sovereignty of the nation state.

The 'upgrading' of rights for third-country residents is not impossible, but it will require, at the very least, a European regulation that is adopted by all the member states.

Secondly, every effort should be undertaken to fight the discourse which has portrayed migrant populations as a problematic group without taking into account their history. Such a discourse only feeds and favours racist explanations. This discourse is rather important, if not hegemonic in the media, in policy statements and in popular thinking, and cannot be changed easily. Europe as a new entity and its member states must bear some responsibility, but they are by far not the only producers of such a discourse. In other words, Europe and its member states only contribute marginally in this production. However, if one recognises that such a discourse stimulates racism, every effort and measure should be undertaken to put a stop to the production and distribution of such discourses. Even with the limited resources and the marginal responsibility of Europe and the member states, a good start could be made at the level of European institutions, at the level of policy and at the level of academic research. For example, no funds should be attributed to a research proposal which takes for granted the problematic character of the migrant populations as an evident fact, without taking into account their social, cultural and economic history. Such a decision would constitute a modest but significant step, because in this way the problematic presupposition concerning the character of migrant populations, is at least critically examined.

Thirdly, and more generally, a conception of Europe as a democratic community of nations should be strengthened. All the forces (parties, associations, etc.) that are engaged in a struggle for a social and truly democratic Europe should be supported. This is, above all, a task for the European citizens and the democratic institutions.

Taking a long term perspective, any initiative which attempts to reduce the inequality in the world merits support, as it is evident that inequality and insecurity in other parts of the world will continue to lead to more or less forced migration. One can think of properly European initiatives against inequality and insecurity. However, given the fact that there are also other conceptions of Europe (the first one conceiving Europe as a new world power, and the third one which is nationalistic and even racist) one should avoid any idealism in this direction, because these initiatives can only be decided on the basis of a consensus between the different European parties and forces involved.

Bibliography

Balibar E., and Wallerstein I. 1991. *Race, Nation, Class. Ambiguous identities*. London: Verso.
Barker M. 1981. *The new racism*. London: Junction Books.
Cole, J. 1997. *The new racism in Europe. A Sicilian Ethnography*. Cambridge: Cambridge University Press.
Commission Nationale Consultative des Droits de l'Homme. 1998. *La lutte contre le racisme et la Xénophobie. Exclusion et Droits de l'Homme*. Paris: La documentation française.
Council Regulation (EC) No 1035/97 of 2 June 1997 establishing a European Monitoring Centre on Racism and Xenophobia.
Commission of the European Communities. Proposal for a Council Directive implementing the principle of equal treatment between persons irrespective of racial or ethnic origin, 1999.
Commission of the European Communities. Draft Communication from the Commission, to the Council, the European Parliament, the Economic and Social Committee and the Committee of the Regions on certain Community measures to combat discrimination, 1999.
Favell A. 1999. 'To belong or not to belong: the postnational question'. In *The politics of belonging: migrants and minorities in contemporary Europe*. A.G., and A. Favell, eds. Aldershot: Ashgate, 209–227.
Fuchs D., Gerhards, J., and Roller E. 1995. 'Nationalism versus Eurocentrism? The Construction of Collective Identities in Western Europe'. In *Migration, Citizenship and Ethno-National Identities in the European Union*. M. Martiniello, ed. Aldershot: Avebury.
Jacobs D., and Maier R. 1998. 'European identity: construct, fact and fiction'. In *A united Europe. The Quest for a Multifaceted Identity*. M. Gastelaars, and A. de Ruijter, eds. Maastricht: Shaker Publishing, 13–34.
Miles R. 1989. *Racism*. London: Routledge.
Nationale identiteit in Nederland. Internationalisering en nationale identiteit. Raad voor Maatschappelijke Ontwikkeling, Advies 9 (1999) Den Haag: Sdu Uitgevers.
Racism and Xenophobia in Europe. Eurobarometer Opinion Poll no 47.1.
Rea A. 1998. *Le racisme européen ou la fabrication du sous-blanc*. In *Immigration et racisme en Europe*. A. Rea, ed. Bruxelles: Ed. Complexe, 167–201.
Staples H. 1999. *The legal status of third country nationals residents in the European Union*. The Hague: Kluwer International.
Taguieff P.-A. 1988. *La force du préjugé. Essai sur le racisme et ses doubles*. Paris: Ed. La Découverte.
———. 1993. Comment peut-on être antiraciste? *Esprit*, mars-avril, 36–48.
Tribalat M. 1999. *Dreux, voyage au coeur du malaise français*. Paris: Syros.
Wiener A. 1998. *European Citizenship Practice. Building institutions of a non-state*. Boulder: Westview Press.

Wieviorka M. 1998. 'Racisme, antiracisme et mutation sociale, l'expérience française'. In *Immigration et racisme en Europe*. Andrea Rea, ed. Bruxelles: Ed. Complexe, 23–44.

Wilson W. J. 1999. *The bridge over the racial divide. Rising inequality and coalition politics.* Berkeley: University of California Press.

Part Two

Different Contexts

REFUGEE AND ASYLUM POLICY INFLUENCED BY EUROPEANISATION

Gudrun Hentges

※

Immediately after the end of World War II, the Allies assumed that the fate of the future Europe primarily depended upon the solution of the refugee problem. In 1946, on the initiative of the United Nations, an international refugee organisation was founded that was meant to take on the fate of the refugees – the millions of 'displaced persons' (DPs) – furthermore, a commission was entrusted with the task of drawing up an agreement on the status of refugees – a treaty text that was to be signed in 1951 as the Geneva Convention on Refugees (GCR).[1]

The central controversy that crystallised, between the British and US American Allies on the one hand, and the Soviets on the other hand, turned on the question of which groups of people were to be considered refugees and so handled correspondingly: the victims of National Socialist rule alone, or also – according to the plea of the Anglo-Saxons – people from the socialist state system as well – 'political dissidents' in the eyes of the British and Americans, 'traitors' and 'collaborators' according to the USSR.

The result of these debates was finally a differentiated listing of the legitimate groups of people: 'Victims of National Socialism, political dissidents, German and Austrian Jews, orphans and finally all *who must fear persecution*'.[2] Excluded from the definition of refugees were North African Jews, Turks expelled from Bulgaria in 1950, two million Asian refugees and those DPs who could be repatriated within Europe. With the introduction of the concept of collaboration in 1946, the 'authentic' refugees were subsequently distinguished from the collaborators and war criminals.[3] The developments and debates of the first postwar years led finally to an international agreement – the Geneva Convention on Refugees. Notwithstanding the current arguments about whether the definition of refugees in the GCR does justice to the demands and developments or not, even 50 years after it came into force it has lost nothing of its relevance.

The Geneva Convention on Refugees

In the sense of the agreement on the legal status of refugees (Geneva Convention on Refugees of 28 July 1951) the expression 'refugee' is applied to a person:

> Who ... owing to well-founded fear of being persecuted for reasons of race, religion, nationality, membership of a particular social group or political opinion, is outside the country of his nationality and is unable or, owing to such fear, is unwilling to avail himself of the protection of that country; or who, not having a nationality and being outside the country of his former habitual residence as a result of such events, is unable or, owing to such fear, is unwilling to return to it ...[4]

In the Geneva Convention (1951) the concept of refugees was limited by time and territory. First, only those people counted as refugees, 'who as a result of events occurring before 1 January 1951', were located outside their country. Second, it was left to the states concluding the treaty to relate to those events which occurred before 1 January 1951 'in Europe' or rather 'in Europe *or elsewhere*'. Consequently, the signatory states had the possibility of undertaking a geographical restriction.[5]

In consideration of the fact that since the acceptance of the Geneva Convention 'new categories of refugees have arisen' that do not fall under the definition from 1951, in January 1967 the Protocol Relating to the Status of Refugees was adopted.[6] With this, the temporal and geographical restriction installed 16 years before became obsolete. Now there was an international agreement whose signatory states obligated themselves to guarantee protection to people who, because of their 'race, religion, nationality, membership of a particular social group or because of their political opinion'[7] have a justified fear of persecution.

'No contracting state', Article 33 of the Geneva Convention on Refugees reads, 'shall expel or return ('refouler') a refugee in any manner whatsoever to the frontiers of territories where his life or freedom would be threatened on account of his race, religion, nationality, membership of a particular social group or political opinion'.[8]

Independently of the concrete formulation of the national differentiated asylum and recognition procedure, with the signing of the GCR the states acknowledged the 'non-refoulement precept'.

The Process Of European Standardisation Of Asylum Law

T.R.E.V.I.

At the beginning of the process of European standardisation of the asylum law – euphemistically also called 'harmonisation' – was the Europeanisation of internal security and the increasingly intensified police cooperation.

'Terrorism, Radicalism, Extremism, Violence International' – this is the full name of the T.R.E.V.I. working group, consisting of representatives of the EC member states, which has existed since 1976. Consequently, long before the adoption of the Maastricht Treaty (1 November 1993), which provided the legal basis for cooperation in internal and judiciary policy, the first forms of international cooperation existed, which from the beginning – sealed off from a democratic public – lacked any democratic control, for example, through the European Parliament or the Commission.[9]

Pilot project Schengen

Although all of the member states of the EC took part in the police cooperation that took place within the framework of T.R.E.V.I. (which resulted in a corresponding lack of political unity), the Schengen[10] Group brought together only the Benelux states, France and the Federal Republic of Germany. The result of the meetings was the Schengen Convention, which was signed in 1985 by the Internal and Justice Ministers of the Schengen states. In this agreement, the Schengen states agreed to dismantle the checkpoints on the common borders – in large parts a practice that was already taking place anyway.

The other side of the coin of dismantling the border checkpoints on the common internal borders was the strengthened control of the common external borders – so-called compensatory measures. The Schengen Implementation Agreement (or Schengen II), which was signed on 19 June 1990 by the five Schengen states, dealt with a tightening and standardisation of asylum and foreigners' rights, with forms of police cooperation and the establishment of a data association (Schengen Information System, SIS).

In concrete terms the Schengen Implementation Agreement governed:

1. Crossing over internal and external borders (Title II, Chap. 1, 2).
2. Granting visas for people from third countries (Title II, Chap. 3).
3. The assumptions under which people from third countries can travel within the Schengen area (Title II, Chap. 4).
4. The deportation of people from third countries (Title II, Chap. 4, Art. 23).
5. Residence papers and writing out of refusal of entry (Title II, Chap. 5).
6. Sanctions against transport firms that transport people from third countries although they do not have the required documents at their disposal (Title II, Chap. 6).
7. Measures against organisations helping illegal aliens (Title II, Chap. 6, Art. 27).
8. Responsibility for handling people requesting asylum (Title II, Chap.7).
9. Prevention of parallel and follow-up applications in the area of the right of asylum (Chap. 7, Art. 30).
10. Cooperation in questions of internal security (Title III).
11. Setting up the Schengen Information System (Title IV).[11]

The Schengen process did *not* take place at EC level first; in the case of the Schengen Convention (1985) and the Schengen Implementation Agreement (1990) it was furthermore *not* a matter of EC law, but of international agreements. Nonetheless, the Schengen process is of the utmost significance for the Europeanisation of the right of asylum, because the essential elements of sealing off borders against refugees are already in the document of 1990, which went into effect five years later. In particular, the undertaking that refugees had to have a valid visa at their disposal in order to travel and submit an application for asylum, and, furthermore, that the Schengen states agreed to a uniform handling of the granting of visas, presents an often insurmountable barrier for refugees. Consequently, the visa policy functions for the potential admitting countries as a means of controlling the entry of refugees. Applicants for asylum have to overcome the first barrier – obtaining an entry visa – in their country of origin, in order to have any opportunity at all of fleeing from the persecuting state and so be able to formulate a demand for asylum.

From the middle of the 1990s, the process of successively accepting the so-called 'Schengen standards' through other member states began.

The Federal Republic of Germany, France and the Benelux states had created facts with the Schengen pilot project; now it was left up to the other EU states to join in with the agreements. The states on the other side of the Schengen area feared a massive increase in the number of applicants for asylum – and, in fact, as a reaction to the restrictive entry, visa and asylum policy of the Schengen states. To this extent, the process of signing moved forward rapidly.

In March 1999, the Schengen Implementation Agreement was in effect in Portugal, Spain, Italy, Greece and Austria in addition to the five initiating states. The Danish, Swedish and Finnish governments had also signed it. In agreement with the Treaty of Amsterdam, Great Britain and Ireland had the possibility of joining in on the international treaty, and Iceland and Norway are so-called associated states.

The Europeanisation of the right of asylum is therefore the result of international negotiation of those countries that call themselves 'the European core'. 'The European core' executive was the starting point for the standardisation of entry and visa regulations; these five countries jointly developed the international treaty that concedes no right to share in the decisions to the other member states, but only gives them the possibility of joining in the agreement. Beyond this, neither the European Parliament nor the national Parliaments, and certainly no human rights or refugee initiatives, participated in the process of working it out.

Not only are the lack of democratic control and participation to be criticised in the Schengen Implementation Agreement, but also the fact that Schengen made it increasingly difficult for refugees to cross the outer borders of the Schengen state system.

Dublin Convention[12]

At the same time as the signing of Schengen II in June 1990, all the EC member states (with the exception of Denmark) signed an agreement that sets the criteria with the help of which decisions can be taken as to which state is responsible for examining an application for asylum made in a member state. According to this, the state that granted the asylum applicant a residence permit which is still valid at the time the application is made or that issued him/her a valid (transit) visa, is responsible. If the applicant is in possession of several residence authorisations or several visas for various member states, then the state that issued the residence permit with the longest period of validity is responsible for examining the application for asylum, or the state that granted the visa that runs out last. If the asylum seeker crossed over the border of a member state illegally, then the country with which the migrant first had 'ground contact' is responsible for the examination of the application.

It had already begun to emerge at the beginning of the 1990s that the draft regulations would create a situation of competition between the EC states. States that handle the granting of resident permits or visas in the most liberal way will – this is in the logic of the Dublin

Convention – have to process the most applications for asylum. With Schengen II and Dublin an EC-wide contest for the most restrictive granting of residence permits, visas and transit visas was set in motion.

Schengen and the Concentric Circles

At the beginning of the 1990s, there was talk in the media of Austrian soldiers securing the green border to Hungary, and in Finland and Norway 'border soldiers became actors in foreign policy'.[13] These observations, to be read in the *Frankfurter Allgemeine Zeitung*, had no critical impetus whatsoever, rather it was considered natural that, after the fall of the Wall, the joint efforts of the EC should be directed at intercepting the new migrants from the East and sending them back. A *cordon sanitaire*, a new 'in-between Europe', had the task of intercepting the expected 'masses of refugees'. In the interests of stemming the immigration from Eastern Europe the EC had to promote and support such initiatives.[14]

The concept of concentric circles was built up further in the course of the 1990s: Agreements to take back refugees were concluded with more and more states, and cooperation between the Bundesgrenzschutz (BGS) (German border police) and the border police of the Eastern European states was further intensified.

Poland

The effect of Schengen was not restricted to only the western European states, but also covered the Eastern European states. On 29 March 1991 the Schengen states concluded a return agreement with Poland for people who stay in the Schengen area for more than three months without the required residence permit. With the signing of this agreement, which went into effect on 1 May 1991, Poland undertook to take in all the people who illegally entered the Schengen area through Polish territory. With this agreement, Poland performed the role of federal border police oriented toward the West.

In the following years, further treaties were concluded between Poland and the Federal Republic of Germany:

1. Treaty of good neighbourliness and friendly cooperation of 17.6.1991.
2. Exchange of notes on setting up a government committee for cooperation regionally and close to the border, also from 17.6.1991.
3. Agreement on cooperation in the fighting of organised crime of 6.11.1991, in effect since 14.8.1992.

4. Agreement on cooperation in respect of the effects of migration movements (Bilateral Return Agreement) of 7.5.1993, in effect since 1.6.1993.
5. International treaty of 5.4.1995 on cooperation of the police authorities and the border police authorities in the frontier areas.[15]

The bilateral Return Agreement of 7 May 1993 represented the first drastic turning-point after the year 1989 and the opening of the borders between East and West. With the signing of this agreement, Poland committed itself to take back 10,000 refugees who secretly crossed the German-Polish border. As a 'consideration in return' the Polish government received 120 million DM to be used specifically for the purpose of building up a system, from 1993 to 1996, for administering refugees, setting up deportation prisons and to seal off the West Polish border.[16]

As the accession of Poland to the EU is linked with the prerequisite of fulfilling the Schengen criteria, it is demanded on the part of the EU that Poland has to introduce an obligatory visa for the neighbouring states to the East – a problematic demand from the Polish point of view, because in this way the economically significant retail trade on the Polish western border would be brought to a standstill.

The year 1996 represented the second drastic turning point. In September 1996 the first major house searches took place in the Warsaw suburbs. Four hundred refugees, to whom it was alleged that they were on the way to western Europe, were taken to detention prison.

1. The legal basis was the passage taken up in the old law on foreigners in September 1995, according to which foreigners could be detained in custody for up to 90 days because of unauthorised residence.
2. The infrastructure prerequisite for the large-scale raids and arrests in 1996 was the setting up of detention prisons (there were 25 in February 1999) as well as the establishment of a so-called guarded camp, located 60km south of Warsaw in direct proximity to the airport.

According to information from the Polish Interior Ministry the building of further detention establishments is planned.

The new Polish law on foreigners, which went into effect in 1998, adopted, in large part, the standards of western European policy for sealing off borders: the concept of safe third countries and safe states of origin, the sanctions against transport firms, building up a central registry of foreigners and stricter entry regulations (required visa, centrally controlled proof of invitation) for Russians and Belorussian citizens.[17]

In principle, the Polish asylum procedure is oriented to the GCR, however, a massive temporal and geographical restriction causes the number of applicants to be reduced massively: asylum must be demanded directly at the border from the border police authorities. In exceptional cases – if it is possible to prove danger to life and limb – an application for asylum can be made within a period of 14 days after crossing the border. The Polish border police decides, though, whether a person may enter or not, and consequently it is at the discretion of the border police whether a person should have the chance to apply for asylum at all.

The new law pursues the objective of preventing transient migrants arrested in Poland from demanding asylum. After an arrest, applications for asylum do not have to be processed at all. Even in the Ukraine, although here the GCR has not yet been signed, legally, nothing stands in the way of deporting arrested transient migrants.

Refugees deported from Germany also have no right according to the current legal situation – strictly interpreted – to make an application for asylum. However, according to the statement of the vice-director of the department for migration and refugee affairs, Maciej Kuczynski, in such cases submission of an application is enabled.

The raids against migrants that began more intensely in 1996 reached a high point in 1998. Under the motto *Akcja Obcy* (Action Foreigners) police and border police carried out joint campaigns.

'We are carefully implementing the regulations of the law on foreigners. The goal of the campaign is to prove the credibility of our country before entry into the EU. After all, our eastern border will be the border of the European Union' – read the reasons of the press spokesman for the Polish border police, Miroslaw Szacillo (29.10.1998).

The victims of the so-called Action Foreigners, and the arrests and deportations connected with it, were, above all, Romanian Gypsies and Tamils from Sri Lanka. An arrest of 294 Romanian Gypsies, among them 126 children, on 28 October 1998 was reported in the Polish media. Journalists and camera teams accompanied the migrants to detention in a sport stadium, through the fingerprinting and photographing procedure and finally to the military airport, where a plane waited for takeoff. On the basis of the media presence and reporting, the massive use of police and the refugee policy à la Schengen met with vehement protest for the first time. Seventy-nine Polish intellectuals made their opinions known in an open letter.

'Before our eyes a total European model of deportation is being developed that answers needs for migration and reasons for flight with repressive measures' – this is the concluding assessment on the Polish refugee policy that is found in the information newsletter of the Deutsch-Polnischen-Gesellschaft Brandenburg (German-Polish Community of Brandenburg).

CSFR

Cooperation between German and Czech border authorities has turned out to be analogous to the intensification of the police cooperation between Germany and Poland. Germany and the CSFR signed a return agreement in October 1994 that went into effect in 1995. Both countries have undertaken to return migrants that have entered illegally to their own country. Just like Poland, the CSFR also received a financial consideration to be used for the purpose: the German government made 60 million DM available to the Czech government for building up the technical infrastructure at the state border, as compensation for the financial burden from repatriation of foreigners taken over from Germany, for the financing of a central system for recording data on foreigners, for training the members of the foreign and border police as well as for obtaining and exchanging information on the countries of origin of refugees. Furthermore, part of this money was earmarked for the organisation and financing of measures for the police to transport, transfer or return foreigners taken over from the Federal Republic of Germany to their countries of origin or homelands, and for constructing facilities for their accommodation.[18]

It was contractually agreed that the payments had to occur in three instalments, and they were linked to the condition that the Czech side had to report regularly on the development of border checks.

Owing to the return agreement with Germany and the build up of the border checks there was a massive increase in arrests in the Czech border region: in 1997, according to information from the BGS, 10,805 people were taken into custody on the Czech border, and in 1998, 19,203 people in all were taken into custody, primarily from Kosovo, Sri Lanka and Afghanistan. The CSFR has concluded return agreements with Austria, Slovakia, Poland, Romania, Bulgaria, Hungary and Canada, as well as with France and Slovenia.

Chains of deportations, according to the results of the research report of the Berlin research group Flucht und Migration (Flight and Migration), are possible, and indeed, very probable based on the international agreements.

In May 1999, the research group Flight and Migration visited the first official deportation prison in the CFSR, which was established in November 1998 in Balková, in the neighbourhood of the German border.[19] Only refugees and migrants who have been pushed back over the German-Czech border by BGS are placed here – regardless of whether they can prove their identity, and also of the reasons that they give for crossing the border. According to the old law on foreigners, refugees could be detained for 30 days; according to the new law that has been in effect since 1 January 2000, it is up to 180 days.

The refugees and migrants detained in Balková, according to the information of the research group Flight and Migration, are not informed that they can submit an application for asylum. In a more recent research report, it says that the FFM Team was able in 'Cerveny Ujezd to speak with several refugees who gave the information that they had made it clear both with the BGS and after being pushed back by the Czech authorities that they wanted asylum. In spite of that they were brought to Balkova usually with the claim of false facts, where they spent several weeks without further explanation. Only hunger strike campaigns of four or five days each led to the transfer to Cerveny Ujezd'.[20]

Those who are successful 'nonetheless' in making an application for asylum are moved to a 'quarantine station' that is located next to the Cerveny Ujezd refugee camp. Only after around three weeks are they then transferred to a refugee camp.[21]

Reporting on the Porous Borders

In connection with the enlargement of Europe to the east there are reflections above all on how it can be guaranteed in the future that the outer border of the EU that has been moved to the east can be sealed off. 'The new outer borders of the European Union should not become a gateway for illegal immigration and drugs': under this headline in October 2000, the FAZ reported about the eastward enlargement of the EU.[22] Within the European Commission, reflections have been initiated on a 'European border police' that is meant to safeguard the 3,000km long future EU external border.[23] They are thinking about whether, from the 40,000 employees of the BGS who will no longer be needed on the German border, around 10,000 officials can be made available for a 'Schengen border troop'.[24] The German border police already 'help', 'colleagues in the Ukraine, and make sure that the border crossings are equipped with computers'.[25]

Here, for example, the Polish government is asked: 'How it plans better to protect the porous border to Belorus and to the Ukraine', Slovakia is criticised for the fact that it obviously, 'because of the still insufficient training and technical equipment ... still cannot guarantee any effective border control'.[26]

On the basis of such reports it becomes clear who needs to be helped according to the FAZ editors: the border protection officials of the East European states and not, for instance, the refugees that are fleeing persecution or civil wars and seeking protection.

The Treaty of Amsterdam

In the Maastricht Treaty (1993) three pillars of the EU were distinguished:

1. European Communities (Decision level: Community policy).
2. Common Foreign and Security Policy (Decision level: Cooperation between governments).
3. Cooperation in internal and legal policy (Decision level: Cooperation between governments).

The Treaty of Amsterdam (1997) stipulates successive structural changes. According to this treaty, the new Title IV (visas, asylum, immigration, etc.) will be set up on a common basis in the future and transferred in steps from the third (intergovernmental) pillar to the first pillar (communitarisation). Within five years of the Treaty of Amsterdam (that is 2002) the right of asylum, visa policy and controls on the external borders are meant to be communitarised. Consequently the so-called Schengen 'acquis' will be integrated into the EU framework.[27]

The step-by-step 'transfer' of the third pillar into the first, however, does not have as a consequence a change in the exclusive competence of the European Council (that is, the Interior and Justice Ministers of the EU states) in questions of migration and refugee policy. In spite of the 'transfer' of internal and justice policy to the first pillar, the European Council will still remain the deciding committee that takes decisions about migration and refugee policy.

In the Treaty of Amsterdam it is stipulated that in the course of the next five years a space of freedom, security and law is meant to be established. The measures required for this will be decided exclusively by the European Council. Under this category fall questions of free movement within the interior, crossing of external borders, standardised granting of visas, and dealings with illegal(ised) migrants.[28]

A communitarisation of asylum and immigrant policies is connected with the assumption that all the governments of the EU states will reach an agreement, 'to grant a right of initiative for this area of policy, to transfer the exclusive competence for decision making to the European Parliament and to allocate authority for control to the European Court of Justice'.[29] Based on the principle of unanimity the full communitarisation of this policy area is considered unlikely.

It can also be assumed that in the future as well – as was already the case in the past – the governments of the EU states, and especially the Interior and Justice Ministers, will determine European asylum and refugee policy to a considerable extent. The central actors of European asylum and refugee policy are consequently neither the Commission nor the European Parliament, but rather the Interior and Justice Ministers of the EU member states. With the example of Schengen (I, II) it has been demonstrated that the initiative of five 'core states' leads around a decade later to an EU-wide adoption of the international treaty. Out of national efforts international agreements arose, and from these in turn, EU law.

The question that is posed here is that regarding the relationship between national, international and EU-wide agreements. Or, to formulate it in a different way: in what way did the governments or the Interior Ministers of the EU states use (and how are they continuing to use) the process of European integration in order to implement projects at national level, that, without reference to European constraints and allegedly required adaptation measures, could not have been implemented at European level?

'Harmonisation of Asylum law' and Massive Restriction of the Fundamental Right of Asylum (Article 16, German Constitution) in Germany

The process of standardisation of the right of asylum at European level was accompanied in the Federal Republic of Germany by a process of restriction of the right of asylum at national level. By the beginning of the 1990s, it was already being demanded by leading politicians that the German right of asylum had to be restricted in order to correspond to European standards in the future.

In 1993, the modification of Article 16 was adopted in the German Bundestag. With the votes of the governing conservative-liberal federal government and the social-democratic party in the Bundestag, the right of asylum anchored in the constitution was massively restricted or distorted to the point of being unrecognisable.[30]

Since 1 July 1993 the new right of asylum has been in effect. In the first paragraph it says:

1. 'Persons persecuted on political grounds enjoy the right of asylum.' In the following paragraphs, however, it becomes clear that the generosity announced in the beginning is taken back again in the following passages, because here the exclusion criteria are found.
2. 'The right of Paragraph (1) cannot be claimed by one who enters from a European Communities country or from another country where the application of the Convention on the Legal Status of Refugees and the Convention to Protect Human Rights and Civil Liberties is ensured.'[31]
3. 'By statute requiring the consent of the Senate, states can be determined in which ... it seems to be guaranteed that neither persecution on political grounds nor inhuman or derogatory punishment and treatment takes place. A foreigner from such a state is presumed not to be persecuted.'[32]

Consequently, Article 16 (2) excludes all those refugees who have reached Germany by the land route and accordingly had 'ground contact' with a safe third country before the intended application for asylum. All the EU states, the Scandinavian countries, Austria, Switzerland, Poland and the CSFR are considered safe third countries. Article 16 (3) stipulates that those refugees that come from so-called nonpersecuting states should go through a very abbreviated procedure. Among those considered nonpersecuting countries or safe countries of origin at this time are Bulgaria, Ghana, Poland, Romania, Senegal, Slovakia, the Czech Republic and Hungary.[33]

The 'asylum compromise' agreed in 1993 has as a consequence that it has become impossible to reach the Federal Republic of Germany by land and apply for asylum. Since the territory of the Federal Republic of Germany is surrounded by safe third countries, refugees are immediately deported to the neighbouring states. To the extent that these countries have made readmission agreements with other states, chain deportations start up or a domino effect begins.

The development of numbers of applicants for asylum after 1993 documents that the new asylum law represents a hurdle for refugees:

Table 5 Application for asylum in the FRG (1991 to 1998)[34]

Year	Total
1991	256,112
1992	438,191
1993	322,599
1994	127,210
1995	127,937
1996	116,367
1997	104,353
1998	98,644

Statistics from the German federal border police are also revealing in this connection: 'Within the year of 1996 about 18,500 Polish citizens were rejected at the German border, 14,500 citizens from the federal republic of Yugoslavia, 6,500 citizens from Turkey, more than 8,000 citizens from the Czech Republic, 2,700 citizens from Bosnia, 2,500 from Macedonia, 2,702 from Slovakia'.

Table 6 Federal Republic of Germany, Rejection at the borders, by nationality (1995 to 1996)[35]

State	1995	1996
Poland	19,546	18,422
Federal Republic of Yugoslavia	18,520	14,412
Turkey	13,121	6,452
Czech Republic	9,795	8,119
Switzerland	8,993	5,292
Denmark	4,971	5,734
Bosnia	4,715	2,737
Austria	4,320	4,352
Macedonia	3,382	2,510
Romania	3,241	–
Slovakia	–	2,702

Section 4 proclaims that the effectuation of measures to end a stay (concerning section 3, or if the claim to stay is considered as obviously unfounded) 'will only be suspended by court order if serious doubts arise concerning the legality of the measure'.

In other words, measures to end a stay will hardly be stopped; there is almost no chance for a refugee to start legal proceedings against deportation.

What use is the definition in the Geneva Convention on Refugees of the 'refugee' as any person who, 'because of their race, religion, nationality, membership of a particular social group or because of their political opinion' is exposed to persecution, if based on hermetically sealed borders, restrictive visa regulations, the concept of the so-called 'safe third state' and so-called 'nonpersecuting states'? It is now hardly possible to reach the territories of those states (or not immediately be turned back again) that have signed the GCR and therefore declared themselves in principle ready to offer protection to refugees.

What use is the non-refoulement-precept (Article 33), that is, the prohibition on deportation into those regions in which the refugee is faced with a threat to life and limb, if those who need protection from persecution are prevented from reaching potential reception states?

The Vienna Strategy Paper, the EU Special Summit in Tampere and German Asylum Policy

In the first half of 1999, the Federal Republic of Germany held the EU Presidency. Otto Schily, the Interior Minister of the red-green federal

German government, presented the 'Guidelines for a European Migration and Asylum Strategy', which was oriented toward the Vienna strategy paper presented a year before by the Austrian government.[36]

In this, the then federal Interior Minister, Karl Schlögl (Austrian Socialist Party) – with the prognosis that western Europe would be subject to immigration of 'a quantitative dimension that had not occurred before'[37] as a starting point – supported the position that 'interethnic persecution and expulsion by nongovernmental power organisations'[38] were the central motivation for flight today. Based on these developments, the GCR had partially lost its applicability, he claimed. In the Vienna strategy paper the conclusion is drawn from this that the GCR should be 'extended, modified or replaced'.[39] For the victims of nongovernmental or interethnic persecution, according to the strategy paper, a 'politically oriented concept of protection' should be developed, which would no longer be based on a subjective individual right, but which would be understood as a political offer from the receiving country.[40]

Following the ideas of the Vienna Interior Ministry, in the middle of 1999 Otto Schily proposed in the future (1) to link the domestic affairs measures of the EU with the common foreign, foreign trade and investment, social and development policy, (2) to regionalise the admission of refugees, that is, to accommodate refugees in their homeland and neighbouring regions outside the EU, as well as (3) to make available a 'complementary protection mechanism', whereby the EU states would have to reach agreement on a binding total quota of refugees to be taken in.[41]

In interviews, the Interior Minister of the red-green government insisted that the subjectively recoverable right of asylum established in the constitution was not compatible with 'European standards', and he argued in favour of replacing the basic right to asylum with an institutional guarantee, that is, to change it to a simple law.[42] (In November 1998, a few weeks after assuming office, Interior Minister Schily had already caused a sensation by noting that 'The maximum tolerance level of the Republic has been exceeded by immigrants'.)[43]

With his demand that the right of asylum anchored in the constitution be repealed, Schily dominated the domestic policy debate in October/November 1999. The decisive argument for repealing Article 16 of the German constitution was the claim that as a result of the EU-wide standardisation of asylum law, the German standard would never be accepted. This line of argument is an unfortunate reminder of the logic of the conservative-liberal government which brought forward the argument in preparation for the drastic change in the basic right of asylum at the end of the 1980s and the beginning of the 1990s, that federal German law had to be oriented to the European 'level'. In other words – with a reference to the supposed generosity of the German federal government's right of asylum – the talk is of emptying the legal standard of content. If one considers, however, that with the beginning of the Schengen process, that is as from the beginning of the 1980s, the German federal government codetermined and codesigned the European asylum policy, then its strategy becomes clear: in international agreements the right of asylum was restricted in its intrinsic content, in domestic policy the international treaties were treated as definite facts and a process of adaptation to the European level was demanded – in the sense of an adaptation to the lowest level.

Green Card, Immigration and Right of Asylum – the Linking of Different Debates

Since the Federal Republic of Germany came into existence, millions of people have immigrated to the federal area: around 15 million refugees, expellees, German natives moving west (from the Soviet-occupied zone and the German Democratic Republic) and resettled people (from East Europe) have settled in the federal German area; in 1993, the number of people living in the federal German area without a German passport amounted to around 6.8 million.[44] Even the conservative-liberal federal government of 1992 granted – with about 450,000 applicants for asylum yearly – a temporary permit to work and live in Germany to 90,000 East European workers with work contracts.[45] Even so, in the past the governments have steadfastly refused to recognise the Federal Republic of Germany as an immigration country. Germany remained the 'denied immigration country', which has had the consequence for the population of foreign residents that immigrants are persistently denied the elementary rights of citizens.

Chancellor Gerhard Schröder (SPD) had hardly announced, at the CeBit computer trade show that takes place yearly in Hanover, the recruitment of 10,000 foreign IT experts and held out the prospect of a green-card decree that went into effect on 1 August 2000, then the debate on Germany's conception of itself as an immigration country was sparked off. The green-card regulation only provided the opportunity for such a debate; the deeper reasons are the complex and tangential questions of the development of the population, the lack of workers in specific sectors, and the interests of the German economy.

On the side of the CDU/CSU – namely from party chairman Friedrich Merz – the readiness for the admission that Germany is an immigration country and needs a corresponding law was promptly linked with the condition that the basic right of asylum also had to be put fundamentally into question. In the end, Merz gave his view to the magazine *Die Woche: his* generation was no longer ready to let itself be taken hostage because of the Nazi past.[46]

CDU member of the Bundestag Martin Hohmann answered the question regarding the 'German reason that we have this right of asylum', as follows: 'But how long do we want to take the German reasons and the history of the unfortunate twelve Nazi years burdening the German as a reason for going a separate way'.[47]

Daniel Cohn-Bendit, for the French Greens in the European Parliament, created an uproar in November 2000 when he gave reasons for abolishing Article 16a of the German constitution as follows: 'The positive German antifascist coming to terms with the past cannot become the guiding European culture. We need a European, humane, antitotalitarian asylum policy, and the German experience should be contributed to this'.[48]

The three lines of argument sketched above refer to the German past and make the demand that now a clean break must be made. Patterns of reasoning like this are of eminent significance when observed in a larger context, because it must be observed that in recent years – under the motto that one must come out of the shadow of the Nazi past – in different policy areas the 'German card' is played in favour of international agreements.

Demands For The Abolition Of The Basic Right Of Asylum

In the course of 2000, an intense debate developed regarding immigration. Parties, trade unions and churches outlined their own political position, the media picked up the 'hot iron' and social scientists made their opinion known. In the centre of the debate were the following aspects: (1) the demographic development of the German population, (2) the interests of the German economy in targeted recruitment of specialists as well as (3) the change in the law on asylum currently in effect.

In particular, the CDU/CSU linked the debate on immigration with the demand for a change in the right of asylum, and also, within the SPD, Bündnis 90 (Alliance 90)/the Greens and the PDS, such voices became loud.

CDU and CSU

'No society can cope with unlimited immigration, if it does not want to risk its internal stability and its identity', it says in the working principles of the immigration commission of the CDU (of 6.11.2000). This assumes that unregulated immigration takes place primarily through the basic right of asylum. A first step toward fighting 'unregulated immigration' is supposed to be the 'reform of asylum law'. Behind this euphemistic formulation is concealed what in plain language is a request directed at the immigration commission that the conversion of the basic right of asylum into an institutional guarantee may no longer be 'a political taboo'.

'Because Germany is not a traditional immigration country and is not meant to become an immigration country in the future'; hence the position of the CSU, that it is necessary to limit immigration. 'Make the immigration of specialists who are useful to us easier, reduce the number of economic refugees who exploit the social welfare benefits' – under this motto, Interior Minister Günther Beckstein made his Bundestag speech on the occasion of the Green Card Debate (of 13.4.2000). The Bundesanstalt für Arbeit (federal labour institute) would have to determine, in coordination with the economy, the need and the public interest regarding the temporary use of highly-qualified experts.

In his speech, Beckstein demands that the basic right of asylum be converted to an institutional guarantee, in order – and here his argument becomes perfidious – to be able to grant admission to all people who are really politically persecuted.

Like the other politicians of the CDU and SPD he puts forward the claim that, of the 100,000 refugees who come into the federal German region every year, only 3 percent are actually politically persecuted.

The majority of the debate within the parties over immigration to Germany is carried out under the sign of national interests. Whilst the CSU 'explicitly' raises the demand for abolition of the basic right of asylum, its sister party, the CDU, hints at such an option under the heading of 'taboo breaking'.

SPD

Interior Minister Schily (SPD) was not able to prevail over his party with his demand for an institutional guarantee; around a year later his advances were taken up by Chancellor Schröder (SPD): 'After ... the CSU at its party conference had demanded the repeal of the individual basic right of asylum, now Chancellor Gerhard Schröder (SPD) seems not averse to a tightening of the asylum procedure within the framework of the existing laws. Certainly he rejects the modification of the asylum rights contained in the German constitution, but speaks of Europeanisation', was to be read in the Kurier.[49]

'Europeanisation' seems to be 'the' magic word. In fact, an elementary fundamental right is being encroached upon and – as happened in

1993 – mutilated to the point of being unrecognisable; in the public debate, however, this action is declared an indispensable reform in the service of the European idea.

How does the National Right of Asylum relate to the European?

In the political debate on the right of asylum it is repeated almost like a prayer wheel: the right of asylum is being misused. As evidence for this, it is cited that only around 3 percent of all applicants for asylum are recognised. The representative responsible for dealing with foreigners, Marieluise Beck, argues that a distinction must be made between the so-called 'recognition quota' and the protection quota. To the argument that amongst the people requesting asylum it is for the most part a matter of 'economic refugees', she counters that in the last five and a half years more than 48.4 percent of all asylum seekers received protection against deportation.[50]

Furthermore, it is claimed over and over again that the German right of asylum is the most liberal in Europe by far. This claim cannot stand up to examination.[51] The federal German legislation demonstrates – in contrast to the other European states – the peculiar feature that, among other things, nonstate persecution is *not* considered relevant to asylum. As a consequence of this, the recognition quota of refugees from Sri Lanka in France turns out to be distinctly higher than that of Germany: in 1996 in France 31.9 percent of all refugees from Sri Lanka were recognised; in Germany, however, only 8.15 percent were recognised as having the right of asylum, and a further 2.87 percent received protection from deportation.[52]

In view of this federal German peculiarity, the UNHCR demanded in its recommendations to the Tampere Summit (October 1999) that, 'A future EU instrument aimed at harmonising the application of the refugee definition should acknowledge that asylum claims resulting from persecution by third parties come within the ambit of the 1951 Convention'.[53] The essential criterion for international protection is meant to be the risk of becoming a victim of serious violations of human rights – independently of whether the persecution comes from the state or not.[54]

In accordance with federal German legislation, gender-specific persecution and female-specific reasons for flight likewise – and here as well, the asylum procedures are more liberal in other states – do not give the right of asylum.

In addition, the invention of 'safe states of origin', which was determined by the federal German government without the agreement of the Bundesrat, goes far beyond the practice in the other EU states.[55]

Standardisation of the differing national rights of asylum – according to my summary – would have to be oriented first of all to the refugee definition in the Geneva Convention. With this as a starting-point, not only would those people who are victims of state persecution have to be recognised as refugees, but also those who are victims of nonstate persecution. People who cannot return to their state of origin because danger to life and limb is threatened there, must be granted the right to accommodation and medical care – corresponding to the standard of living of the admitting country. Furthermore, the still existing prohibition on work for refugees must be repealed.

Moreover, it must be guaranteed that refugees have the possibility of reaching potential admitting countries in the first place. The current entry and visa regulations, along with the concept of safe third states and countries of origin, considerably limit the possibility of finding refuge.

Establishing a 'Fortress Europe' is not the appropriate answer to the world refugee problem and the phenomenon of international migration. On the contrary, the GCR must again be established in its full meaning and must become the guideline for national asylum policies and procedures.

Notes

1. Cf. Gérard Noiriel: Die Tyrannei des Nationalen. Sozialgeschichte des Asylrechts in Europa, Lüneburg 1994, p. 103 ff.
2. Gérard Noiriel: Die Tyrannei des Nationalen. Sozialgeschichte des Asylrechts in Europa, Lüneburg 1994, p. 107.
3. Cf.: Gérard Noiriel: Die Tyrannei des Nationalen. Sozialgeschichte des Asylrechts in Europa, Lüneburg 1994, p. 107.
4. Abkommen über die Rechtsstellung der Flüchtlinge, in: Menschenrechte. Ihr internationaler Schutz, Munich 1985, 2nd revised edition, pp. 147–163, here p. 147.
5. Cf. on this: Gérard Noiriel: Die Tyrannei des Nationalen. Sozialgeschichte des Asylrechts in Europa, Lüneburg 1994, pp. 123–138.
6. Protokoll über die Rechtsstellung der Flüchtlinge, in: Menschenrechte. Ihr internationaler Schutz, Munich 1985, 2nd revised edition, pp. 164–167.
7. Abkommen über die Rechtsstellung der Flüchtlinge, in: Menschenrechte. Ihr internationaler Schutz, Munich 1985, 2nd revised edition, p. 148.
8. Abkommen über die Rechtsstellung der Flüchtlinge, in: Menschenrechte. Ihr internationaler Schutz, Munich 1985, 2nd revised edition, p. 158.
9. Cf. zu Trevi: Otto Diederichs: Trevi – ein standardbildendes Pilotprojekt?, in: Bürgerrechte & Polizei / Cilip No. 40, 3/1991, pp. 35–40; Heiner Busch: Europäische Innere Sicherheit – Möglichkeiten parlamentarischer Kontrolle?, in: Bürgerrechte & Polizei / Cilip No. 57, 2/1997, pp. 58–67.
10. The five EC States met for the first time in the Luxembourg city of Schengen.
11. Cf. on Schengen: Dokumentation (Abschrift) des Schengener Abkommens, published by BürgerInnen kontrollieren die Polizei et al., Hamburg 1990, Heiner Busch: Schengener Abkommen – Ausdehnung, Umsetzung und Folgen, in: Bürg-

errechte & Polizei / Cilip No. 40, 3/1991, pp. 9–13; Basso-Sekretariat Berlin: Europäische Asylpolitik: Zwischenstaatliche Vereinbarungen und Asylrechtsstandards der EU- und EFTA-Staaten im Überblick, in: Basso-Sekretariat Berlin (Ed.): Festung Europa auf der Anklagebank. Dokumentation des Basso-Tribunals zum Asylrecht in Europa, Münster 1995, pp. 244–251.
12. The correct designation for the Dublin Convention is 'Convention determining the State responsible for examining applications for asylum lodged in one of the Member States of the European Communities'.
13. FAZ of 19.6.1990.
14. Ibid.
15. Helmut Dietrich: Deutsch-polnische Polizeikooperation. Flüchtlingspolitik als Schrittmacher, in: Cilip No. 59, 1/1998.
16. Cf. below: Polnische Flüchtlings- und Migrationspolitik, in: Transodra – Informationsbulletin der Deutsch-Polnischen-Gesellschaft Brandenburg, February 1999.
17. As a result of the introduction of required visas for the neighbouring states the local east Polish economies cooperated. Cf. Helmut Dietrich: Deutsch-polnische Polizeikooperation. Flüchtlingspolitik als Schrittmacher, in: Cilip 59, 1/1998, pp. 32–41.
18. Cf. below: Recherchebericht der FFM zur Situation von aus Deutschland zurückgeschobenen Flüchtlingen und MigrantInnen in der Tschechischen Republik – Background report, Berlin, 15.6.1999.
19. At present four additional deportation prisons are planned on the Austrian and Polish Slovak borders.
20. Report on the situation found in Balkova, the first deportation prison in the Czech Republic, by a team from the research society Flight and Migration (Flucht und Migration) (FFM) on 25.4.2000.
21. Rückgeschoben aus Deutschland, interniert in der Tschechischen Republik. Short report on the visit of the FFM in Balková, the recently (1.11.1998) established Czech deportation prison, and Cerveny Ujezd, a 'Reception Center' for asylum seekers.
22. FAZ of 11.10.2000.
23. The following scenarios of EU eastward enlargement and the external borders resulting from it were played out in FAZ (of 11.10.2000):
Scenario I (3000 km): Estonia, Latvia, Lithuania, Poland, Slovakia border to the Russian Federation, Belorus, Ukraine.
Scenario II (4000 km): Estonia, Latvia, Lithuania, Poland, Slovakia, Bulgaria, Romania border on the Russian Federation, Belorus, Ukraine, Rep. Moldau, Turkey.
24. Ibid.
25. Ibid.
26. Ibid.
27. Vertrag von Amsterdam, ed. Thomas Läufer, Bonn 1999.
28. Cf. Claudia Roth/Mark Holzberger: Europäischer Flüchtlingsschutz heute, in: Christoph Butterwegge/Gudrun Hentges (Eds.): Zuwanderung im Zeichen der Globalisierung. Migrations-, Integrations- und Minderheitenpolitik, Opladen 2000, pp. 91–104.
29. Ibid., p. 92.
30. Bettina Höfling-Semnar: Flucht und deutsche Asylpolitik. Von der Krise des Asylrechts zur Perfektionierung der Zugangsverhinderung, Münster 1995, pp. 202–203.
31. Translation of the 'Grundgesetz' of the FRG: http://www.uni-wuerzburg.de/law/gm00000_.html, 1st june 2000.
32. Translation of the 'Grundgesetz' of the FRG: http://www.uni-wuerzburg.de/law/gm00000_.html, 1.6.2000.

33. http://www.emz-berlin.de/start.htm.
34. Source: von Pollern: Die Entwicklung der Asylbewerberzahlen im Jahre 1997; in: ZAR 3/1998 (documented by: Berliner Institut für Vergleichende Sozialforschung: http://www.emz-berlin.de/start.htm.
35. Source: Federal Border Guard, KL 4.
36. Cf. on the Vienna strategy paper: Claudia Roth/Mark Holzberger: Europäischer Flüchtlingsschutz heute, in: Christoph Butterwegge/Gudrun Hentges (Eds.): Zuwanderung im Zeichen der Globalisierung. Migrations-, Integrations- und Minderheitenpolitik, Opladen 2000, pp. 92–94.
37. Vienna strategy paper, cited ibid., p. 92.
38. Vienna strategy paper, cited ibid., p. 92..
39. Ibid., p. 93.
40. Cf. Thomas Uwer/Thomas von der Osten-Sacken: Wie Deutschland und Österreich die Genfer Flüchtlingskonvention zu Makulatur machen, in: Jungle World of 1.9.1999.
41. Cf. Claudia Roth/Mark Holzberger: Europäischer Flüchtlingsschutz heute, in: Christoph Butterwegge/Gudrun Hentges (Eds.): Zuwanderung im Zeichen der Globalisierung. Migrations-, Integrations- und Minderheitenpolitik, Opladen 2000, p. 94 ff.
42. Cf. Die Zeit of 28.10.1999; Der Spiegel of 21.11.1999; cf. Schily: Pitt von Bebenburg: Schily denkt über Asyl bei nichtstaatlicher Verfolgung nach, in: Frankfurter Rundschau of 27.7.1999; Jochen Baumann: Türkischer Dreiteiler, in: Jungle World of 20.10.1999; same author: Alle Macht dem Staat, in: Jungle World of 10.11.1999.
43. Cf. Gudrun Hentges: Irreale Bedrohungsszenarien und reale Politik: 'Eine Gespenst geht um in Europa – das Gespenst der multikulturellen Gesellschaft', in: Christoph Butterwegge/Gudrun Hentges/Fatma Sarigöz (Eds.): Medien und multikulturelle Gesellschaft, Opladen 1999, pp. 29–44.
44. Cf. Klaus J. Bade: Homo Migrans. Wanderungen aus und nach Deutschland. Erfahrungen und Fragen, Essen 1994, p. 53 ff.
45. Cf. Vera Gaserow: Tastende Schritte auf unsicherem Terrain, in: Frankfurter Rundschau of 4.4.2000.
46. Interview with Friedrich Merz, in: Die Woche of 23.3.2000.
47. Interview with Martin Hohmann, in: Fuldaer Zeitung of 23.11.2000.
48. TAZ of 27.11.2000.
49. Kurier of 19.11.2000.
50. Marieluise Beck: Mythen im deutschen Asylrecht [http://www.bundesauslaenderbeauftragte.de/ aktuell/mythen.htm] Between 1995 and 1999 the yearly recognition quota was between 9 and 13.5 percent. Refugees are considered 'recognised' if there are compelling hindrances to deportation according to the German constitution or according to agreements under international law. Beck points out that refusal for 'formal reasons' may not be included in the calculation of the protection quota, and furthermore the 'legal decisions' must be included. If the quota of these two factors is taken into account in the calculation, then it would be determined that almost half of the applicants for asylum are in need of protection.
    In the first seven months of the year 2000 in Germany, 2.7 percent of applicants were recognised as having the right of asylum, 6.5 percent received protection from deportation. FAZ of 4.8.2000.
51. Gudrun Hentges: Asyl in Europa, in: Blätter für deutsche und internationale Politik, 5/1992, pp. 519–523.
52. Jochen Baumann: Alle Macht dem Staat, in: Jungle World of 10.11.1999.

53. Festlegung der europäischen Asyl-Agenda: UNHCR-Empfehlungen zum Tampere-Gipfel (Oktober 1999).
54. In August 2000 the German Federal Constitutional Court revoked two decisions of the German Supreme Administrative Court. In these Afghan applicants for asylum who saw themselves threatened by the Mudschahedin were denied a claim to asylum. The constitutional court held to the fact that a claim to asylum exists in principle only with 'state persecution',' but the judges loosened the assumptions under which 'quasi-state' persecution relevant to asylum can be assumed. cf. FAZ of 23.8.2000; cf. furthermore: FAZ of 24.8.2000; 26.8.2000; 28.8.2000.
55. Norman Paech: Abgestimt, Abgeurteilt, Abgeschoben, in: Frankfurter Rundschau of 24.8.1998.

Bibliography

Agreement on the legal status of refugees (Abkommen über die Rechtsstellung der Flüchtlinge). In *Human rights: their international protection (Menschenrechte. Ihr internationaler Schutz)*. München 1985, 2nd revised edition, pp. 147–163
Bade, K.J. 1994. *Homo Migrans. Migration from and to Germany. Experiences and questions (Homo Migrans. Wanderungen aus und nach Deutschland. Erfahrungen und Fragen)*. Essen.
Basso-Sekretariat. 1995. European asylum policy: an overview of international agreements and right of asylum standards of the EU and EFTA states' (Europäische Asylpolitik: Zwischenstaatliche Vereinbarungen und Asylrechtsstandards der EU- und EFTA-Staaten im Überblick). In *Fortress Europe in the dock. Documentation of the Basso court on asylum law in Europe (Festung Europa auf der Anklagebank. Dokumentation des Basso-Tribunals zum Asylrecht in Europa)*. A. Rea, ed. Berlin: Münster, pp. 244–251.
Baumann, J. 1999. 'All power to the state' (Alle Macht dem Staat). In *Jungle World of 10.11.1999*.
———. 1999. 'Turkish three-parter' (Türkischer Dreiteiler). In: *Jungle World of 20.10.1999*.
Beck, M. 2000. 'Myths in German asylum law' (Mythen im deutschen Asylrecht). [http://www.bundesauslaenderbeauftragte.de/aktuell/mythen.html]. Report on the situation found in Balková, the first deportation prison in the Czech Republic, on 25.4.2000 by a team from the research organisation Flight and Migration (FFM) (Bericht über die von einem Team der Forschungsgesellschaft Flucht und Migration (FFM) am 25.4.2000 vorgefundene Situation in Balková, dem ersten Abschiebegefängnis in der Tschechischen Republik). [http://www.berlinet.de/mh/ffm/].
Busch, H. 1997. European internal security – possibilities for parliamentary control? (Europäische Innere Sicherheit – Möglichkeiten parlamentarischer Kontrolle?) In *Citizens' rights and police (Bürgerrechte & Polizei)*. Cilip Nr. 57, 2/1997, pp. 58–67.

———. 1991. 'Schengener Abkommen – Ausdehnung, Umsetzung und Folgen'. In *Citizens' rights and police (Bürgerrechte & Polizei)*. Cilip Nr. 40, 3/1991, pp. 9–13.

Diederichs, O. 1991. 'Trevi – a standards forming pilot project?' (Trevi – ein standardbildendes Pilotprojekt?) In *Citizens' rights and police (Bürgerrechte & Polizei)*. Cilip Nr. 40, 3/1991, pp. 35–40.

Dietrich, H. 1998. German-Polish police cooperation. Refugee policy as pace-maker (Deutsch-polnische Polizeikooperation. Flüchtlingspolitik als Schrittmacher). In *Cilip* Nr. 59, 1/1998, pp. 32–41.

Documentation (copy) of the Schengen Convention (Dokumentation [Abschrift] des Schengener Abkommens). Ed., by BürgerInnen kontrollieren die Polizei u.a. (Citizens controlling the police), Hamburg 1990.

Dublin Convention: 'Convention determining the State responsible for examining applications for asylum lodged in one of the member states of the European Communities'

Gaserow, V. 2000. 'Tentative steps in uncertain terrain' (Tastende Schritte auf unsicherem Terrain). In: *Frankfurter Rundschau of 4.4.2000*.

Hentges, G. 1992. Asylum in Europe (Asyl in Europa). In *Blätter für deutsche und internationale Politik*. 5/1992, pp. 519–523.

———. 1999. Unrealistic threat scenarios and realistic policy: 'A spectre is going around in Europe – the spectre of the multi-cultural society' (Irreale Bedrohungsszenarien und reale Politik: 'Eine Gespenst geht um in Europa – das Gespenst der multikulturellen Gesellschaft'). In *Media and multi-cultural society (Medien und multikulturelle Gesellschaft)*. Christoph Butterwegge, Gudrun Hentges, and Fatma Sarigöz, eds. Opladen pp. 29–44.

Höfling-Semnar, B. 1995. *Flight and German asylum policy. From the crisis of the right of asylum to the perfecting of the hindrance of access. (Flucht und deutsche Asylpolitik. Von der Krise des Asylrechts zur Perfektionierung der Zugangsverhinderung)*. Münster.

Interview with Friedrich Merz. In: *Die Woche of 23.3.2000*

Interview with Martin Hohmann. In: *Fuldaer Zeitung of 23.11.2000*

Leuninger, H. 1995. 'From legal subject to object of the state. The new right of asylum as depriving refugees of their rights' (Vom Rechtssubjekt zum Objekt des Staates. Das neue Asylrecht als Entrechtung des Flüchtlings). In *Fortress Europe in the dock. Documentation of the Basso court on asylum law in Europe (Festung Europa auf der Anklagebank. Dokumentation des Basso-Tribunals zum Asylrecht in Europa)*. Basso-Sekretariat Berlin, ed. Münster, pp. 74–81.

Noiriel, G. 1994. *The tyranny of the national. Social history of asylum law in Europe' (Die Tyrannei des Nationalen. Sozialgeschichte des Asylrechts in Europa)*. Lüneburg.

Paech, N. 1998. Voted, condemned, deported (Abgestimt, Abgeurteilt, Abgeschoben). In *Frankfurter Rundschau of 24.8.1998*.

Polish refugees and migration policy (Polnische Flüchtlings- und Migrationspolitik). In *Transodra* – Information newsletter of the German-

Polish community of Brandenburg (Informationsbulletin der Deutsch-Polnischen-Gesellschaft Brandenburg). February 1999 [http://www.berlinet.de/mh/ffm/]

Protocol on the legal position of refugees (Protokoll über die Rechtsstellung der Flüchtlinge). In *Human rights. Their international protection* (Menschenrechte. Ihr internationaler Schutz). Munich 1985, 2nd revised edition, pp. 164–167.

Research report of the FFM on the situation of refugees and migrations sent back from Germany to the Czech Republic – background report (Recherchebericht der FFM zur Situation von aus Deutschland zurückgeschobenen Flüchtlingen und MigrantInnen in der Tschechischen Republik – Hintergrundbericht). Berlin, 15.6.1999 [http://www.berlinet.de/mh/ffm/].

Roth, C., and Holzberger, M. 2000. 'European refugee protection today' (Europäischer Flüchtlingsschutz heute). In *Immigration under the sign of globalisation. Migration, integration and minority policy* (Zuwanderung im Zeichen der Globalisierung. Migrations-, Integrations- und Minderheitenpolitik). C. Butterwegge, and G. Hentges, ed. Opladen, pp. 91–104.

Sent back from Germany, interned in the Czech Republic. Short report on the visit of the FFM in Balková, the recently (1.11.1998) established Czech deportation prison, and Cerveny Ujezd, a 'Reception Center' for asylum seekers (Rückgeschoben aus Deutschland, interniert in der Tschechischen Republik. Kurzbericht über den Besuch der FFM in Balková, dem seit kurzem (1.11.1998) eingerichteten tschechischen Abschiebegefängnis, und Cerveny Ujezd, einem 'Reception Center' für Asylsuchende). [http://www.berlinet.de/mh/ffm/].

Setting the agenda for European asylum policy: UNHCR recommendations to the Tampere Summit (Festlegung der europäischen Asyl-Agenda: UNHCR-Empfehlungen zum Tampere-Gipfel) October 1999.

Translation of the 'Grundgesetz' [constitution] of the FRG: http://www.uni-wuerzburg.de/law/gm00000_.html, 1st June 2000.

Treaty of Amsterdam (Vertrag von Amsterdam). Ed., Thomas Läufer, Bonn 1999.

Uwer, T., and von der Osten-Sacken, T. 1999. 'How Germany and Austria turned the Geneva Convention on Refugees into rubbish' (Wie Deutschland und Österreich die Genfer Flüchtlingskonvention zu Makulatur machen). In *Jungle World of 1.9.1999*.

von Behenburg, P. 'Schily reflects about asylum in non-state persecution' (Schily denkt über Asyl bei nichtstaatlicher Verfolgung nach). In *Frankfurter Rundschau of 27.7.1999*.

von Pollern. 1998. 'The development of numbers of asylum applicants in 1997' (Die Entwicklung der Asylbewerberzahlen im Jahre 1997). In: *ZAR 3/1998* (documented by: Berlin institute for comparative social research [Berliner Institut für Vergleichende Sozialforschung]) [http://snake.cs.tuberlin.de:8081/~bak/fachinfo/FIB_INS/Berliner_I__Dr_ _Thomas_SchwarzPostfach_3.html]

Ethnic Relations in Local Contexts:
Beyond a Dualist Approach to Identities and Racism

Maykel Verkuyten

It was on a Thursday morning in a 'Social Studies' lesson for 15 and 16-year old students in a multiethnic school in the inner city of Rotterdam. The teacher had prepared a lesson on racism and discrimination. He talked about colonialism, the Second World War, and ethnic minority groups being discriminated against in the Netherlands. He argued that racism and discrimination not only blocks opportunities for minorities, but would leave its 'psychological mark of oppression'. The students were not very involved. After noticing this, the teacher asked them why they were not interested. One of the ethnic minority group students said: 'Well we all know that stuff, but what has it got to do with us, eh, here it is all different'.

The teacher responded by arguing that also in Rotterdam, and in their inner city neighbourhood, ethnic minority youth are being discriminated against and face everyday racism. First, the students agreed and they came up with examples of discrimination at disco's, shops, etc., but very quickly their thinking became more complex. They mentioned examples of racism and discrimination between and within minority groups, and of ethnic Dutch youth being discriminated against and being marginalised. The outcome of the discussion about their everyday lives was that you could not say in advance who was discriminating who, and who was more powerful. The scheme of perpetrators being white (Dutch) and victims being black (minorities) was questioned At the level of society this scheme was accepted, but not in relation to their local lives and experiences. According to the students, it all depended on a lot of things. They certainly did not see themselves as passive victims marked psychologically by discrimination and racism. The students claimed an active and constructive role for themselves and their group. An interpretation in terms of only being defined and not as defining or an agent was rejected as one-sided.

This is one example from the research that we have been conducting over a number of years in the inner city of Rotterdam (e.g., Verkuyten 1997a, 1997b, 1997c, 1998a, 2001: Verkuyten et al. 1994, 1995). In this research we use observations, documents, interviews and focus group discussions in examining old neighbourhoods and local schools. The example illustrates the issue that I want to address. My focus is on ethnic minority identity, and I am interested in connecting with, or making sense of, the experiences and definitions of people living in old neighbourhoods. Hence, I focus on the more subtle processes affecting local situations, and not so much on the general structural patterns in society or on intellectual ideologies and discourses.

My central argument is that ethnic minority identity is dependent on a range of constructive processes and is certainly not only shaped by a simple overarching factor: that is a majority-minority dualist model of racism. In this model, racism is understood in terms of power differences whereby the indigenous group is more powerful, and minorities define themselves predominantly in relation to this group. At the level of society, this model is adequate, but it can not be applied self-evidently to the local lives of people in many urban quarters. My argument is based on our research in the inner city of Rotterdam, but our findings are by no means particular for this city. Based on empirical studies, similar arguments have been made in, for example, the United States, the United Kingdom and Germany (e.g., Back 1996; Conquergood 1994; Dannenbeck et al. 1997; Hewitt 1986; Mac an Ghaill 1999; Marshall et al. 1999). In the following I will address two issues. First, the question of comparisons and identity constructions, and, second, the question of group relations and power differences.

Identity Comparisons

The unfavourable social position is often seen as the defining principle of ethnic minority groups and as the central issue for understanding minority identity (e.g., Tajfel, 1978). The focus is on power and status differences and in particular on the question of the self-defining and psychological effects of the threat to social identity that a minority position imples. One of the implicit assumptions here is that ethnic minorities define their identity predominantly in relation to the majority group, which is implicitly considered the main significant other. At least three critical points can be made to this line of thinking.

First, in concentrating on the minority aspect of ethnic minority identity the ethnic aspect tends to be ignored. Attempts of ethnic minority groups to preserve their cultural traditions and to establish a positive self-definition are seen as a response to perceived inferiority. Ethnic awareness would be a reaction to the frustrations of not being granted access to the dominant group. Such a reactive or oppositional identity is, of course, quite possible and has been described in the literature (e.g., Ogbu 1993; Waters 1994). With oppositional identities, self-defining traits, norms and beliefs are in the opposite direction of what the majority group values.

However, many ethnic minority groups have a rich (imagined) culture and history and they do not have to define themselves in reaction and opposition to the majority group. For self-definition, the majority group is often not central or a significant other. An exclusive analytical focus on the majority group seriously ignores and underestimates the importance of group continuity and the history and culture of these groups. Ethnic minority groups are 'ethnic' from the 'inside' because a common imagined origin and culture are used for self-understanding (Hutnik 1991; Roosens 1994). The fact that many ethnic minority groups are endowed with a culture, tradition and structure of their own should be taken into account. For example, for ethnic minorities, many identity issues have to do with differences and similarities 'within' their own ethnic group and in relation to the situation in their country of origin. Cultural characteristics and traditions have self-defining meaning and discussions, and arguments often centre around issues of cultural change and stability. Several studies have shown that in-group hassles are often more stressful and problematic than relations with the majority group (e.g., Lay & Nguyen 1998).

Second, the implicit assumption is that ethnic minorities compare their situation predominantly with the Dutch. However, in multi-ethnic societies there is a variety of groups in relation to whom people construct their own identities. Ethnic minority identity is depended on a diversity of comparisons that are being made and their relation to each other. For example, among Turkish people in the inner city of Rotterdam a self-definition as Turkish often involves Moroccans living in the area. In fact, many Turks are keen to differentiate themselves from the Moroccans who are said to be aggressive and criminal. Also, the Turks see themselves as more European and Moroccan culture as Arabic and archaic (Verkuyten 1997c).

Similarly, South Moluccan youth not only define their identity in relation to other Moluccans, and to a lesser degree in relation to the Dutch, but also in comparison to what they define as 'foreigners', meaning Turks and Moroccans (Verkuyten et al. 1999). The South Moluccans do not wish to be defined as similar to other minority groups. They claim a separate position because they have a different history with the Netherlands and a different culture. They also use familiar racial and cultural discourses in presenting an essentialist Moluccan identity. In making distinctions with other ethnic minority groups, biological justifications are given and assumed cultural differences are made natural and absolute. So their self-definition very much involves a contrast with other ethnic minority groups illustrating the limited value of a majority-minority model for understanding identity constructions.

Third, the predominant concern with status and power implies a tendency to place ethnic minorities members in the position of helpless victims denying them an active and constructive role. In fact, however, many minority group members make it clear that their identity is *not* derived from that of the majority group, who is doing the defining. In our studies, people present themselves not only as victims but also as agents or actors who have their own responsibilities and who can draw upon a rich culture and tradition in defining themselves in relation to other groups.

In addition to social considerations there are important psychological reasons for claiming such an active and self-determining role. There are many studies showing that the experience of discrimination and racism has serious negative effects on psychological well-being and self-esteem in particular (e.g., Branscombe et al. 1999; Kessler et al. 1999; Verkuyten,1998). The predicaments of racism and discrimination have clear negative psychological implications. However, discrimination can also have positive effects on well-being. For example, when discrimination offers an external explanation for not being successful at school or in the labour market. Well known is a 'blaming the system' interpretation that has been found to have a positive effect on self-esteem and feelings of self-worth (Gurin & Epps 1975). Moreover, being successful despite discrimination is even more admirable.

However, a 'system blame' interpretation has psychological costs. It implies that the control over one's life is (partly) in the hands of others. The result is feelings of helplessness and of being a victim who can do little to change his or her situation. So there is a sort of psychological 'trade-off' whereby an attribution to discrimination and racism protects feelings of self-esteem and self-worth, but threatens feelings of personal control. Interestingly, some studies have examined what minority group members consider more important: self-esteem or personal control (Ruggiero & Taylor 1995, 1997). These studies show that, in general, feelings of personal control are more important and that therefore, minorities are quite 'reluctant' to use discrimination as an explanation of their situation. Hence, there is not much support for the view that minorities are oversensitive to racism or predisposed to make discrimination attributions. On the contrary, psychological research shows minorities to be hesitant do so because such attributions lead to feelings of helplessness and lack of control. This reluctance has positive psychological effects, but it may have more negative social consequences. Minimising personal discrimination can imply that actual discrimination is ignored or not used for mobilisation and social change.

Category Relations and Power

The distinction between majority and minority that, in society, is used as a standard scheme or a social representation for interpreting relations is present and evident in local situations. Local situations are not immune to relations at the level of society. The scheme of the majority group being dominant and discriminating, and minority groups being subordinate and discriminated, does play a role in the everyday thinking of local people. For example, I asked a Cape Verdian boy whether there is discrimination at his school. His answer was: 'No, I do not experience it, but of course there are only foreigners here'.

Here the little word 'but' is interesting because it introduces an explanation and defines the Dutch as the discriminating group. Because there are very few Dutch there would be little discrimination. Another example is when, during a gymnastics lesson, the Dutch teacher was annoyed about a Surinamese boy who was slow and the teacher almost let his tongue run away with him by saying 'come on blac ... '. Afterwards, the class spoke about the incident. Both Dutch and minority group students were angry, but the minorities were inclined to place this event in the context of a pattern of racism and as evidence that the Dutch cannot be trusted. The Dutch children, on the other hand, were more likely to see it as specific for this teacher. So societal definitions of majority-minority relations (discriminating and discriminated at) are known and used for interpreting local situations. However, actual power relations and differences are often not self-evident.

For example, the standard scheme defining majority-minority relations can have power implications because it places 'ethnic minorities" in an advantageous position compared to the Dutch. The charge of racism is one of the strongest moral condemnations of the present day. The taboo on racism and its strong moral meaning make, for example, the teachers, very sensitive to possible racism. In the schools we studied it was clear that ethnic minority students were sometimes able to interpret their experiences in terms of racism and discrimination and get these interpretations accepted by teachers. For the Dutch students such an interpretation is less obvious. After all, the Dutch are typically seen as the perpetrators and the Dutch students had much more difficulty in convincing teachers that they sometimes faced discrimination or racism. So the taboo on racism and the dualist majority-minority model presents a power resource for ethnic minorities.

Language is another example of such a resource. Many schools have the policy that only the Dutch language is to be used in school. This has practical reasons, because the lack of a common language hampers interactions and causes misunderstandings and conflicts. It limits the possibility of shared understandings which makes it very hard to develop a certain modus vivendi in schools. However, there are also other aspects involved. For example, the obligation to speak Dutch can be interpreted as an act of majority group domination that ignores diversity and ethnic identities. Furthermore, stressing the lack of a command of the Dutch language is a strong argument because it can be used as a socially acceptable and understandable reason for expressing negative feelings and arguing for assimilation (Verkuyten 1997a). Teachers sometimes use the topic of language in this way.

However, using one's own language also plays a role in group relations among youth themselves. It gives ethnic minorities a position of power whereby they can exclude others, in particular the Dutch. Not being able to understand what others are talking about means being defenceless and unable to have influence, and it leads to suspicions and feelings of exclusion. In schools, we encountered various examples where ethnic minorities used their own language, making the Dutch feel excluded (Verkuyten 1997a). The Dutch themselves are not able to use their language as a power resource because ethnic minority students speak Dutch.

Although asymmetrical power relations in favour of the ethnic Dutch are often assumed, in many local situations the Dutch have lost much of their power. The Dutch have increasingly becoming a numerical minority in old neighbourhoods and schools. In inner city quarters Dutch inhabitants make up around 25 percent of the residents and only 10 percent at schools. Hence, ethnic minority groups are increasingly becoming numerical majorities, which finds expression in the fact that shops, provisions and institutions become orientated towards these groups.

In terms of unity and groupness the Dutch have also become relatively powerless in many inner city neighbourhoods and multiethnic schools (De Jong & Verkuyten 1996). There is relatively little social cohesion because the mutual ties and the sense of fellow-feeling, have weakened considerably. In contrast, the level of solidarity and groupness is higher among many ethnic minority groups, which may be due to shared experiences with discrimination and racism, but which is also related to their sometimes more collectivistic cultural worldview.

Institutionally, housing corporations, neighbourhood organisations, community centres and schools used to see the ethnic Dutch population as their main group of reference. However, in comparison to some twenty-five years ago this situation has changed substantially (see De Jong & Verkuyten 1996). Community centres and neighbourhood organisations have shifted their attention to supporting, advising and promoting the interests of ethnic minorities. There are different reasons for this. Studies showed that ethnic minorities were more disadvantaged than the indigenous population. Furthermore, numerically, the ethnic minorities became a majority, certainly regarding families and children. In addition, governmental priorities were in favour of the integration of ethnic minorities, and community centres are subsidised institutions which get financial assistance when they meet the criteria formulated by the government.

Thus, in many situations the Dutch have lost much of the local power which would enable them to put their racist views into practice. The existence of these views in which the Dutch are considered (culturally) superior and as having more rights has been documented in various studies (e.g., van Dijk 1997; Essed 1991). However, in many local situations this increasingly seems to have become a racism without viciousness, because ethnic Dutch residents have lost much of their influence and have become one of the many. This does not mean that the Dutch are the new subordinated group or that they accept this situation and do not use their origin for claiming status and rights, but power is being dispersed. The perspective of (some) ethnic minority groups has become important, and these groups have institutional means to get their interpretations and definitions accepted and diffused.

Discussion

Racism and discrimination are pervasive and highly problematic phenomena. Racism is diversified, changing and subtle. It exist on the institutional and structural level of society, it is communicated in the media and by politicians, and it is a feature of many situations in everyday life. Racism has many forms and is closely related to power relations. Racism is also related to local circumstances that may differ from relations at the level of institutions and society at large. Drawing on our research in Rotterdam, I have tried to argue that a 'simple' dichotomy between domination (ethnic Dutch) and subordination (ethnic minorities) is of limited value for interpreting and analysing many local situations. Studies in other European cities and countries have presented similar findings and arguments (e.g., Back 1996; Dannenbeck et al. 1997; Hewitt 1986; Mac an Ghaill 1999; Marshall et al. 1999). Thus, in addition to the unique and particular conditions in neighbourhoods and cities, there are also more general circumstances and processes that affect ethnic relations in various local situations.

These studies show that it is necessary to have a more detailed understanding about how people define and negotiate about themselves and their everyday life. The common-sense dichotomy of majority-minority or perpetrator-victim cannot be applied self-evidently, particularly not to the lives of younger generations. With this dichotomy it is difficult to make contact with the experiences of people who are in the process of arguing about belonging, exclusions and self-definitions, and in doing so make all kinds of comparisons and distinctions.

The need for careful studies of local situations does not, of course, undermine analyses of structural and institutional racism in society. Racism is evident in many spheres of society and the domination-subordination model is often very useful for understanding ethnic relations. In addition, and as I have argued, local situations are affected by existing representations and group relations in society. However, localities have also their own characteristics and dynamics that should be taken into account.

Failing to do so and applying the dualist model to local situations may, in part, be responsible for the often limited success of antiracism (see Bonnett 1999). This model is the implicit frame of reference in different forms of antiracism, making it in practice less than adequate for changing local situations. A frequently observed risk is that strategies aimed at reducing racism are not effective because they aim at either too restricted goals or too generic areas (Goldberg 1993). That is, a too generic theory or 'solution' may prevent one from grasping the specific nature of, and answers to, racism in concrete settings, whereas the understanding of a very specific aspect, expression or condition of racism may lose sight of the wider implications. Using local analyses for criticising structural racism is an example of the latter, whereas simply applying the common-sense dichotomy to a local situation is an example of the former.

The dualist model tends to turn identities and group relations into fixed, essential and homogenous entities, rather than examining how power relations and identities are being locally produced and played out. We cannot unproblematically equate one group with power and others with powerlessness or subordination. There are numerous situations where this equation is valid but there are also situations where it distorts our understanding of events and thereby hampers attempts at successful interventions.

The existence of power and dominance should not be treated as a priori, or as a backdrop for analysis. In most studies, processes of racialisation, racism, and identity constructions are seen as flexible, changing and situationally contingent, whereas power differences are typically treated as unproblematically given. Power tends not to appear as an object of investigation, but as an analytical foundation providing direction and coherence. Thus, in studying racism, one central analytical category is left unexamined whereas other assumptions and implications are critically examined. However, the issue of power and status differences should be studied in relation to the wider social situation as well as in relation to local circumstances. Power relations need to be understood as being actively (re)produced, involving global, national, regional and local circumstances, resources and boundaries. There is a range of discourses and practices that place individuals and groups in subordinate or dominant positions, but there are always competing constructions and challenges possible. Examining the (re)production of racism and power also offers the possibility for acknowledging personal agency. Studies on racism have the danger of portraying individuals as passive recipients of socially dominant ideas or as rather helpless victims. However, ethnic minority group members claim an active and constructive role for themselves. For social and psychological reasons, they present themselves not only as victims but also as agents who have their own responsibilities.

Studying local situations in detail is important for improving our understanding of racism in its different forms, and for trying to improve group relations. These studies are also important for another reason. Politicians in several European countries are inclined to focus on working class people in urban areas when discussing racism. Basically, what is presented is an image of society that is not racist as a whole but only has some racism localised in old urban quarters. This racism would exist in response to material disadvantages, feelings of insecurity, and conflicts over scarce resources because of the increasing number of immigrants. However, local situations and relations are much more complex than as presented in these images. Systematic studies of relations, discourses and practices in local situations are important for challenging public images about inner-city areas. These images are being used to justify restrictive policies and can have the effect of ignoring and obscuring racism among, for example, employers and other more institutionalised forms of racism.

Bibliography

Back. L. 1996. *New ethnicities and urban culture: Racisms and multiculture in young lives*. London: UCL Press.

Bonnett, A. 1999. *Anti racism*. London: Routledge.

Branscombe, N.R., Schmitt, M.T., and Harvey, R.D. 1999. 'Perceiving pervasive discrimination among African Americans: Implications for group identification and well-being'. *Journal of Personality and Social Psychology*, 77: 135–149.

Conquergood, D. 1994. 'For the nation! How street gangs problematize patriotism'. In *After postmodernism: Reconstructing ideology critique*. H.W. Simons, and M. Billig, eds. London: Sage.

Dannenbeck, C., Losch, H., and Esser, F. 1997. 'Adolescents in a culturally mixed environment: Multiculturalism as an everyday learning process'. Paper presented at the VIIIth European Conference on Developmental Psychology, Rennes, France, 3–7 September.

Essed, P. 1991. *Understanding everyday racism*. Newbury Park, CA: Sage.

Goldberg, D.T. 1993. *Racist culture: Philosophy and the politics of meaning*. Oxford: Blackwell.

Gurin, P., and Epps, E. 1975. *Black consciousness, identity and achievement*. New York: Wiley.

Hewitt, R. 1986. *White talk, Black talk: Inter-racial friendship and communication amongs adolescents*. Cambridge: Cambridge University Press.

Hutnik, N. 1991. *Ethnic minority identity*. Oxford: Clarendon. Press.

Jong, W. de, and Verkuyten, M. 1996. Urban renewal, housing policy, and ethnic relations in Rotterdam'. *New Community*. 22: 689–705.

Kessler, R.C., Mickelson, K.D., and Williams, D.R. 1999. 'The prevalence, distribution, and mental health correlates of perceived discrimination in the United States'. *Journal of Health and Social Behavior*, 40: 208–230.

Lay, C., and Nguyen, T. 1998. 'The role of acculturation-related and acculturation non-specific hassles: Vietnamese-Canadian students and psychological distress'. *Canadian Journal of Behavioral Science*, 30: 172–181.

Mac an Ghaill, M. 1999. *Contemporary racisms and ethnicities: Social and cultural transformations*. Buckingham: Open University Press.

Marshall, H., Stenner, P., and Lee, H. 1999. 'Young people's accounts of personal relationships in a multi-cultural east London environment: Questions of community, diversity and inequality'. *Journal of Community and Applied Social Psychology*, 9: 155–171.

Ogbu, J.U. 1993. 'Differences in cultural frame of reference'. *International Journal of Behavioral Development*, 16: 483–506.
Roosens, E. 1994. 'The primordial nature of origins in immigrant ethnicity'. In *The anthropology of ethnicity*. H. Vermeulen, and C. Govers, eds. Amsterdam: Spinhuis.
Ruggiero, K.M., and Taylor, D.M. 1995. 'Coping with discrimination: How disadvantaged group members perceive discrimination that confronts them'. *Journal of Personality and Social Psychology*, 68: 826–838.
Ruggiero, K.M, and Taylor, D.M. 1997. 'When minority group members perceive or do not perceive the discrimination that confronts them: The role of self-esteem and perceived control'. *Journal of Personality and Social Psychology*, 72: 373–389.
Tajfel, H. 1978. *The social psychology of minorities*. London: Minority Rights Group.
van Dijk, T. 1987. *Communicating racism*. London: Sage.
Verkuyten, M. 1997a. *'Redelijk racisme': Gesprekken over allochtonen in oude stadswijken*. Amsterdam: Amsterdam University Press.
———. 1997b. 'Cultural discourses in the Netherlands: Talking about ethnic minorities in the inner-city'. *Identities*, 4: 99–132.
———. 1997c. 'Discourse of ethnic minority identity'. *British Journal of Social Psychology*, 36: 565–586.
———. 1998a. 'Personhood and accounting for racism in conversation'. *Journal for the Theory of Social Behaviour*, 28: 147–167.
———. 1998b. 'Perceived discrimination and self-esteem among ethnic minority adolescents'. *Journal of Social Psychology*, 138: 479–494.
———. 2001. 'Abnormalization' of ethnic minorities in conversation'. *British Journal of Social Psychology*, 40: 257–278.
Verkuyten, M, van de Calseijde, S., and de Leur, W. 1999. 'Third-generation South Moluccans in the Netherlands: The nature of ethnic identity'. *Journal of Ethnic and Migration Studies*, 25: 63–79.
Verkuyten, M, de Jong, W., and Masson, C.N. 1994. 'Similarities in anti-racist and racist discourse: Dutch local residents talking about ethnic minorities'. *New Community*, 20: 253–268.
Verkuyten, M, de Jong, W., and Masson, C.N. 1995. 'The construction of ethnic categories: Discourses of ethnicity in the Netherlands'. *Ethnic and Racial Studies*, 18: 251–276.
Waters, M.C. 1994. 'Ethnic and racial identities of second-generation black immigrants in New York City'. *International Migration Review*, 28: 795–820.

ECONOMIC GLOBALISATION AND RACISM IN EASTERN AND WESTERN EUROPE

Béla Greskovits

Introduction

Has economic globalisation been breeding xenophobia and racism in Europe? I shall argue that during the 1990s it has, but its most striking effects occurred in places commonly held to be less prone to these kinds of threats, and were mediated by new and not yet fully explained mechanisms. While racism was not absent in Eastern Europe, the accelerated process of global and European economic integration brought about more racist political mobilisation in some western European countries than in much of Eastern Europe. Furthermore, in the East, racism and its kin – ethnic and religious discrimination and strife, xenophobia, and ethnic wars – have been more characteristic to the least globally integrated countries – of the Caucasus, Central Asia or the eastern part of former Yugoslavia – than to the west of East Central Europe. These outcomes may tell about truly puzzling relationships between globalisation and racism during the 1990s.

In the first section of my essay I shall review the standard expectations of the transformation studies concerning the political dynamics of the postsocialist transformation. An influential body of this literature developed various scenarios of political destabilisation and democratic breakdown – among them the turn to populist, authoritarian and racist regimes – in postsocialist Eastern Europe. The many losers of Eastern Europe's globalisation – bureaucrats, displaced workers, nationalist intellectuals and the masses of marginalised poor – were expected to revolt by mass protest, strikes, riots, demonstrations, and by supporting populist, xenophobic and racist politicians. In contrast, in these theories western Europe was typically seen as the only significant counterweight against the danger of a continent-wide loss of political and economic control and stability. The second section contrasts these expectations with the realities of the 1990s. Surprisingly, while their countries have rushed towards economic globalisation, the citizens of the most Westernised countries of Eastern Europe have remained remarkably patient despite the immense economic hardship and social dislocation they had to face. Riots or populist authoritarian turnabouts occurred only in exceptional cases, there was no more, or perhaps even less, disruptive social and political action than in the consolidated Western democracies. Thus, a number of politicians and academics who wrote about the political dynamics in the New Europe may be wrong both ways: while by their gloomy prophecies they generalised the image of an unstable and xenophobic East, they underestimated the threats of globalisation inside the Western core of Europe.

Still, racist-xenophobic populism was present in Eastern Europe as well, and, in some countries gained, while in others lost, popularity by the late 1990s. What accounts for the political career of xenophobic populism in the East? The third section offers an elaboration on the case of Hungary's Party of Hungarian Justice and Life. In the last section I briefly summarise the lessons for our understanding of the politics of economic globalisation in an all-European context.

A Nationalist and Xenophobic East?

In the 1990s, most analysts expected that economic globalisation would lead to xenophobic and racist politics in postsocialist Eastern Europe. Why have scholars arrived at such gloomy prophecies? How did they see the Western role in Europe's economic and political stability?

From Economic Frustration to Populist Authoritarianism

Most analysts of the postsocialist transformations linked the perspectives of economic globalisation and racism in the East to the missing cultural and institutional preconditions of tolerance and liberalism in the region and the social costs of neoliberal transformation strategies. In the accounts of the above type, xenophobia and racism were seen as part and parcel of broader pessimist scenarios combining the most diverse array of political phenomena: labour strikes, protest votes, nationalism, authoritarian turnabouts, ethnic and religious strife, secession and civil war. John Walton and David Seddon wrote that:

> Conflict over the pace and character of economic reform contributed to ethnic and national divisions, and to the disintegration of existing states (e.g., the Soviet Union, Yugoslavia and Czechoslovakia); in others, popular protest against the social costs of government economic policies began to give way to, or take the form of, ethnic and racial violence directed particularly against 'foreigners' and other minority groups (e.g., Hungary, Romania, Poland and East Germany) (Walton and Seddon 1994: 320).

In David Ost's view also, racism and religious and ethnic intolerance directly resulted from the economic frustrations with the neoliberal transformation, as a form of protest by losers who felt excluded from building the new society. (Ost 1992: 49–50). While Ost proposed more inclusive democracy to avoid losers' support going to racist authoritarianism, Jadwiga Staniszkis argued that it was precisely too rapid democratisation that would bring about growing hostility against domestic minorities and foreigners, because 'As long as the economic foundations for a genuine civil society do not exist, the massive political mobilisation of the population is only possible along nationalist or fundamentalist lines' (Staniszkis 1991: 326 quoted by Offe 1991: 876).[1] Most extreme along the same lines was Ken Jowitt's suggestion, that: 'A form of liberal authoritarianism like the bourgeois regimes of nineteenth-century western Europe is a desirable alternative to the religio-ethnic, militant nationalist, even fascist (sic) regimes that might emerge from the maelstrom; and it would be a more practical response than the utopian wish for immediate mass democracy in Eastern Europe' (Jowitt 1992: 223).

Historical experience did not seem to work in favour of the perspectives of a democratic East either. In the view of Iván T. Berend it magnified the threat of degrading into racism and xenophobia.

The lost security and dissatisfaction is a fertile soil for demands of 'law and order', for a strong and attentive power, and for the rise of hatred against 'others', especially stigmatised minorities. Oppression of minorities and aggressive anti-Semitism has characterised the entire modern history of Central and Eastern Europe. 'Recycled' ideas are reappearing in the periphery of Central and Eastern European society (Berend 1997: 363).[2]

Europe is the Only Hope

In most accounts Western Europe and the European Union (EU) appeared as the single or most important factor of hope in political stability. The EU was presented as a model, a disciplining force, a life belt, a generous aide and an active ally in democratisation. Adam Przeworski believed that: 'Geography is indeed the single reason to hope that Eastern European countries will follow the path to democracy and prosperity. There is no place in Europe today for nondemocratic politics; democratic institutions are a sine qua non for any country that seeks to become a member of this community' (Przeworski 1991: 190). To 'check the increasing frustration, depression, fragmentation and anger that will lead to country and region-wide communal-like violence in Eastern Europe' Jowitt went further by advocating 'to attempt in East Europe and parts of the Soviet Union what West Germany is attempting in East Germany: adoption' (Jowitt 1992: 224). More earthbound, neoliberal policy advisers expected grants and loans backing currency convertibility, the abolishment of trade restrictions, finance for a social safety net for the region, debt relief, generous grants rather than loans for infrastructure and environmental projects and, last but not least, economic and political integration with Western Europe. To achieve this, 'more leadership and vision, and far more generous financial support' were required (Sachs 1990: 21). Eastern European academics joined Western analysts by putting their faith in 'Europe as the only hope' and pushing for rapid and financially supported full integration. If East Central Europe cannot become a part of the European integration process 'or only marginally, then we can expect a protracted process of deepening crisis with a possible return to authoritarian rule ... The re-emergence of the right-wing dictatorship as a new edition of the traditional type from the period between the two world wars will be very likely' (Ágh 1991: 115–116).

Finally, common to these advocates of the West as the ultimate safeguard of Eastern Europe's future was their pervasive doubt in the possibility that the latter could mobilise any resources of stability on its own, and their assumption of a faultless Western Europe. The uniform image of affluence, democracy and solidarity failed to include real-world Europe's shadows. Jean Marie Le Pen's racism, the United Kingdom of Ulster, Italian democracy plagued by Mafia, corruption and recurrent crisis, and the existence of Western Europe's own peripheries – less developed countries, de-industrialised regions, or explosive immigrant slums in a number of metropolises – did not get much attention.

How did the above presented prophecies fit the political dynamics of the 1990s in the East and the West?

Globalisation without Contention – National and Ethnic Hostility without globalisation

The 1990s passed, and brought about what Peter Murrell called 'the most dramatic episode of economic liberalisation in economic history' in Eastern Europe (Murrell 1996: 31). Many, but not all of the Eastern European applicants to the European Union, became fully integrated with the West on the dimensions of economic institutions, foreign trade, foreign direct investment, banking and external debt. In the context of one of the deepest economic crises of the twentieth century, this unprecedented rush towards globalisation resulted in grave socioeconomic consequences: large drops in GNP, living standards, substantial unemployment and a deterioration and erosion of social organisation.

Rapid Economic Globalisation on all Dimensions

Measured by their various indicators of economic freedom – such as freedom of the foreign trade regime, of flows of capital and foreign direct investment and of the financial sector – most of the 10 potential exsocialist EU-members caught up with the rest of Europe at a remarkable speed in the 1990s. In these terms, Eastern Europe's 'europeanisation' seems, by and large, to have been completed, and the economies of many exsocialist EU-applicants do not appear as either less 'capitalist' or less 'internationalised' than those of Western Europe. Rather than trading with other exsocialist countries, the new membership candidates shifted towards foreign trade with the EU. European investors often provided dramatically high shares of investment in the East (Transition Reports 1998 and 1999). In this respect, a few countries, such as Hungary, the Czech Republic, Estonia and Latvia appear as significantly more 'global' in the sense of having more foreign domination in their business class than many EU-members. The latter comparison applies to another crucial area, the degree of internationalisation of the financial sector. While banking is still, to a large degree, nationally owned in most EU-member states, foreign (mostly European) banks own and operate much of the banking sectors (and occasionally the related services such as insurance) of Hungary, Poland, the Czech Republic and Latvia.[3] Moreover, much of the East is globally integrated through debt. The high debt/GDP, or debt/export ratios reflect not just another international dimension of their development, but rather the specific kind of their paths towards internationalisation: their location next to the 'lower ends' of global economic interdependence. Finally, the developments at the Western Rim of Eastern Europe exhibit an accentuated international institutional dimension as well: they have become increasingly integrated into international economic and political organiational structures such as the IMF and the World Bank, the OECD, WTO, NATO and, of course, the European Union.

Economic and Social Costs

Far beyond even the most pessimistic expectations, the recession of the Eastern European countries resulted in very high economic and social costs. Data on aggregate economic performance reflect a large gap between Western and Eastern Europe. In 1997, in terms of per capita GNP in US dollars controlled for purchasing power parity (USD at PPP), Eastern Europe is not just lagging far behind the rest of Europe, but this region's economic backwardness seems to have significantly increased in the course of the past decade.[4] Available accounts tell of a striking degree of deteriorating living standards, increasing poverty and inequality, associated with sky-rocketing unemployment and high degrees of social marginalisation.

The Dog that did not Bark

Yet, crisis and globalisation failed to bring about the predicted dramatic consequences. There was relatively little disruptive social protest, and most new democracies did not turn to populist authoritarianism. Nor do we find much evidence for the expected political success of racism, xenophobia, ethnic or religious hostility and strife – at least, not in the parts of Eastern Europe most exposed to, and affected by, economic globalisation.

To elaborate on this striking puzzle, let us recall Offe's expectation concerning the potential factors of protest against social losses in the East. In societies that have become used to comparing themselves to the West and are now involved in the project of imitating Western political and economic institutions, the threshold of patience with poverty and insecurity is likely to be much lower even than it is assumed to be in the contemporary, newly industrialised societies of South Asia or South America ... [In the absence of reforms of social protection and security] the aggregate medium term effect is likely to be any combination of disruptive social conflict, symptoms of social disorganisation, and emergent longings for the more attractive aspects of the old regimes (Offe 1993: 657).

Did the apparently 'low thresholds of patience with poverty and insecurity' indeed shape the dynamics of social contention? In the important field of labour protest this does not seem to be the case. Instead, in the first half of the 1990s, Eastern European labour rather passively tolerated the process of its own economic and political marginalisation. Forecasts of frequent and massive strikes involving large numbers of workers and threatening both the paralisys of economic activity and the impasse of political process, have mostly proved to be failures. Instead, Eastern European workforces remained remarkably patient.

The striking degree of patience is supported by the surprising finding that during the first half of the past decade many of the consolidated and relatively affluent and/or dynamic European market societies experienced much more labour militancy than the presumably 'fragile' and crisis-ridden systems of the East. In the crucial period of 1990-1995, labour movements in Western Europe proved to be much more contentious: in comparable terms, and at an average, they organised twice as many strikes and lockouts, with the participation of ten times more workers, and caused fifteen times more economic damage in terms of lost workdays. Poland, once (in)famous for her contentious labour traditions, has occupied only the sixth place on Europe's strike list, while Romania, with all the violent and spectacular actions of her miners, appears at the bottom of the list, and joins the camp of the champions of labour peace in Europe: Hungary, Austria, Slovakia and the Czech Republic (Greskovits 1999, based on World Labour Report 1997–1998).[5] Nor have other forms of disruptive protest become much more popular in the eastern part of Europe. (Ekiert and Kubik 1998). While spectacular outbursts of contention – such as the Hungarian taxi-drivers' blockade of 1990; the repetition of violent miners' marches to Bucharest; the Bulgarian food riots, or the Albanian mass-revolt triggered by the scandalous collapse of the Vefa Holdings pyramid-scheme in the second half of the 1990s – conquered the headlines of mass media, these unique events had been all too sporadic to alter the overall balance of protest and patience in the East. Social science definitely has to ask the question: 'Why have East Europeans – unlike their fellow-citizens in the West – not protested more by strikes or other direct action against their worsening life conditions'.

This is all the more a puzzle given that the method of avoiding the threat of 'religio-ethnic, militant nationalist, even fascist' authoritarianism by reform-dictatorships, as suggested by Jowitt (1992) has not been adopted in Eastern Europe. Instead, economic liberalisation often went hand in hand with political liberalisation.

However, while neither the 'Leninist legacy' nor the inheritance of a racist past, nor antisystem social mobilisation resulted in excessive political instability or democratic breakdown, economic hardship did bring about widespread social anomy and disintegration. This is the basis of Ost's concern that racist and xenophobic populism, as a perverse expression of social anomy, may still arrive. The reality is that people support neoliberal economic reform 'and' that they don't like what neoliberal reform is bringing about. This state of affairs is quite dangerous to democracy, because it describes a situation in which people are 'unable to express their economic grievances in economic ways. Labour in particular suffers as a class, but does not protest as a class: this only means that its grievances are more likely to be expressed in noneconomic, nonclass ways – in other words, by gravitating to the policies of the political illiberals who offer substitute satisfactions for people's dashed hopes. Labour represents the potential base of support for illiberalism because it constitutes the majority of the population and is full of anger. The political future will be shaped in large part by the way labour's anger is mobilised (Ost 1995: 178–181).

However convincing this argument may turn out to be in the future, for the time being we do not have much evidence of a trade-off between the 'class-based' and ethnically, or racially based, perverse forms of social protest. True enough, during elections, East Europeans furiously sought to punish those who supposedly caused injury to their interests, and their protest vote resulted in the specific pattern of alternating incumbents much more rapidly than in the rest of Europe. However, until now, voters in most of the EU-applicant countries generally have not favoured the extreme right. While racist and xenophobic political forces are not absent in the East European political arena, their mobilisation capacity measured in terms of electoral success – with one recent exception – remained modest.

Specifically, in Hungary, the maximum electoral support of 5 percent for the extreme right racist and xenophobic Party of Hungarian Justice and Life (MIÉP) led by István Csurka was achieved in 1998. While the anti-Roma and antiforeigner Republican Party (SPS-RSC) got about 10 percent of the votes in the 1996 June elections in the Czech Republic, and was, at that time, the most successful extreme right party of the East, their influence was on the wane by the late 1990s, and, finally, they could not pass the parliamentary threshold. Similarly, Romania's Greater Romania Party (PRM), and PUNR (a no less extreme nationalist and anti-Hungarian party based mostly in Transylvania, and currently absorbed by PRM) – have, together, attracted a maximum of 10 percent of the votes during most of the 1990s. However, in the autumn 2000 elections, PNR achieved a shocking 20 percent, and its leader and presidential candidate Corneliu Vadim Tudor, a one-third support of the Romanian electorate: a frightening signal of the limits of social peace in Eastern Europe.

Bulgaria has not got strong extremists at all, whereas the influence of the once moderately attractive nationalist or racist extremist parties of Poland, Russia, or Slovakia seem to be on the decline.[6]

Upsurge of Ethnic, Racial and National Hostility in the East and the West

Is, then, racism and xenophobia, national, ethnic or religious intolerance and strife generally weak in the transforming postsocialist World? We know this is not the case. However, the countries which suffered most from the devastating effects of such hatreds and hostilities – Albania, Croatia, Bosnia-Herzegovina, Yugoslavia, Macedonia, Moldova, Georgia, Armenia, Azerbaijan and Tajikistan – are not the most, but the least globalised countries of the excommunist East.

Their advance with the neoliberal reforms opening their economies to external trade and, competition, foreign investors, technology imports and capital flows had been much less impressive than the extent of internationalisation in other countries. Foreign owners, investors and bankers are largely absent in their elite, thus, whatever kind of capitalism they achieved is mostly operated by national elite groups, often of doubtful origins, skills and aspirations. They are poorly integrated with the international institutions, and have often suffered from extreme economic and political isolation imposed by the international community, or by their hostile neighbors. Clearly, hasty democratisation cannot be blamed for their dominant pattern of political mass-mobilisation along lines of nationality, religion, or ethnicity either. Many of these countries maintained or reinstalled authoritarian political systems with limited or absent political and civil rights.

The in-depth analysis of these political developments is beyond the scope of my essay. However, I believe a proper interpretation should focus more on the political determinants of these countries' economic and political fiascos than on the economic factors of their political failure. The recent histories of the Balkans (or the Caucasus) seem much less to represent cases of political catastrophe rooted in economic globalisation than of failures of economic (and political) integration originating in forceful nation- and state-building.[7]

Surprisingly, while the above striking manifestations of ethnic and national hostility in the postsocialist East can hardly be seen as the results of economic globalisation, the intensified cross-European integration seems to have brought about more discontent with globalisation, and more disruptive protest against it in Europe's Western core.

In part, the response involved strong labour protest and changes in the political affiliation of the electorate. This in the 1990s resulted in the failure of some ruling coalitions – Conservatives in the UK and Germany, Socialists in Spain, and alternating Christian Democrats and Socialists in Italy – to keep their hold on power for another term. However, parallel to these changes, racist and xenophobic parties achieved remarkable political successes. These include the Freiheitliche Partei

Österreich's (FPÖ) 27 percent of support and government participation, the success of the Swiss Peoples' Party (SVP) to form the Swiss government in 1999, the presence of the extreme right in the Italian government, the ongoing attraction of the French Front National for about 15 percent of the electorate, and the political advance of extremists, prominently in Belgium, but also in the Netherlands, Denmark, Sweden and Norway. To analyse the factors of the extreme rights' success in the West is not a subject of this essay. The only observation I want to stress is that, apparently, some of the most adverse political effects of economic globalisation occurred in places commonly held to be the least prone to these kinds of developments, and these effects were mediated by new and not yet fully explained mechanisms, such as the extreme rights' capacity to bring together coalitions of potential winners and losers of globalisation under the same party banner.

Specifically, analysts of the west European extreme right have found:

> Radical right-wing populist parties are radical in their rejection of the established sociocultural and sociopolitical system and their advocacy of individual achievement, a free marketplace, and a drastic reduction of the role of the state ... What distinguishes most radical right-wing populist parties from the established parties is not only their militant attacks on immigrants but also their pronounced neoliberal program. Although varying in emphasis and importance, radical right-wing populist parties have tended to hold strong antistatist positions. They find articulation in a sharp criticism of high levels of taxation, of the bureaucratic state in general, and of welfare outlays (Betz 1993: 417–8).

In the brief cross-European survey above, we registered successful racist parties in a number of the richest, and truly global, EU member states, their moderate attraction in the most globalised but much less affluent western part of Eastern Europe, and the explosive presence of racist and xenophobic politics in the least integrated states of the postsocialist world. This demonstrates anything but a clear-cut link between xenophobia and racism on the one hand, and economic globalisation on the other, and predicts specific types of the racist-xenophobic project currently present in the European political landscape.

How does globalisation at the 'lower end' influence the politics of racism and xenophobia in Central Europe, where, unlike in the Balkans, the urgency of nation- and state-building is not widely perceived by the electorate? To account for the political career of this 'mixed' type of extreme right populism it is helpful to take a closer look at the rhetoric, ideology and economic strategy of the leader of Hungary's most successful racist populist party, István Csurka's Party of Hungarian Justice and Life (MIÉP).[8]

Populist Extremism in Eastern Europe: a Case Study of MIÉP[9]

In the critics' view, contemporary Hungarian populism more often than not appears to be an outdated phenomenon. Interpretations of its xenophobia and anticapitalism stress the close kinship with prewar right- wing extremism (Bozóki and Sükösd 1993, Bozóki 1994). According to some writers, it is thus the tradition, rather than an ideological transfer or innovation, that is most instructive in deciphering the xenophobic populist political-ideological formula under postcommunism. I think this portrait is not entirely false, but it is far from being precise or complete.

Csurka's rhetoric undoubtedly resounds with prewar accusations of the 'alien element' for the misery of Hungary. His political anti-Semitism, conspiracy-theory, concern about the 'genetic decline' of the nation and the Hungarian 'Lebensraum' are obvious proofs of a rhetorical kinship with prewar national socialist parties.[10]

Rhetoric and Economic Program

There is, however, an important reason why the pure identification of postsocialist and prewar racist populism would be a mistake: their economic program is different. In the 1930s, both Böszörmény's national socialists and Meskó Zoltán's National Socialist Hungarian Workers and Agrarian Party formulated their demands as follows. '[A] proportional distribution of material wealth'; 'state provision of jobs to every worker, and free distribution of land to agrarian labourers'; 'immediate nationalisation of large department-stores which have to be parceled out for rent to small artisans; the latter should get priority in government procurements as well'; 'nationalisation of all socialised firms'; or 'nationalisation of all large firms and mines'; 'profit-sharing arrangements in large firms'; 'economic planning aimed at production control, and a rational distribution of goods produced'; 'a moratorium on the interest on usurious loans of international capital'; 'nationalisation of creditors' activity' and 'of financial institutions'; 'leaving the Union of Nations, which is nothing but an organisation representing the interests of Jewish freemasonry, and cosmopolitan capital'; and 'just, socially sensitive and progressive taxation, elimination of turnover and consumption taxes on wage goods'.

However, the economic program and the foreign policy of Csurka's movement and party represent a significantly different ideology. While Csurka kept arguing the Hungarian situation would not improve unless 'economists' and 'narrow-minded financial experts' were replaced by 'national strategy thinkers' in top policy-making positions (Csurka,

1992), the program of the MÚKM did not reveal strong antimarket, or statist backgrounds. Rather, they seem to have adopted a variant of the chic neoliberal slogan on the advantages of a lean and cheap (but efficient) state apparatus. (Csurka 1993: 20). In contrast to the suspicion that Hungarian populist extremists wanted a moratorium on debt service is the remarkably moderate view expressed in Csurka's programs.[11] There have also been widespread fears in Hungary that extremists would oppose and try to block the country's EU-membership. Surely, by the late 1990s, MIÉP's rhetoric became more and more anti-European, and Csurka and his followers suspected that the EU was motivated merely by greed, fear and absent solidarity in their politics towards the East and Hungary. However, in the first part of the 1990s, Csurka and his followers still had wanted to join Europe.[12]

Similar to the liberals (and postcommunist socialists), Hungarian populist extremists have been proponents of privatisation rather than of (re)nationalisation and announced a warfare against corruption accompanying privatisation. Their criticism against foreign capital was mainly directed against policies and practices favouring certain foreign investor groups to other interests, and the national bourgeoisie. To be sure, they expressed a positive bias for a would-be national bourgeoisie of noncommunist origin and suggested that their emergence be supported. However, this demand, again, was not in contrast with other parties' programs. Finally, while Csurka and his advisers have passionately attacked fiscal and monetary restriction and blamed it for the rapid impoverishment of Hungarians, they have not, in fact, demanded society-wide redistribution from the richer to the poorer classes by expansive aggregate demand. Instead, they shared with most other parties the platform of upper-middle, and middle-class oriented supply-side measures.

Belying their reputation as irresponsible, anticapitalist Third-Way-believers and unreliable debtors, Hungarian extremists' economic programs have not been radically different from the mainstream of Hungarian socialist and liberal views of what was to be done concerning economic transformation. How to explain the remarkable convergence of economic ideas between these extremes? What accounts for the absence of antagonistic economic strategy conflict between opposite political poles?

Constraints and the Social Base

In part, the explanation may lie in the constraints on the freedom of policy choice. Due to the grave macroeconomic situation, crucial early political choices and a significant degree of external influence, a sort of subordination of politics to economic conditions could be observed in the transition countries at the Western Rim of Eastern Europe.

Equally convincing, however, is to argue that in terms of their economic policy preferences, Csurka and his followers were influenced by the tastes and ideas of their ideological kin – in Western Europe. Undoubtedly, the Hungarian populist extremes have been actively seeking international contacts and recognition. This is demonstrated by István Csurka's highly publicised meetings with right-wing movement leaders, including Jean Marie Le Pen, who spoke on the Hungarian national holiday October 23 1996. Other parties of the West European New Right – Austria's FPÖ, the Lega Lombarda, or the German Republikaner have also been contacted by MIÉP. While transnational political alliances may lend their support to their ideological kin, the European New Right would hardly identify with equity-oriented classic populism, given its statist, protectionist and redistributive economic program.

While populist extremists appeared to tacitly share the European (and worldwide) consensus regarding many general aspects of economic transformation, it is the redistribution of wealth, income and jobs within the elite, specifically from foreigners and domestic 'alien elements' to the new national bourgeoisie and bureaucratic corps that appears to most concern the Hungarian extreme right. All in all, István Csurka's extremist populist formula combined a modern dependency ideology in a local Hungarian – anti-Communist, anti-Semitic and nationalist – 'orchestration' with an economic program largely respecting the neoliberal revival. No surprise, then, that in addition to some losers of the transformation, this mixed appeal may attract certain elite or middle class groups who are not losers at all but fear losing influence relative to others, although they feel capable of implementing similar transformation scenarios with dramatically different consequences for the upper and middle social strata. This is a similarity with the multiclass appeal of a number of Western extreme-right parties.

The Attraction of the Populist Rhetoric

The improving political position of the extremists in Hungary indicates that well-accentuated populist rhetoric presented by talented political entrepreneurs might have considerable chances for success. Such chances may originate in the condition that extreme right populists address problems, which, not long ago, were considered real dilemmas by all political forces, including their major rivals. Hence, in many respects, the actual transformation scenario and its populist criticisms stem from closer roots than suggested by their recent antagonism. Grievances, such as the lack of elite change, unjust privatisation and pervasive corruption had been identified mainly by the extremist populists by the mid-1990s. While from time to time other parties, too, have raised these issues, it is only in the extremist agenda where they appear as central themes. In this respect, their rhetoric has become a kind of 'ideological nature reserve' of a number of sensitive and crucial problems, which both the left and liberal sides seem to have failed to articulate convincingly and coherently.[13] In sum, the strength and attraction of populist rhetoric may come from the fact that debate on the above crucial issues finished far too quickly for broader groups of the electorate. In many cases, it ended before socially and morally satisfactory, generally acceptable solutions were reached. After all, it is the everyday observation and belief of many Hungarians that the country is corrupt, taxes are crippling, public services are eroding, privatisation has been full of injustice and immorality, and, while some of the same elite is still in power, most of the society paid hard for the transformation.

In virtue of the characteristics detailed above, MIÉP, the extreme right party of the economically globalised Hungary, comes closer to its ideological kin in Austria than to the nationalist extremists in Yugoslavia. It is becoming an advocate of a Western type of racism and xenophobia on the European periphery where some of the 'targets' of their Western fellow-extremists – large masses of immigrants and political asylum seekers – are still to arrive.

Brief Lessons

In the literature on the postsocialist transformation, racism and xenophobia as the dead-ends of these processes were assumed to originate in economic globalisation and its negative effects, exacerbated by the institutional weakness and the unfavorable historical legacies of the emerging new societies. They were seen as the perverse but likely avenue of losers' protest. A return to Europe was suggested as the remedy for the threatening sociopolitical catastrophe.

One lesson of my review of the recent interaction between economic globalisation and racism is that the economic losses in the poor countries integrating in the economic and political space of Europe have not resulted in the political success of racist or xenophobic projects. However – connected to forceful attempts at nation building – politics was more strongly influenced by ethnic hostility and racism in the least globalised parts of the post-socialist world. Can we conclude that, against every expectation, economic globalisation – rather than fuelling racism and xenophobia – is actually the best strategy for avoiding such catastrophes? Such a conclusion would be a mistake, because, as I argued, the relative affluence and the liberal democratic culture of the EU-member states have not automatically turned into safety belts against extremist political mobilisation either. Thus, we seem to be in need of less economic determinism and less 'loser-focused' analyses of the links globalisation and political extremism.

A way of breaking with the narrow economic determinist explanations of politics would be to give more weight to alternative theoretical perspectives, such as Karen Remmer's suggestion 'that in the less politically stable regions of the world, "democratic goods" may factor heavily in the calculus of citizens' (Remmer 1991: 779). The reverse suggestion would be that citizens of liberal, democratic and rich societies may fail to realise that, ultimately, their political economic status may be more threatened by its alleged – racist and xenophobic – 'defenders', than by the newcomers in Europe, against whom they seem to be increasingly mobilized.

As to our understanding of the incidence of racism and xenophobia in an all-European context, my tentative suggestion is to think in possible variants, and their different combinations in East and West. Specifically, those who predicted a strong racist component to Eastern European politics foresaw losers of European globalisation mobilised by frustration over their experience of being excluded from building the new society, as the main audience of racist-xenophobic demagoguery. However, the Western experience may highlight the appeal of racism and xenophobia for those actual winners of globalisation who feel threatened by the inclusion of, and sharing with, others – immigrants, minorities, or new member states of the EU.

The next lesson concerns the perspectives of Central Europeans' remarkable political patience beyond the 1990s. To the extent that their tolerance was also due to their hopes and expectations related to their countries' 'Return to Europe', indirectly, the stability of the East is clearly threatened by the turn to xenophobic and exclusive political moods in some Western countries. Leaders who built their political capital on a prodemocratic, procapitalist, and pro-European project may be weakened while nationalist and xenophobic demagogues are strengthened by a potential shift of the EU towards exclusion. Conversely, to the degree that the potential fulfillment of the Eastern hopes in an EU-membership raises the fears and insecurity manipulated by the extreme right in the West, fighting racism, xenophobia and destabiliszation in Europe seems to be a difficult task indeed.

Finally, the intensity of political extremism and ethnic violence in Eastern Europe's least integrated and globalised regions suggests that there are worse scenarios on Earth for a nation than becoming part and parcel of the European globalisation project. Being left isolated and trapped in national and ethnic conflicts, or being exposed to all the risks of a global economy and politics, without any access to its opportunities, definitely does not offer a superior alternative. Thus, there remain important reasons for Eastern Europeans to put their faith in 'returning to Europe'.

Notes

1. Claus Offe also pointed at the '*amorphous* or *atomized*' structures of the postsocialist societies as a source of heightened regional or ethnic conflict (Offe 1993: 674–675).
2. Similarly, in Jowitt's view it was the past – specifically the unfavorable precommunist legacy preserved and even worsened by the communist condition – which reappeared after the collapse as the, 'Leninist legacy' inimical to any attempt at democratic capitalism after state socialism (Jowitt 1992).
3. In general, foreign penetration of the financial sector measured by the number of foreign banks relative to all banks, and by the share of foreign bank assets in total bank assets appears to be much more accentuated in the 'Europeanised' countries of the East than in the European West (Várhegyi 1998, Claessens et. al. 1998, Transition Report 1998).
4. Even worse, in 1997, in the above terms Eastern Europe is significantly lagging behind any other relatively industrialised region of the Third World. Much of South-East Asia, but even many Latin American countries have surpassed many of the ten leading exsocialist reformer states in the course of the 1990s (World Development Report 1998–1999, and 1999–2000).
5. The inclusion of Ex-Soviet Union – Belarus, Moldova, the Ukraine, and Russia – does not change the picture. To the contrary, it poses even bigger puzzles: in comparable terms, workers of Finland protested roughly ten times stronger – in part, presumably, against their losses associated with the collapse of Finnish-Soviet trade – than the Russian workers who had lost about one-third-to-one-half of their whole economy. It is not the task of this essay to explain why western European labour was so much more contentious in the first half of the 1990s than Eastern European workers, yet, it is striking to realise the distinctly 'non-European' nature of labour responses to economic hardship in the exsocialist states (Greskovits 1999, based on World Labour Report 1997–1998).
6. Overall, the political influence of racist and xenophobic parties in the most globalised countries of Eastern Europe seems to be more modest than the degree of presence of these types of forces in the European Parliament (altogether about 10 percent of all mandates). Thus, in this respect, the political dynamics of most Eastern European applicants to the EU seems to be luckily 'non-European', and may, in fact, help to stabilise European politics.
7. To what extent the above cases represent a perverse deviation from European development rather than a belated repetition of western Europe's history 'by assuming and emulating the homogenous European nation state as the normative force of social organization' (Todorova 1997: 13) is a highly controversial question. As a matter of fact, multiethnic, and multireligious states do not abound in the EU, and where such cleavages are important (in Spain, Belgium or the UK), they contribute to political tensions.

8. Founded in 1993 as a splinter of Hungarian Democratic Forum (winner of Hungary's first democratic elections) MIÉP, under the leadership of former dramawriter István Csurka, became the major political organisation of extreme forces in Hungary. While MIÉP lacked popularity initially, recently, its electoral support is increasing.
9. This section is based on Greskovits (1998 Chapter 7).
10. If we compare the rhetoric of the leader of the Movement of Hungarian Way Circles (MÚKM, the movement which predated the party) and of the MIÉP with the views of Zoltán Böszörmény, leader of the National Socialist Hungarian Workers Party in the early 1930s, we find close similarities even from a philological viewpoint. For instance, there is much in common in the way the prewar, plebeian national socialists and the postsocialist racist populists thought about issues of Hungary's dependence from 'the cosmopolitan superstructure' of financiers and their domestic servants, the reasons behind 'the nation's misery', the methods of subordination and it's beneficiaries, the 'alien elements' of Hungarian capitalism in the 1930s and 1990s. (See Gergely, Glatz and Pölöskei, eds. 1991 for the former, and Csurka 1992 and 1993 for the latter).
11. 'What should be the guiding principle of the new economic policy of the Hungarian Way? Should we announce a moratorium on debt payments? Should we ask for debt-rescheduling? It's out of question! To trick national forces into it might be the aim of the nomenclature which is pulling the strings' (Csurka, 1993: 19).
12. 'of course, we have to participate in the political and economic process of European unification, however, it is not somebody else's but our task to create the conditions for Hungary's suitable and harmonic adaptation' (A Magyar Út Körök Mozgalom Programja: 1993).
13. In addition to elite change, corruption, and the shortcomings of privatisation, there were other issues such as the future of agriculture, and the danger of foreign dependency. Other parties' fairly oblivious attitude to the above issues may be explained by their assumption that after the early, crucial political choices were made, the revolution was essentially finished.

Bibliography

Ágh, A. 1991. 'Transition to Democracy in East Central Europe: a Comparative View'. In *Democracy and Political Transformation. Theories and East-Central European Realities*. György Szoboszlai, ed. Budapest: Hungarian Political Science Association: 103–122.
Betz, H.-G. 1993. 'The New Politics of Resentment. Radical Right-Wing Populist Parties in Western Europe'. *Comparative Politics*. 25, no. 4: 413–28.
Berend, I.T. 1996. *Central and Eastern Europe, 1944–1993. Detour from the Periphery to the Periphery*. Cambridge University Press.
Bozóki, A. 1994. 'An Outline of Three Populisms: The United States, Argentina and Hungary' (Vázlat három populizmusról: Egyesült Államok, Argentína és Magyarország). *Politikatudományi Szemle* 3. no. 3: 33–69.
Bozóki, A., and Sükösd, M. 1993. 'Civil Society and Populism in the Eastern European Democratic Transitions.' *Praxis International* 13, no. 3: 224–41.
Claessens, S., Demirgüc-Kunt, A., and Huizinga, H. 1998. 'How does Foreign Entry Affect Domestic Banking Market?' *World Bank Policy Research* Paper (June).

Csurka, I. 1992. 'Bitter Hinterland' (Keserű Hátország)., *Magyar Fórum* (December 31).
_____. 1993. 'Gondolatok a Magyar Út Körök Mozgalom kszülö programjához.' *Magyar Fórum* (June 3).
Ekiert, G., Kubik, J. 1998. 'Contentious Politics in New Democracies: East Germany, Hungary, Poland, and Slovakia, 1989–93.' *World Politics*. Vol. 50, No. 4. July 1998.
Gergely, J., Glatz, F., and Pölöskei, F. (eds.). 1991. *Party programmes in Hungary 1919–1944 (Magyarországi Pártprogramok 1919–1944)*. Budapest: Kossuth Könyvkiadó.
Greskovits, B. 1998. *The Political Economy of Protest and Patience. East European and Latin American Transformations Compared*. Central European University Press. Budapest.
_____. 1999. 'Social, Economic, and Political Transformation of Central and Eastern Europe. Processes, Results, and Perspectives for Research.' Prepared for the Conference on Rural development in Central and Eastern Europe, Cornell University, and Nitra Agricultural University. Poprad, Slovakia.
Jowitt, K. 1992. 'The Leninist Legacy'. In *Eastern Europe in Revolution*. I. Banac, ed. Ithaca and London: Cornell University Press: 207–24.
Murrell, P. 1996. 'How Far has the Transition Progressed?' *Journal of Economic Perspectives*. Vol. 10, No. 2 (Spring), pp. 25–44.
Offe, C. 1991. 'Capitalism by Democratic Design? Democratic Theory Facing the Triple Transition in East Central Europe'. *Social Research*. 58, no. 4: 865–92.
_____. 1993. 'The Politics of Social Policy in East European Transitions: Antecedents, Agents and Agenda of Reform'. *Social Research*. 60, no. 4: 649–84.
Ost, D. 1992. 'Labour and Societal Transition'. *Problems of Communism*. (1992–6: 48–51).
_____. 1995. 'Labor, Class, and Democracy: Shaping Political Antagonisms in Post-Communist Society'. In *Markets, States, and Democracy. The Political Economy of Post-Communist Transformation*. Beverly Crawford, ed. Boulder: Westview:177–203.
Przeworski, A. 1991. *Democracy and the Market. Political and Economic Reforms in Eastern Europe and Latin America*. Cambridge and New York: Cambridge University Press.
Remmer, K. 1991. 'The Political Impact of Economic Crisis in Latin America in the 1980s'. *American Political Science Review* 85, no. 3: 777–800.
Sachs, J. 1990. 'Eastern Europe's Economies: What is to Be Done?' *The Economist*. January 12. pp. 19–24.
Sedelmeier, U. 1999. 'Eastern Enlargement: Risk, Rationality, and Role-Compliance'. In *The State of the European Union, Volume 5: Risks, Reforms, Resistance and Revival*. M. Green Cowles and M. Smith, eds. Oxford University Press.
Stallings, B. 1992. 'International Influence on Economic Policy: Debt, Stabilisation and Structural Reform'. In *The Politics of Economic*

Adjustment. International Constraints, Distributive Conflicts, and the State. S. Haggard, and R. Kaufman, eds. Princeton, New Jersey: Princeton University Press: 41–88.

Staniszkis, J. 1991. 'Dilemmata der Demokratie in Osteuropa'. In Demokratischer Umbruch in Osteuropa. Deppe et al., eds. Frankfurt: Suhrkamp.

Todorova, M. 1997. Imagining the Balkans. New York, Oxford: Oxford University Press.

Walton, J., and Seddon, D. 1994. Free Markets & Food Riots. The Politics of Global Adjustment. Oxford: Blackwell.

Várhegyi, É. 1998. Bankprivatizáció. Állami Privatizációs és Vagyonkezel Intézet. Budapest.

'World Development Report 1996. From Plan to Market., World Development Report 1998–1999. Knowledge for Development'. And 'World Development Report 1999–2000. Entering the 21st Century'. Published for the World Bank. Oxford University Press.

'World Labour Report 1997–1998. Industrial relations, Democracy, and Social Stability'. ILO. Geneva.

Part Three

Avenues to Remediation

THE ROLE AND FORMS OF EDUCATION

Giovanna Campani

Introduction

Can education reduce or prevent racism? And if so, how?

In order to answer these questions, we have to consider, on the one hand, racism and its causes, and, on the other hand, the role of education systems in western liberal societies as well as the forms of education.

However, the present debate on racism, questioning even its definition, makes the search for an answer difficult. What, in fact, is racism? Is it a consequence of the universal phenomenon of ethnocentrism, which can be considered a sort of protoracism? Or is it an ideological and sociopolitical phenomenon which appeared in Europe and in the United States at the beginning of modernity (Taguieff 1997)? Or might it be the ideological justification of the division of labour (Wallerstein 1988)?

What are the causes of racism? Ignorance, stereotype, prejudice, lack of information? Or, on the contrary, is it the non-egalitarian structure of society which needs an ideology to keep in place a system of discrimination?

If the main causes of racism can be found in ignorance, then education should easily overcome racism. If racism is an ideology which supports a social organisation, then things are, of course, much more complicated.

It has happened that, in some countries which were submitted to totalitarian fascist regimes, racism was taught at school. This was the case in Nazi Germany and in fascist Italy. However, the recent examples of the ethnic republics created in former Yugoslavia show that, even in our time, racism can be part of the curricula. We should then learn to identify education systems which are the expression of a political organisation, and distinguish them from education as pedagogical thought. The latter can sometimes be opposed to what is taught in schools.

There is a clear connection between racism and fascism; racism and ethnonationalism. In totalitarian regimes, school systems push to racism and not the opposite. However, considering that the growth of racism in Europe has corresponded to the rise of the nation states, we might wonder whether, here, the risk of racism, or at least of protoracism, is not contained in the idea of 'nation state', which is a peculiar 'european invention' (Pomian 1990) and in the process of dividing the nationals from the foreigners and of excluding the strangers from citizenship.

In order to clarify this issue, the role of the education systems in nation states has to be considered. For the nation state, education is not an accident, but a structural element. According to the definition of Gellner (1983): a nation state is a society whose construction needed a unified education system, which disseminates the national culture, repressing traditional and folkloristic cultures.

Education systems are an instrument to keep unity inside the nation state: in order to keep this unity, internal diversity has been repressed and the 'foreigners' and 'strangers' have been excluded.

The relationship between education and the nation state has been theorised within pedagogical schools of thought. One of the clearest examples of theory is given by the italian philosopher Giovanni Gentile, who was the Italian Minister of education in the 1920s and realised a reform of the education system (not completely abandoned even today). Inspired by Hegel's thought, Gentile held that the goal of the education process is the unification between the individual wills and the general will of the nation state.

Of course, Gentile had in mind the idea of an authoritarian, nondemocratic state (he supported the fascist governement). The subordination of the individuals to the state proper to the totalitarian systems is generally justified by a discourse of extreme nationalism. Nevertheless, Gentile's ideas have also been adapted to democratic Italy.

In contradistinction to the totalitarian societies, liberal democratic societies are characterised by the fact of not monopolising the production of ideology. Precisely because of this, in liberal democracies, education systems can reflect the pedagogical tradition of universalism and criticism, inherited from the Enlightenment, and Utopian and Marxist thought. Education has to produce critical minds, capable of searching for freedom and justice. The function that education systems should fulfill in the nation states, i.e., to form 'closed identities' of citizens ready to defend the borders and to kill the enemy, may enter into contradiction with the universalistic and critical contents of pedagogical thought. These latter contents can challenge an education model which is too nationalist or too authoritarian and thus prone to producing racism.

However, if education systems have to form people who can adapt themselves to non-egalitarian society, do they have the possibility of eliminating racism completely? According to Wallerstein (1988) the causes of racism lie in the structure of the economic system, namely the capitalist economy, which needs racism for keeping the present division of labour.

If it is like this, education alone can neither prevent nor eradicate racism, unless a larger social movement takes place, pushing forward the contradictions between the discourse and the structure, and finally changing the economic system. According to this approach, antiracist education can only be an instrument to promote and deepen the contradiction between the apparently universalistic Western ideology and the structural need of racism for the division of labour. Antiracist education can be part of a larger movement to change the society, which, necessarily, discriminates against some groups.

In this paper, we will consider those contradictions that are provoked by:

1. The presence of racist thought inside the same paradigms of Western culture since the beginning of modernity.
2. The functions and role of education in the nation states.

We will then consider the development of multicultural, intercultural and antiracist education as an answer to racism and as a possible critical pedagogical school of thought.

Racism[1] as a Modern Phenomenon

This article is not going to recapitulate the history of racism and racist ideas. However, to develop our topic, it is important to underline, along with other authors such as Taguieff (1997), that racism is a product of modern Western history. Racist thought cannot be reduced to the work of marginal thinkers such as Gobineau and Chamberlain during the nineteenth century and in the first half of the twentieth century. It has influenced, in different measure, biology, psychology, anthropology, ethnology, and many other natural and social sciences Uprooting the racist heritage from the Western paradigms in general, and from each discipline in particular, still remains a task for the twenty-first century.

Racism is opposed to the principle of universality, which means the acceptance of the basic idea of the unity of the human species, the natural equality among human beings and, as a consequence, the necessary fraternity which should unite them. This idea is already present in the ancient world: *Homo sum*, nothing of what is human is strange to me ... (as the latin writer Terence states) and is common to the great philosophical and religious systems –not only Western ones (Christianity, Islam and Buddhism as well as Stoicism, and Kantian and Marxist philosophies) (Lévi Strauss 1952).

The universalist idea has been opposed by 'naive' ethnocentrism,[2] which rejects that which doesn't correspond to the life norms of the group from the sphere of culture, and projects it onto nature (Lévi Strauss, 1952). It has also been denied by well structured social and political organisations (slavery, the cast system, the colonial system set in place by the European countries, the Nazi state, the fascist states and the apartheid system in South Africa, and, even, more recently, states like Croatia ...).

To justify these systems of discrimination, different ideologies have been used: modern European societies have developed a system of categorisation which has used biology, nature or culture to divide human beings.

Claude Liauzu (1992), in an extremely interesting book, *Race and Civilisation*, analyses the representations of difference: the 'sauvage' (savage), the barbarians, the black, the traditional societies, the immigrant, the Jew, as well as the notions of civilization, nation, etc. Through his research, Liauzu shows how racist ideas have permeated the basic paradigms of the Western culture. It is possible to find racist ideas in the development of biology in authors like Philippe de Broca, of psychology in authors like Alfred Binet and Stern (who develops the notion of I.Q., which is used in American psychology to show a presumed difference between e.g., white, black and chinese children), of psychiatry (the Jewish nervosis, theorised by some psychiatrists; North African native violence, theorised by professor Porrot).

It is not by chance that the notion of race is generally accepted in the nineteenth century: even a rationalist like Ernest Renan is forced to use the notion of 'linguistic races', although he specifies that the divisions among human groups based on languages have nothing to do with the anthropological division of races.

The same evolutionist paradigm suggests the division of societies between those with a history and those without history, situating the latter close to 'nature'. Colette Guillemin has tried to show how, in modernity, social relations have been naturalised and some social groups (ethnic groups, but also women for example) have been reduced to 'nature'.

Because of the presence of racism inside the Western paradigms through the project to analyse the world, civilization, evolution, progress, etc., in the framework of the 'naturalisation' of the social relations, education can spread racist ideas. This is not only the case in totalitarian states explicitly based on racism or in racist systems like apartheid, but also in our liberal democracies.

The work on geography, history and biology textbooks that has been done in the last twenty years, in countries such as Canada, the United States and the United Kingdom, represents an effort to eliminate elements which are still present in the 'common sense' of the teachers. Unfortunately, not all the European countries have started this work of analysis and of rewriting of textbooks.

The task is particularly difficult, because it is not enough to eradicate the 'biological racism' that is considered by some authors to be the only 'real' racism; today, biological racism is generally considered to be just one among many forms of racism. Taguieff has pointed out the development of the so-called differential racism, which focuses mainly on cultural difference. The issue is, in fact, the naturalisation of social relations that hides behind differentialist or culturalist racism.

If we only consider the biological approach, we can see that it has been legitimised by European colonialism, by the totalitarian fascist regimes, by segregationist models (in the South of the United States) and by the apartheid system. If we consider differentialist racism, the racism based on cultural difference, we should agree that it has been largely legitimised all over the world. Even the liberal democratic countries have given it space through the production of a national culture. Forms of this type of racism are so spred out across the world, including in the liberal democratic societies, that it is necessary to be constantly vigilant in the fight against them.

The emergence of new forms of racism shows the limits of a Western universalistic worldview that is unable to eradicate forms of discrimination based on a system of categorisation that 'naturalise' the victims (as naturally inferior, biologically or culturally). It has shown a common matrix between a system of ideas that is openly racist and one which, apparently, is not, but nevertheless cointains racist elements. This system of ideas is still transmitted in Western schools.

As we have mentioned, Wallerstein attributes the impossibility of eradicating racism to the type of division of labour in which some groups are left in a position of being discriminated against.

The Role of Education Systems in the Modern Nation State

Liberal democratic societies are mainly structured in the form of the nation state. For the social sciences, national industrial societies are the modern form of social and political organisation, corresponding to the industrial economy, in opposition to the world of (organic) community and of tradition.

Still, nation states are the result of a long process, and didn't start as democracies. On the contrary, the experience of absolutist governments was shown to destroy the ethnocultural diversity existing inside the national borders which were defined, very often, through wars. During the development of the nation states, a certain degree of linguistic and cultural homogeneity has appeared to be favourable to the organisation of the nation state itself and to the development of social boundaries in the civil societies. The school was one of the institutions which was charged to establish such linguistic and cultural homogeneity.

The Canadian writer John Saul (1999) points out that since the beginning of the nation state, the majority of countries tried to manage their internal diversity by creating 'simplicity': one language, one culture, one ethnic group or a dominant group. This dominant language and this dominant culture are the basis of the school curriculum. In this vision, a citizen of a nation state is a person who is not only part of a political organisation, but also of a language, of a culture, or of an ethnic group.

As a consequence of this vision, minorities were often discriminated against and foreigners became the noncitizens coming from outside, who could even become the enemies. Considering that in a nation state the task of the education-system was not only that of transmission of knowledge and values and the development of attitudes necessary to the implementation of a social life, but also that of the shaping of citizens loyal to the state and the 'Homeland' (and eventually ready to die for their country against an enemy, who did not belong to the nation state), patriotism had to be transmitted by the school through national myths and through national history. The latter do not always portray noncitizens sympathetically. Sometimes, patriotism would be taught, clearly resulting in hatred for the peoples of other nations.

The avenue of creating 'simplicity' with a view to managing internal diversity through homogeneity, is, of course, very different from a nationalism based on blood or ethnic nationalism. Old European democracies – France and Great Britain – have rejected the 'ethnic' nation state (the racist one of Nazi Germany and Fascist Italy) for a civic nation state: in the discourse, the Western democratic nation states have looked first of all for the political consensus. That is to say, a political consensus accepted as a basis for nationhood by the citizens. Still, they have tried to impose homogeneity, promoting a hegemonic culture the 'national culture' through their institutions, and first of all, through the schools. Political consent and creation of a hegemonic culture based on national elements (myths, literature, art, etc.) have hence been both present in, and necessary to, the formation of the European nation state.

There are different ways or levels of imposing homogeneity: we could consider that there is both a more inclusive and a more exclusive way of conceptualising the nation state, according to different concepts of nation, national culture and homeland. These alternatives will eventually fight each other in the political arena. A more inclusive idea – open to, for example, immigration, multiculturalism, etc ... corresponds generally to the left and a more exclusive one to the parties of the right. Often, this distinction between left and right is complicated, because, one finds different positions within, as well as between the left and the right.

For example, in France, there are two different conceptions of the Republic. One is more inclusive and is based on the values of the French Revolution, a second is more exclusive. It was defended by the parties of the right and degenerated in the collaboration with the Nazis during World War II and the Pétain government (Liauzu, 1996).

Of course, the exclusive theory can, in its extreme forms, develop into fascism: in this case nationalism is opposed to liberalism, as was the case in France at the time of Pétain. Fascism included racism as part of its ideology. Because, in contrast to the liberal democracies, the state in the totalitarian regimes has a monopoly of the production of ideology (in the 1930s, in Nazi Germany and in Fascist Italy), the school had the task of teaching and disseminating racist theories as if they were scientifically valid. For instance, textbooks had titles suggesting that Jews always lie and that Aryans always have noble qualities.

The exclusive concept of the homogeneous nation state can be very close to an ethnic concept of the nation state, even in liberal democracies. This was clear before World War II, when racist theories were hidden under an evolutionary idea of civilisations (with the Western white civilization at the pinacle and, the black one at the bottom. The responsibility for the white nations was seen as civilizing the world). Still, even today, too exclusive a conception of the nation state discriminates against immigrants and encourages de facto forms of racism.

The way colonisation has been justified in the majority of the European countries until recently is a clear example. The European nation states were experiencing, inside their borders a fight for democracy, but in the whole outside process of colonisation, they were practising racism, allowing even for genocides.

The Swedish writer Sven Linquist (1999, 2000) details the different genocides that were committed in Africa by the Belgians and the British. Sven Linquist, taking a position in the debate on the unicity of the Shoah, suggests that such genocides may have been a model for Hitler, who considered Eastern Europe the 'Lebensraum' for the German colonisation. However, in Linquist's view, Hitler only reproduced the same genocidal model of conquest which the European nation states had applied to the African colonies.

I think that in the Shoah, other specific elements can be pointed at. For example the bureaucratic order and the industrial organisation of death which have been so well pointed out by Zygmund Baumann – are particular features. Still, Linquist's book is interesting because it has the undoubted merit of raising the issue of the 'forgotten genocides' committed by the Europeans in Africa.

These forgotten genocides should certainly be part of antiracist education in European schools, to keep alive the memory of what Europe did at the time of colonisation.

Just a little example: in the years between 1943–45, in the islands of Cap Verdia, west of Senegal, 23,000 people died of hunger. The international organisations did not have the possibility of reaching the islands because of the war. Although the inhabitants were also victims of the awful massacre of World War II, nobody ever mentions the cost of this conflict, nor of the other massacres, to the African and Asian colonies.

To give another example, in Italy, there has been no real critical work about the horrors of the Italian colonisation in Lybia or in Ethiopia. A film which showed the cruelties of the Italians in Lybia (*The Lion of the Desert*) has never been distributed.

The European experience of colonisation, which has definitely influenced European policy and thought, should not be forgotten; it deserves the painful work which has been done on the tragic experience of fascism and Nazism and the Shoah. The experience of colonisation allows us to better understand the influence of racist ideas in all of European history. It would show precisely that they were not marginal, but hegemonic, until they became political and institutional practice in fascism and Nazism. In the same nationalistic policy, in Italy, the racial laws against the Jews were precedeed by laws forbidding marriages between Italians and natives in the colonies of Lybia, Somalia and Ethiopia.

Another important point is the attitude that nation states have developed in the face of migration. In this regard the difference between the immigration countries of America (United States, Canada, but also Argentina, Brasil, etc.) and the European countries is evident. The latter have not considered themselves immigration countries, in spite of their high percentage of immigrants.

Education, Nation State and Pedagogical Thought

There is a contradiction between seeing the role of education systems as the formation of citizens faithful to the nation state and teaching the national culture, which had to be preserved as static, and the Utopian perception of education as contributing to the creation of a better world common to all human beings.[3] Pedagogical thought has often contained an element of utopianism. In the modern era, from Rousseau through to Marx until relatively recently, education has been characterised by prefigurations and the construction of projects for human beings. Even if the revolutionary paradigm with its idea of emancipation, equality and integral promotion is said to be going through a crisis, pedagogy cannot be reduced to a mere training technique. On the contrary, the crisis of the revolutionary model has identified education as a factor of change (the learning society, presented in the UNESCO Report by Faure in 1968, Apprendre à être), in view of a better society (Cambi, 1998).

The universalistic pedagogical approach was always in contradiction with the idea of forming citizens loyal to the nation state, ready to kill the others to defend the nation's borders. Universalism can be opposed to the national culture. Montesquieu wrote these lines in the eighteenth century:

> Si je savais quelque chose qui fut utile à ma patrie et qui fut préjudiciable à l'Europe et préjudiciable au genre humain, je la regarderais comme un crime.[4]

Still, this principle wasn't really taught in schools in periods when nationalism was dominant. After the tragedies of nationalism in the nineteenth and twentieth centuries – the terrible combination of nationalism and racism – the notion of race has been rendered illegitimate, but this does not means that racist ideas have suddenly disappeared.

It has taken a long time to see how deeply racism was embedded in Western culture: decolonisation, civil rights movements in the United States in the 1960s, new ethnicity and feminist movements are all relatively recent attempts to denounce and break away from racism.

Thanks to these movements, antiracist education has started. One of the first examples of antiracist education – at least of 'declared' antiracist education – was the experience of Jane Elliot in Iowa in

1968: shocked by the killing of Martin Luther King, she felt that she had to do something, and that education had to become part of the movement for civil rights. She divided her class between the blue-eyed and the brown-eyed children, making them experience the hard meaning of discrimination.

From then on, the debate on multiculturalism, interculturalism and antiracism started, and a new education model emerged, implying the function of promoting a new system of social relations.

The Development of Multicultural, Intercultural and Antiracist Education in the past Thirty Years

The battle for the rights of the blacks is one of the movements which different groups of citizens traditionally discriminated against have started in the second half of the twentieth century to affirm their identity and defend their rights and interests. Black people; women; homosexuals; linguistic minorities; ethnic groups (immigrants, migrant minorities, depending on the definition – in France they are called, minorités immigrées); regional or territorial minorities like the Scottish and the Welsh in Great Britain; Corses in France; French-speakers in Québec, were all involved. Because of these movements, nation states have been forced to look at their internal diversity.

At the same time, ethnocultural diversity has been increased by a growing number of immigrants directed to the Western countries from all corners of the world. In the age of migration (Castles and Miller 1993), the presence of immigrants transforms a great number of countries, including the ones which, up until the 1970s, have never been countries of immigration. Such is the case of Southern Europe, the Gulf countries and Japan.

National and cultural minorities on the one hand, and immigrants on the other, represent two aspects of the present cultural pluralism existing inside the nation states (Kymlicka 1996): the multinational and the poly-ethnic dimension. The 'ethnic mobilisation' of both the national minorities and of the migrants has been a line of action to affirm their specificity and to defend 'cultural rights', and has had a real impact on education, in the years when the 'right to difference' seemed the goal to achieve for any social movement (not only migrants and minorities and black people, but also feminists, homosexuals etc.). In fact, the debate on multiculturalism, interculturalism and antiracism began at the end of the 1960s under this pressure. I have mentioned the experience of the teacher Jane Elliott in 1968. If we are looking for a birthplace for multicultural and antiracist education, that place is

North America: the United States where, in the 1960s, the Afro-American civil rights movement and the new ethnicity movement of the ethnic communities were developing; and Canada, where the French-speaking Canadians, after their quiet revolution, were looking for a new model of living together with the other groups, and where multiculturalism became official policy in 1971.

In Europe, intercultural education was developed as an answer to the issue of immigration, after the settlement of the migrants' communities in the 1970s (which had followed the closing of the borders and the introduction of strict control policies for migration) and of the growing presence of the so-called 'second generation' children. Only later did intercultural education appear as a possible education model for all in a changing world. This world shows, as a main characteristic, that of 'globalisation'.

As far as the issue of the education of immigrant children is concerned, in the 1970s and 1980s, the assimilationist perspective has been abandoned, and has given way to the ideas of cultural pluralism and the recognition of difference – and the right to difference. In this connection, the pioneering work of the Council of Europe must be mentioned, which, from the 1970s on, promoted a variety of studies and projects on intercultural education, defining a completely new curriculum for the schools, attentive to difference, refusing nationalism, and at the same time taking into account varying languages and cultures.

In the late 1980s, the impossibility of applying cultural relativism to everyday life – both in society and schools – has opened a new debate on how to 'manage the cultural difference', within a possible common framework of values and on education for citizenship.

The European unification and the search, which is just beginning, for a new European education model, has provoked a debate on the possible interaction between multicultural or intercultural education and the European dimension of education.

I am not going to enter into the terminological debate here on multicultural and intercultural education which terms are used differentially in different cultural areas (Anglo-Saxon is one, French and French-Canadian the other) and different conceptions of state, education and society.

Multicultural, intercultural and antiracist education are, of course, bound to each other, and their combination is more efficient than their division (Grinter 1985); still, their development shows a certain opposition among them. We agree with Leicester (1992), that a dichotomy is wrong. Still, we should point out the differences in the paradigms. Multiculturalism corresponds to the liberal ideology, which supports the freedom of thought and action of each individual, allowing for a type of multicultural education, which looks for the mutual understanding between cultures and the change of society through education. Intercultural education is focused more on the critique of the dominant paradigm, in order to produce new forms of culture. Antiracist education represents a more radical ideology, insisting on the divisions in society and looking for a change based on the liberation of oppressed groups and the elimination of institutional discriminations, in which education is part of a more general political action. We have seen that the famous experience of Jane Elliott in Iowa was suggested by the murder of Martin Luther King. It was in fact part of a movement.

Antiracism can represent a radical political discourse in which the fight against racism is part of the fight against capitalism, of which racism is a structural part, as Immanuel Wallerstein states, for example. We could say that antiracist education starts from an analysis of the role that racism has in society: not only irrational prejudice, but also the power system of the whites, the ideology that keeps the class system intact and an instrument of domination, etc.. Our societies are, in fact, racist societies, and school helps to reproduce this structuring and structural racism, according to this school of thought.

Following that reasoning, for antiracist education the main task of the education system should be precisely to fight this ideology – racism – which is still regularly transmitted in the education system. One of the main differences between intercultural or multicultural education as nonracist and an openly antiracist education lies precisely in the passage from difference to inequality, in the construction of categories and in the practice. For the nonracists within the multicultural approach, the passage from difference to inequality is caused by prejudices, by ignorance. For them, racism is only a question of discrimination which can be overcome through education, in the sense of the transmission of the right values and of the necessary capacities in order not to produce racism. On the contrary, for the antiracists, the explanations of this transformation are not of a psychopathological type, but of an ideological type. For this reason, it is necessary to have a global strategy. Antiracist education represents something different in the sense that the emphasis is put on the form in which differences are used to produce inequality (Moodley 1986).

Still, the three forms of education appear as an attempt to answer to some of the new challenges the school has to face, such as the growing presence of foreign (migrant) children or of children of ethnic minorities, who are more conscious of their specific cultural needs and the necessity of forming (or at least of proposing) a new national, postnational and international identity in order to prevent ethnocultural conflicts.

They also appear as a way to eradicate a racism which appears again and again in spite of the end of Nazism and the progressive disappearance of all the fascist regimes (at least in Europe; Spain, Portugal and Greece), showing, as Primo Levi once wrote, that the matrix which produced Auschwitz can still produce monsters. Antiracist education as such insists more on the specific aspects of racism and discrimination, but can be complementary to multicultural and intercultural education.

In the next section, we will show some approaches which have been suggested to implement multicultural, intercultural and antiracist education in different countries, making a selection of some of the authors I consider more interesting. These approaches represent suggestions to the teachers and indications for good practices. They also depend on the selection of the main goals that education should accomplish.

Some Approaches in Multicultural, Intercultural and Antiracist Education

Multicultural and intercultural education are considered an instrument to assure equality in education (Sleeter and Grant 1988): in this approach, what is most important is to offer to any child (independently of the culture she belongs to) the same opportunities in education. The idea behind this is that the children, being culturally different, will experience difficulties in apprenticeship in schools characterised by dominant values. On top of that, there is the presence of racism in schools. For this reason, it is important (even through systems of compensatory education) to give those pupils the same opportunities. The supports can be different (classes of language of the receiving country, but also classes on the cultures of origin). This approach will have as its main target the pupils of migrant origin.

Another approach focuses mainly on the importance of offering to every pupil an education which will allow her to understand and to appreciate cultural differences. Multiculturalism should be part of the curriculum. Students must learn to live in harmony in a multiethnic society. For this reason, in the classroom we have to face differences and similarities among the groups (Garcia 1978; Seifer 1973; Wynn 1974; Solomon 1988). Multicultural education means to learn about different cultural groups who are in the city and in the country (Hilliard 1974), to learn to accept and appreciate differences (James 1971; Banks 1986).

The goal of multicultural education is, in this case, to overcome stereotypes of which minority groups are victims (Laferrière 1985). If students have to respect the values of minorities, a multicultural philosophy has to enter into all aspects of school-life (Kehoe 1983). School will have to consider the heterogeneous sociocultural background of immigrants when it has to plan their education. Teachers should become aware of sociological factors having an influence on migrant children's educational experience and take them into account in the curriculum (Cohen 1986). According to this approach, teachers and students have to face both differences and similarities. This can be done by clarifying values, norms and beliefs, through topics like racism, sexism, prejudice, cultural negation, etc. Becoming aware of the contribution that each cultural group can offer to society can help to overcome racial prejudices. In order to do this, it is possible to use theories of social psychology, the analysis of prejudice, and so on. We will try to offer a synthesis of the most common approaches in intercultural education.

One approach focuses on the role the school can have in the development of cultural pluralism, once the practices of acculturation and assimilation have been rejected by the ethnic minorities. How can a school preserve and extend cultural pluralism? Taking the example of the US, Perlmutter (1981) insists on the necessity of having teachers of different origins. Diversity must be reflected in the teachers, that is why the importance of teacher training is so great in view of educating children with cultural differences. When the school does not reflect cultural pluralism, there is the risk that the cultural community will seek separate education for its own children. The role of the director is particularly important: he should be bilingual, have a multicultural knowledge, an open mentality and so on. Teachers have to become aware that not all cultural groups give the same importance to different contents of curricula and must take into account the aspirations of different groups.

Cultural pluralism as an educational approach is based on sociological and anthropological theories. According to Newman (1973, quoted in Sleeter and Grant 1988), there would be four types of processes for the co-citizenship of different groups in a society: (1) Assimilation (A+B+C=A), where A, B and C represent different social groups, A being the dominant group; (2) Fusion (A+B+C=D), where D represents the synthesis of different groups in a new one; (3) Classical Cultural Pluralism (A+B+C= A+B+C); (4) Modified Cultural Pluralism (A+B+C = A1+B1+C1), according to which different groups assimilate partially to a dominant group, but in different ways according the nature of each group. The last option is the most important one for multicultural education: a school should recognise and teach the existing diversity.

This approach uses the anthropological theories on acculturation and cultural communication in the frame of anthropology of education. Theoretical anthropological models explain processes by which the members of a human group transmit their knowledge, beliefs and values to the younger generation. We can also affirm that all programs of intercultural education have been influenced, in one way or another, by the anthropological concept of culture, even if many of them have oversimplified the concept.

Another approach considers education as an instrument or a process to develop the levels of consciousness of minority students and the community in general in order to make them capable of social actions to change the social reality. It is a sort of 'radical paradigm', as Banks calls it. The empowerment model is part of this approach. As Sleeter and Grant (1998) say, in this approach, education must be considered as an instrument for social change and emancipation. Banks (1986) suggests that students have to learn critical thinking. Sociological theories of conflicts and resistances inspire this approach (Sleeter and Grant 1988).

We cannot forget the role of language in multicultural and intercultural education as a bridge between two cultures (Brennan and Donoghue 1974). Hoffman (1989) suggests that language not only has the role of safeguarding one's cultural identity, but also to establish an inter-bi-cultural point of reference, where the meanings and the values of the mainstream culture are translated in the vision of the minority.

The issue of language brings us to the idea of the possibility of having a bicultural competence. Is it really possible and how does it function? Different studies suggest hypotheses on the different levels of bicultural and bilingual competences depending on the contexts (Paulston 1978).

Beyond these different approaches, the issue is to determine up to which point the education system has to be opened to multicultural, intercultural or antiracist education strategies and which approach is more convenient for the 'management of ethnocultural diversity'. Far from being idealistic aspirations, it seems today that the issues of multiculturalism, interculturalism and antiracism have become quite pragmatic, as the notion of management of ethnocultural difference idicates. Old nation states have accepted the differences, but are looking for new forms of homogenisation. This is exemplified in the idea of citizenship education, which risks becoming a new form of assimilationism.

Intercultural Education, Antiracist Education and Citizenship Education in Europe

Even though there is an urgent need in Europe to find an answer to the existing ethnocultural diversity and growing racism, and in spite of the large amount of work done by educators in the different European countries, multicultural, intercultural and antiracist education are still controversial issues.

If it seems relatively simple for the education systems to get rid of the remnants of biological racism, things are much more complicated when it is a question of eradicating differentialist racism based on culture, to recognise the value of all cultures and to tackle perceptions of Western superiority, let alone to propose a new common model of education for the global world as UNESCO, and Edgard Morin for UNESCO, have tried to do in the past few years. Education systems resist major changes that threaten to put the national culture approach too much into question.

In the 1980s, the OECD accused intercultural education, and, more generally, the intercultural discourse – to be vague, general and utopian, in other words, to be a discourse of 'good will', without any real potential of being applied to reality.

A similar critique was raised by Tzetvan Todorov, who accused the intercultural perspective of simplifying existing conflicts in the name of good will: as if it were enough to teach people respect for the other to prevent conflicts.

Another critique concerns the normative aspects of the intercultural discourse. Intercultural education is proposed almost as an ideology, and it would merely have taken the place of previous ideologies which have disappeared or are going through crisis (like, for example, class ideology).

In the 1980s, Micheline Rey – a famous expert of intercultural education at the Council of Europe – accused the proponents of intercultural education of being Manichaean. In the 1990s, Mary MacAndrew accused them of being almost a sect.

Another set of critiques concerns the disciplinary approach to intercultural education. The theoretical roots of intercultural education were found in anthropology. Only later were they integrated into psychology, and finally incorporated in sociology and political science.

The anthropological approach, which was dominant in the beginning, produced two risks, or, better, two perverse effects. The first of these was culturalism, which can be the origin of stereotyping and is an essentialist point of view. Culturalism considers cultures to be static and closed entities. Cultures are not seen as processes undergoing perpetual change and containing internal difference.

The result of culturalism in education practices was the so-called folklorisation of ethno-cultural difference in schools: the 'pédagogie cous-cous' in France, or the 'Sahri, Samosas and Steel bands' in Great Britain.

Moreover, the fact of insisting too much on cultural difference can support a slip into differentialist racism, which has taken the place of biological racism (Taguieff 1997). The second risk bound to the anthropological approach is cultural relativism, or rather an extremely relativistic approach, accepting everything for the sake of the cultures. Can cultural relativism be a way of managing ethnocultural difference in a society? Of course not. There are already numerous examples of the difficulties that can arise in the common life of populations having different social practices and social rules who have to share a territory and limited resources. I contend that poly-ethnic rights cannot be in contradiction with general human rights and with the national right system.

The case of the 'foulard' (scarf) in France[5] is just an example: the problem with this affair is that it has often been presented in terms of islamophobia, rejection of the Islamic culture (an attitude which was certainly present in some of the actors of the affair) or what is supposed to be islamic culture, and not in terms of the difficult relationship between secularism and individual choices in school, or specific cultural traditions and women's universal rights (which were, in my opinion, the real question).[6]

Other issues are much more dramatic in fact: sexual mutilations (among African women), early marriage and early pregnancy (for example among Gypsies), family codes as far as divorce and children are concerned (in the countries of origin, mainly muslim).

In fact, cultural relativism, which is the epistemological basis of intercultural thought, is unable to suggest a solution in the face of cultural conflicts which arise when different peoples have to share a common space.

The anthropological approach, which is at the basis of intercultural education, presents clear limits, which have to be met and overcome by other approaches. The 'deconstructionist' approach, considering any culture as a social construction, which is primarily the result of power relationships, allows a critical insight into one's own culture.

Neither cultural relativism nor deconstructionism can offer any single model, however the deconstruction of one's own cultural patterns can help to develop social action and formats for dialogue. Still, starting from the approach based on cultural relativism and deconstructionism, practical and concrete solutions have been found in what are called the 'Reasonable' accomodations (which, in Québec, are 'les accomodements raisonnables'). What do they mean? A sort of compromise, allowing people to live together, around some common rules freely chosen by the social actors, sharing responsibility.

This idea of reasonable accomodations represents a shift which has taken place, first in Canada, and now in Europe as well, from intercultural education to education for citizenship.

The passage from intercultural education to education for citizenship means that the culturalist and relativist approaches, which have been dominant in intercultural research in the past, should be forgotten. The acknowledgement of diversity is not a goal in itself (the right to difference), but it is an instrument to make equality real and to build a new type of citizenship, where everybody can recognise themself.

The common framework should not be the result of an ethnic culture (the dominant culture in the nation state), but it should be represented by the conditions which make actual pluralism – political, cultural and social pluralism – possible. Democracy is, of course, a key concept in this idea of citizenship education. In this way, the new vision of society may allow racism to be overcome.

Education has a major role to play here, citizenship education being one of the main instruments to prepare people for this new plural society. Still, this project has a few limitations. The first is the fact that the construction of a pluralist society is only at the earliest stages. Citizenship education can refer only to *in fieri* experiences and not to a structured model. The other limitation is that the references to human rights, individual rights and even democracy, are certainly looking for universalism, but are, at the moment, exclusively dominated by Western thought. If cultural relativism has to be criticised, the research of unversal values has to be the result of a renegotiation involving the points of view of other cultures.

Only after this process, which will definitely be long, might the concept of citizenship assume a new meaning. At the moment, the advantages and the limitations of citizenship are still fixed in the frame of the nation state.

Conclusion. Management of Ethnocultural Difference, New Citizenship and New Perspectives for Education

The acknowledgement of ethnocultural diversity inside the nation state is now considered by the majority of the democratic forces to be an 'added value'. The European Union, for example, holds an official discourse favourable to cultural pluralism. We speak of the majority of the democratic forces. There are still political forces, which are, by the way, growing in Europe (think of Haider in Austria and of the Italian right parties, such as the Ligue, Forza Italia, etc.), who consider the multicultural society a danger, a source of decadence, thus repeating, more or less, the discourses of Gobineau on hybridity.

Still, even if ethnocultural diversity is considered to be an 'added value' for any modern pluralist society, the notion of 'management of the ethnocultural diversity', as it is described today, comes down to a form of adaptation of the public and private organisations to a more and more diversified public than to a real questioning of the structure and the basis of the nation state. It has not yet the meaning of a shared culture, nor the idea of new forms of citizenship. The principle of adaptation is a much more prominent social agent today than that of, structural change, even for schools.

The diversity is there, the adaptation is necessary, but the structures are not questioned. This is the sense of the 'reasonable' accomodations proposed in one of the countries where intercultural education has reached the highest degree of implementation, Québec. Different people and groups have to learn to live together, accepting the idea of common citizenship, which means the adherence to democratic values and participation in society. This common citizenship (which is only a real common citizenship in immigration countries like Canada or the United States, but not in Europe) should make it possible to eradicate racism, and education could contribute to this. Is this reasonable? We have seen that the causes of racism are extremely complex. We know that racism is part of Western culture, of the Western process of expansion, which brought us to the present era of globalisation. Education can only help to promote the contradictions between universalism and discrimination, universalism and racism, which characterise the whole history of the Western civilization. Therefore, it is very possible that racism will not disappear over the next few years.

Notes

1. If I should define racism in this paper, I would consider it a system of ideas and practices which denies the principle of basic equality among human beings and the necessary fraternity which should unite them (Levi Strauss and the idea of Edgard Morin, Ierre-patrie), a system of categorisations which tend to affirm inequality, and a process of naturalisation of social relations (through biology – biology is destiny – but also through culture – culture is destiny; or maybe the genetic approach in the future).
2. To show what naive ethnocentrism means, in the famous text, *Race and History*, Lévi Strauss refers to the parallelism between the attitudes of the Spanish at the time of the discoveries, who sent commissions to the Caribbean Islands to inquire if the natives had a soul, and the attitudes of the natives, who left the bodies of the Spanish in water to see if they were submitted to putrefaction. Theoretically, this type of ethnocentrism could, of course, be abolished through education (being a product of ignorance) and through the reciprocal transmission of knowledge

between the groups. In fact, things are much more complicated, because each group also reacts according to the type of relations the groups have established among themselves. When we are faced with a structured sociopolitical system and a structured ideology, things are even more complicated.
3. I am not talking here of another function of the education systems: selection. In the 1960s, students used the slogan, 'school is twice a school of class', because it discriminated against the children of the working class and transmitted class values. The French sociologist Pierre Bourdieu focused on these aspects of the school in 'Les Heritiers' and in 'Reproduction'.

Things are in fact more complicated: still, the official tasks of the school in our liberal democratic societies are to select the pupils, according to their capacities. Everywhere, privileged children succeed better than underprivileged children.
4. If I knew something which was useful to my country and would bring prejudice to Europe and to the human species, I would consider it as a crime.
5. For those who don't remember: there was a big debate in 1988, in France, in relationship to the refusal of a school director to accept into his class three young Moroccan girls who wanted to go to school wearing their headscarves.
6. In the United States, the Amish have the right to take their children away from school before the age of 16. This is an old right, which was granted before the time of multiculturalism, that they have preserved ...

The debate between public school, private school and parents having the right to educate the children as they want is a far larger debate (which is going on all over Europe) than the debate over the headscarf.

It is in this context that the 'querelle' should also be considered.

Bibliography

Balibar, E. and Wallerstein, I. 1988. *Race, nation, classe. Les identits ambigues.* Paris: La Découverte.
Banks, J.A. 1986. 'Multicultural education : Development Paradigms and Goals'. In J.A. Banks and J. Lynch, eds.
Brennan, P. andDonoghue, A.A. 1974. 'Biculturalism through experimental. Multicultural education in Western Societies. Language Learning'. *Council of Anthropology and Education Quarterly*, Vol. 5, No. 2. New York: Rhinehart.
Brunsvick, Y. and Danzin, A. 1998. *Naissance d'une civilisation.* Collection DEFIS, UNESCO, Paris. Morin, E. 1999. *Les sept savoire nécessaires à l'éducation du futur.* Paris: UNESCO.
Cambi, F. 1998. 'Profetismo in educazione, in Profetismo e Pedagogia'. Convegno, Università degli Studi di Firenze, octobre 1998.
Castles, S. and Miller, M. 1993. *The Age of Migration.* London: Macmillan Press.
Cohen, Ch.B. 1986. *Teaching about ethnic diversity.* Bloomington: ERIC.
Garcia, R.L. 1978. *Fostering a pluralistic Society through Multi-ethnic education.* Bloomington: PHI Delta Kappa, educational Foundation.
Gellner, E. 1983. *Nations and Nationalism.* Oxford: Basil Backwell.
Grinter, R. 1985. 'Multicultural or anti-racist education? The Need to choose'. In *Cultural Diversity in the School. Education for Cultural*

Diversity. *Convergence and Divergence*. J., Lynch, C., Mogdil, and S., Mogdil, eds. Vol. I, London: Falmer Press.
Guillamin, C. 1992. *Sexe, race et pratique du pouvoir, Côté –femmes*. Paris: Syros.
Hilliard, A.G. 1974. 'Restructuring Teachers' Education for Multicultural Imperatives'. In Hunter, W. ed. *Multicultural Education Through Competencies-Based Teachers Education.*. Washington D.C., AACTE.
Hoffman, D.M. 1989. 'Language and Cultural Acquisition among Iranians in the United States'. *Anthropology and Education Quarterly*, vol. XX, No. 2.
James, R. 1971. *Directory of Multicultultural programs in Teachers' Education*. Washington DC: American Association of Colleges in teachers' Education.
Kehoe J. 1983. 'Enhancing the Multicultural Climate in the School'. *History and Social Science Teacher*, Vol. 19, No. 2.
Kymlicka, W. 1996. 'Démocratie libérale et droits des cultures minoritaires'. In *Pluralisme, citoyenneré et éducation*. F., Gagnon, M., MacAndrew and M., Pagé, eds. Paris: L'Harmattan.
Laferrière, M. 1985. 'Education interculturelle et multiculturalisme'. In *Education Canadienne et Internationale*, Vol. 14, 1.
Leicester, M. 1992. 'Antiracism versus New Multiculturalism. Moving forward an Interminable Debate'. In Lynch, Mogdil, Mogdil. M. Leicester, ed. Vol. 3.
Lévi Strauss, C. 1952. *Race et histoire*. Paris: UNESCO.
Liauzu, C. 1992. *Race et civilisation*. Paris: Syros.
———. 1996 'Migrazioni nella ricerca e nell'insegnamento storico in Francia'. In *La rosa e lo specchio*. G., Campani, ed. Napoli: Ipermedium.
Linquist, S. 1999. *Sterminate quelle bestie*. Roma: Associate.
Moodley, K. 1986. 'Canadian Multicultural Education: Promises and Practices'. In *Multicultural Education in Western Societies*. J.A., Banks, and J., Lynch, eds. New York: Holt, Rhineheart and Winston.
Montesqieu, de. 1780. *Les lois*. Paris.
Paulston, CH.B. 1978. 'Biculturalism: Some Reflexions and Speculations'. *TESOL Quarterly*, Vol. 12, No. 4.
Perlmutter, P. 1981. 'Ethnicity, Education and Prejudice'. In *Ethnicity*, Vol. 8, No. 1.
Pomian, K. 1990. *L'Europe et ses nations*. Paris: Gallimard.
Saul, J. 1998. *Réflexions d'un frée siamois*. Québec: Boréal.
Seifer, N. 1973. 'Education to new pluralism, A Preliminary Survey in fifty States'. Annual Meeting on National Coordination Assembly on Ethnic Studies, Detroit.
Sleeter, C.E. Grant C.A. 1988. *Making Choices for Multicultural Education. Five Approaches to Race, Class and Gender*. New York: Macmillan.
Solomon, I. D. 1988. 'Strategies for Implementing Pluralistic Curriculum in the Social Studies'. *Social Studies*, Vol. 79, No. 6.
Taguieff, P. 1997. *Le racisme*. Paris: Flammarion.
Rey Von Allmen, M. 1984. 'Pièges et défis de l'interculturalism'. *Education Permanente*, No75, pp.11–21.

Wallerstein, I. 1988. *The politics of the world-economy: the states, the movements and the civilizations*. Cambridge: Cambridge University Press.
Wynn, C. 1974. 'Teachers' Competences for Cultural Diversity'. In *Multicultural Education Through Competencies-Based teachers Education*. W.A., Hunter, ed. Washington DC: AACTE.

RACISM, DEVOLUTION AND EDUCATION IN THE EUROPEAN UNION

Jagdish S. Gundara

Introduction

There are complex processes taking place in Britain at the present time. On the one hand, power has been devolved to assemblies in Cardiff and Belfast and a parliament in Edinburgh. On the other hand, processes of centralisation within Europe are taking place. Neither devolution nor a centralised European Union are, by definition, guarantors of democratic and human rights or of the negation of racism. They present a challenge in educational terms because inclusions and exclusions are both possible. There are also at the present time no coherent European perspectives, policies and strategies which can help us in dealing with racism in education. Education largely remains a matter for national educational systems and these national traditions are very different from each other. For instance, British research and practices are informed by English speaking countries, especially the United States. In non-English speaking European countries there may be a common terminology of 'interculturalism' but not all member states of the European Union assume that they have to firstly counteract racism before the positive aspects of intercultural education can be actualised.

The second problem in the context of the European Union is the way in which the principle of subsidiarity is used by national governments to maintain political control over any educational policies. This continues to perpetuate facets of educational inequalities, especially of the weakest group, if the national governments choose to ignore these. In any case, education is not always delivered at the national level but is often devolved to provinces, landers, state, local or school level. Issues are further complicated because centralising states and devolving states may represent diverse political and educational realities. The differences are also partly illustrated by the way in which different foci and different disciplines contribute to discussions about education and anti-discrimination policies in this field. Academic discussions, joint research and publications can help to develop some shared understandings on issues of intercultural education and to initiate developments which would enable the field to become better defined. There is a greater need for interregional and cross-national discussions so that racial, linguistic, curricular and cultural divides within the education sector can be minimised and lead to developments which are more coherent and rational within and across national boundaries. Such cross-fertilisation of ideas across current divides requires a great deal of coherence in, and rationalisation of, anti-discriminatory educational policies.

Terminology and Focus

The differences in the various foci and disciplinary bases are reflected by the way in which terminology is used in this field. English speaking researchers have tended to use the terms 'antiracist' and 'multicultural', while non-English speaking European educators use the term 'intercultural'. Likewise, there is a continued usage of the term 'ethnic minority' without any clarity about this category. Terminology is problematic and in itself raises issues of how it can be rationalised and used more uniformly, especially to develop better anti-discriminatory policies in education.

There have been attempts across English/European divides to develop common learnings and understandings. For instance, the name of the Centre where the author works has been changed from the Centre for Multicultural Education to the International Centre for Intercultural Studies (ICIS). The term 'multicultural' is increasingly being seen to reflect the nature of societies and used in descriptive terms, while the term intercultural is indicative of the interactions, negotiations and processes within societies. While racial discrimination is seen as being central within many education systems, issues of discrimination against other languages, social classes and religions also present new challenges. This further highlights the complexity of dealing with racism in education.

Given the breadth of issues of discrimination on linguistic, religious, social class and racial bases, complex rather than single issue policies are necessitated. The ICIS at the Institute of Education at the University of London was involved in the establishment of the International Association of Intercultural Education in 1984. This Association is currently based in Sweden and publishes the Journal *Intercultural Studies*. Over the years, a number of research and development projects have been undertaken which do not demonstrate a divide, but an attempt to bring about shared understanding of issues of discrimination in education under the umbrella term of intercultural education to develop appropriate educational strategies within the European Union. In two of the issues of the *Intercultural Studies*[1] there was an examination of the types of policies and conditions of intercultural education within the member states of the Union, and these were subsequently published in the United States in the *Journal of Ethnic Development*.[2] It is perhaps fair to state that despite the differences in the foci of policies, practice and research, there are also attempts to learn from each other's experiences.

Collaboration and Definition of Issues

It is very likely that a more concerted effort in the European Union would lead to the development of anti-discriminatory and intercultural research collaboration which would be an extremely productive undertaking. Since the field is relatively new, not only can educators learn from the mistakes made in the field in different national contexts, but also from the advances. At a more basic level, this collaboration can help in providing a map of the needs within member states of the European Union. For instance, while there are statistics about legal immigrants in the European Union there is hardly any statistical and factual evidence to help provide a clearer picture of these presences in schools. Hence, to deal with discriminatory practices and evaluate quantitative and qualitative features which inhibit equality, it is important to have factual and statistical information for effective non-discriminatory policies. Tackling institutional racism, therefore, requires a sound collation of such information, practices, customs and procedures. Policies need to be developed sensitively and with delicacy to ensure that institutional practices are successfully dismantled and not dealt with simply at a rhetorical level. Furthermore, all policies and practices need to be monitored to ensure that their implementation is effective.

National and Academic Differences

One of the major problems in developing intercultural education has been the way in which the malaise of racism permeates education and the different ways in which researchers have developed research paradigms. In most states, the issues have tended to increase in scope and intensity, and despite some international conventions and national laws, these issues of racism have a very complex pattern. Even before any type of comparative or collaborative policies are embarked upon, a stocktaking of the realities and discourses in our diverse contexts needs to be considered. During the period of European unification, matters of education are excluded from the purview of the EU on the basis of subsidiarity principles as argued by national governments.

One of the criticisms which needs to be addressed is that, in English speaking countries, interculturalism has been racialised. This is partly because racism as a pervasive phenomena has brought about resistance. This issue has preoccupied some educators and occasionally been projected into ideological directions. At another level, the state has attempted the containment of interculturalism by racialising it.

Within many educational institutions there have been numerous funded and unfunded projects, which have examined the role of racism in education. Yet, there is very little collation and utilisation of any good models that emerge from these projects, particularly to inform policy, practice and development of teaching, learning and the curriculum.

The demands that British universities should teach more and research less[3] have less relevance in a field like antiracism and intercultural education in particular. This is partly because there is very little good academic research to inform learning and teaching strategies as it is. Hitherto, both research and teaching in this field has been informed by the practice of teachers within the classrooms and has largely been seen as resulting from problems presented by immigrant students. Much of this work has focused on language issues, especially as teachers felt that children were not competent in learning the dominant or second language. The field is therefore informed by a problem-centred approach and has few academic underpinnings. At a time when devolution is leading to the teaching of languages of the territorially based nationalities, the languages and cultures of immigrant minorities may be further undermined. Paradoxically, processes of centralisation can lead to the privileging of dominant languages like English, French and German to the exclusion of all smaller languages. Unless inclusive national and multilingual policies are devised, the languages of immigrants in Europe could face a bleak future.

The academic developments that have informed the field have largely been conducted by sociologists of education. There is now a need for reflection on how to develop a more comprehensive understanding of issues both within a contemporary as well as a historical frame, which involves academic historians and social scientists. Such broadly based intellectual contributions would be very useful within the field of education in improving responses to discrimination by focusing on intercultural curricula, teaching and learning, and a focus on these issues would, in turn, raise new researchable questions. Therefore, the earlier deficit oriented language focus ought to be changed and issues of linguistic diversity and their impact on appropriate multilingual school policies need to be examined from perspectives of difference, not deficit. Secondly, Eurocentric on Anglocentric curricula have led to certain problems that disadvantage students from immigrant communities who may now face further exclusions in education systems in the devolved regions or nations.

Experiences from English Speaking Contexts

Anti-discriminatory practices in English speaking contexts have tended to examine the nature of educational provision for those who were considered to be citizens. Governments have tended to interpret education for its citizens as being different from that of those who are not citizens. These policies tend to suggest that despite the fact of citizenship rights, those who were either black or were colonial citizens tended not to have equality of educational outcomes. If one examines evidence from three English speaking countries: Britain, Canada and the US, then the pattern of educational outcomes for the African-American population in the US and the Afro-Caribbean population in Britain reflects patterns of low educational outcomes. Yet, an important factor of racism has complex manifestations. What is not explained by the evidence is why some black groups do better. Hence, of the African-Caribbean population which migrated to Britain, Canada and the US, those who migrated to Canada and the US have better educational outcomes than in Britain, despite the fact that the Afrio-Caribbeans migrated to Britain much earlier. Do racisms function differentially and disadvantage different groups, or are there other variables which are operative in making the situation more complex? How does one explain the differences of educational performance within each group? Does the factor of forced or voluntary migration contribute to the issues of subsequent educational outcomes?

The openness to immigrants despite racism in the US and Canada can provide some explanations. What has not been clear is that the African-Americans who migrated from the American south to the industrialised urban north have, for decades, not done well in northern schools. However, more recent evidence demonstrates that there are increasingly higher numbers of them completing school and doing better. However, given their long historical presence and their citizenship rights they have not acquired educational equality on a par with other American groups.

Research evidence, which describes low levels of performance, does not always lead to dismantling the causes of low performance. There may be various reasons for this. There exists, for instance, within the education system, a long legacy of eugenic science and psychological deficit which needs to be understood in many countries, including Sweden,[4] before appropriate inclusive and intercultural educational strategies can be developed. Another problem lies in the way in which racism, both in its historical and contemporary manifestations, has deep and complex roots in societies, structures and societal institutions.

Hence, the working class or underclass situation of the African-Americans locks them in structural and institutional terms, while the migrating African-Caribbean population may have greater levels of fluidity in social class terms. What, then, explains the more hardened African-Caribbean class position in Britain compared to Canada? The more rigid British class and institutional structures compared to those in Canada may partly explain this. It may also be the widening gaps between rich and the poor. Even in the devolved Canadian context, the position of the historic black community in Nova Scotia differs from that of Caribbean immigrants in English speaking Ontario. Furthermore, in Quebec the French speaking immigrants from the Caribbean, especially Haiti, represent an even more complicated picture.

The differentials which occur even between different migrating groups can cause tension amongst such groups. Hence, if racism is a major factor inhibiting educational performance, those who do worse, turn not on the racists as their enemies, but on other racialised groups who may do better academically than them. Hence, the differentials in educational outcomes between the very complex category defined as Asians in Britain and the US are seen as the real problem by certain sections of the black community.[5] One of the questions which needs considering in devising policies in the field is whether notions of differential 'ethnic' performances (despite their conceptual inadequacies) and without social class correlation are the best way to devise educational initiatives. What is not clear is whether there are characteristics inherent within each 'ethnic' group which are relevant to the education systems, or whether educators should isolate characteristics within the educational institutions, structures and systems which would provide better analysis of what needs to be done to improve educational outcomes for those who are performing badly. If both categories are relevant, how are appropriate educational policies to be devised which ensure that institutions and communities are apportioned relevant responsibilities for action and change. Furthermore, how do the conditions of migration and the subsequent processes of settlement lead to differential educational experiences and outcomes?

Group Identities and Education

The current modalities of research do not provide answers about why groups who have different family structures, languages and religions from those of the dominant groups perform better despite racial and cultural discrimination and stereotyping. Hence, in English speaking countries, Asians are seen to be doing better than the largely Christian, English speaking black groups.

Furthermore, the focus which defines African-Americans, Asians and Afro-Caribbeans could be construed as being in itself flawed, because such groups are highly complex and differentiated. The Asian category includes for instance, the Chinese – which, in turn, includes Chinese of various nationalities. The educational outcomes for an 'uptown' Chinese and a 'downtown' Chinese in many European cities are markedly different. Hence, if the ethnic categorisations are to be used, they have to be more carefully defined to provide greater clarity, as well as a textured and layered analysis of their social class and positioning in society. Are there distinctive features of diasporic groups which hold across different national boundaries or are the differences within the groups so complex that categorisations used at the present time do not hold sway? In other words, are all immigrants considered to have come from the same social class in their countries of origin, or are they classified (or stereotyped) as such in the country of settlement. What are the consequences in the European context of constructing all Iranians as Muslims or as fundamentalists, if they are a variegated and differential community and therefore raise complex issues for devising educational policies and strategies?

Complex strategies in education are necessary because of the changing patterns and natures of identity over a period of time. This might be demonstrated by the development of longitudinal surveys which can map the changing patterns of identities as immigrants become settlers and develop hybridised identities, multiple identities or narrow 'siege mentalities' which inform the ways in which social structuring and positioning may be operationalised. Over a longer period, the patterns of social positioning of Afro-Caribbeans or Asians in different parts of the same city, or in different regions, develop in ways which would provide a more complex but realistic map of educational experiences and outcomes. At the present time, there is very little clarity about how to apportion social positioning as a consequence of social structures or of the sense of agency of the groups in question. There are also very complex generational differences as immigrants become settlers and their children and grandchildren are totally socialised in countries of settlement.

The national or federal government policies may or may not have an impact on the educational outcomes of those who are citizens. Since education in federal systems is largely provided by state, provincial or local authorities, there are variations in educational performances given the types of policies and practices applied and resources expended. Hence, evidence suggests that Afro-Caribbeans in southern England would have greater potential for better education/skills/life chances than in northern England, where the economies are increasingly de-industrialised and poorer, and educational resources more limited. The long settled black and Afro-Caribbean community in Merseyside has not done well in educational terms. Despite the fact that they have Merseyside identities and affiliations they nevertheless, still, experience deep seated institutional racism and multiple forms of social exclusion. In other European contexts, would the immigrants and settlers be better placed in a successful environment or in poorer areas, where they would lead economically and professionally depressed lives like other groups who are unemployed? In both richer and poorer parts of Europe, what role does racism and exclusivity play in marginalising the life chances of different groups? In these complex and devolved educational contexts how are identity and generational differences taken cognisance of?

If intercultural policies and practices at the state, provincial, local or school levels are superficial and not antidiscriminatory or integrated into the mainstream educational provision, they perpetuate the notions of groups that are seen as 'the others'. This status continues to be perpetuated and the issue of social differences tends to get constructed as one of social disadvantage and deficit. Future educational policies ought to take cognisance of these patterns to ensure that educational policies contain an adequate understanding of these factors. It is especially important that difference is not constructed as deficit and certainly not as a eugenic deficit, as mentioned earlier.

Educational Interventions and Meritocracy

There are complex issues for educational research within the European Union, which pertain to developing overall policies within the Union, but can also relate to issues of devolution and local differences. In this case, one of the major educational interventions has been projects like Head Start and programmes of Affirmative Action developed in the United States. Both of these initiatives have been extensively criticised in the United States. Therefore, before they are used within the European context they need to be analysed and evaluated for their effectiveness and applicability within the European context.

Head Start programmes did not lead to major interventions in all areas of public and social policy to improve the life chances of those who have been subjected to prolonged racism within the United States. These programmes represented educational interventions of a limited nature and were in general successful in raising literacy, numeracy and educational achievement and performances of children from disadvantaged and disenfranchised communities and areas.

The issue of difference articulated as disadvantage and racial deficit has also been highlighted after the Civil Rights struggle in the US, when President Johnson instituted Affirmative Action Programmes to help the African-American population acquire greater levels of equality. They were increasingly seen in most of the educational institutions as being special beneficiaries. The legacy of the long history of racism and exclusions was forgotten by those who went to school or university with them, and they were seen to be advantaged. Poorer whites particularly saw this to be the case, because they argued that they too were poor. Therefore, antidiscriminatory educational policies which operate within racialised paradigms and discourses while attempting to reverse racism may lead to unintended consequences. There is, however, little critical thinking about developing genuinely intercultural frameworks which are antiracist but avoid the possibility of further victimisation of disadvantaged groups. Such policies which racialise groups further may also not allow groups that are discriminated against from establishing solidarities with the disadvantaged members of dominant or majority groups.[6]

At an international level, the issue of equality for women in education was given force by the UN Convention of Discrimination against women, and is articulated in Article 10. Women from subordinated groups who have benefited from Affirmative Action become victims of double jeopardy, because women from dominant communities who come from poorer families see themselves as not receiving special benefits which are accorded to women from minority communities. Article 4 of the UN Convention allows for affirmative action, yet there are hardly any optimum strategies, informed by good research and sound policies which avoid internal tensions between groups of women who are discriminated against in educational terms.

Most European states have not developed a complex programme of affirmative action. Although, where access courses, or special language provision has been made, then students who benefit from these are seen to be special beneficiaries. It is, therefore, necessary that educational institutions appraise the ways policies for inclusion are operationalised, and their benefits, disadvantages or consequences for such groups.

The onslaught by the forces of marketisation in many countries has led to the dismantling of special provisions for benefiting disadvantaged groups because of the ideology of meritocracy. An issue which does need to be reflected upon is how to provide help for those who have been historically oppressed and whose educational achievements are seen to be lower than others, without them being constructed as special beneficiaries. This issue is not only relevant to English speaking countries, but also in the member states of the European Union: there are deep levels of inequalities, hence the question of how to provide educational equality to all groups without them being seen as receiving special benefits. I addition, how does one deal with the meritocratic argument given that very high levels of inequality still exist in society? Meritocracy assumes that there are greater levels of equalities in starting points than there actually are. One issue is whether such arguments exist within European Union and what are the responses of national education systems. It is possible that the meritocratic argument is particularly relevant in English speaking countries. It has been suggested that meritocracy and marketisation are viruses carried by the English language. Is this the case, or are other member states in the European Union afflicted with the same virus? Issues of neoliberal economic ideas may no longer be the privilege of those who live in English speaking countries because globalised economic and institutional changes in education may have transcended the linguistic divides.

Multilingualism and Education

Issues of discrimination can be racial, but they also have other dimensions and aspects. In educational terms, the way in which linguistic diversity is construed can play a major role in raising or depressing equalities of educational outcomes.

In English speaking countries, researchers have paid more attention to the acquisition of the English language by immigrant children to provide them with an access to the curriculum. Despite this major similarity between the approach to research in English speaking countries, the directions in which the countries have gone have not been similar. In Britain, the notion of a largely monolingual nation is still predominant and there is continued emphasis on English as an additional language. Yet, the extensive practice and research undertaken by teachers, advisers and others on first and other languages in educational practice has been diminished. This is despite the enormous amount of work done by teachers and schools to implement research findings. In Britain, the work of the Linguistic Minorities Project[7] is a case in point. The use of funding from the Home Office (Ministry of Interior) has provided funding in the past for the education of bilingual children in schools. This funding traditionally came from the

Urban Aid scheme under Section 11 of the Local Government Act 1966. Recently it was changed to the Ethnic Minority and Traveller Achievement Grant (EMTAG) to be administered by the Department of Education and Employment. There is an urgent need to appraise how such activities can be continued and even strengthened if education of children is not to suffer, especially by ensuring that multilingual school policies are not confused with the issue of acquiring competence in the dominant language.

The Canadian situation in general is different, at the bilingual federal level (French, English) but varies across provinces, depending on provincial policies and the strength of the multilingual communities. Generally, however, in Canada and Australia, policies and practice on multilingualism has a much higher profile. The change in Australian government to one which is now very conservative – in fact even racist – has reversed some of these policies. Mechanisms to combat anti-Asian and anti-Aboriginal sentiments previously implemented by the Directorate of Multiculturalism in the Prime Minister's Office have now been abolished. In many EU countries, first language teaching has received a priority, but what is the relationship between first language learning and the dominant second language acquisition? Is there a research collation of the multilingual programmes in schools in the EU and their implications for the educational performance of students who have received such education? Future policies can only be meaningful if they are based on learning from the mistakes made in the earlier phase and in different countries. Similarly, good and successful practices can be, and need to be, replicated within devolved regions so that autochthonous and allochthonous languages do not lead to greater levels of educational inequalities by racialising languages.

In the largely monolingual British context, linguistic inequalities have been intensified with migration of second language learners from nonmember states and all the research evidence, policies and practices have been brushed aside. In reality, children in school playgrounds and within the community continue to speak languages other than dominant languages. Whether subsequent generations will do so is an open question. The field is largely informed more by practitioners than by research, and this has been the case for a long time. In countries like the Netherlands where languages are taught more systematically there might be useful pointers to develop future work.

The divisions between what might be dissimilar educational policies and those which may have similarities are somewhat arbitrary. For instance, it may be possible to develop educational research projects which examine the educational position of colonial citizens in France, Britain and the Netherlands. Both had colonies, and have had citizens from the colonies living within their jurisdictions. To develop intercultural multilingual policies further, France presents a different set of realities. France as a nation subscribes to equality, fraternity and liberty. Nevertheless, it represents the greatest levels of resistance to intercultural ideas and their implementation in education systems because it defines citizenship rights as accruing to all citizens in constitutional terms, whatever their origin. Therefore, the state does not question notions of what it means to be French. Hence, what might ostensibly appear to be surface similarities between Britain, France and Netherlands and the education for their ex-colonial citizens may not be as similar as one might expect. It can be suggested that in the case of Germany, which considers itself as a non-colonial, non-immigration country, the position of settled communities might face the continual denial of educational rights. However, since education is provided by the Länder, the substantive realities for educational experience of those settled in Germany would be very complex and may not represent a situation of exclusion and marginalisation across the board. Hence, children in Rhine Westphalia may have totally different experiences from those in Bavaria. In the EU, Sweden presents yet another reality and model of migration and settlement. What are the particularistic issues of home language teaching within Sweden and what effect have they had on providing educational equalities for the children of immigrants? The educational realities in Sweden and Germany may also be (more) complex than they might initially appear.

Exclusionary Treatment

Exclusionary treatment accorded to refugees, asylum seekers and illegal immigrants makes the issues of discrimination even more complex in most European states. Increasingly powerful attempts to take away rights from these groups is reflected by the late Cardinal Hume's statement that in Britain they provide: 'a useful scape-goat for those who wish to appeal only to other people's self interest or who promote a narrow nationalism'.[8]

The Archbishop of Canterbury Dr George Carey, in his Christmas address, compared the arrival of asylum seekers with the plight of the Holy Family in the Nativity story. This was seen by conservative politicians in all political parties as an attack on the charged debate on the issue of refugees and asylum seekers.[9]

They have now largely been excluded from main social policy provision. While warnings are being given in Britain about the legally sanctioned exclusion of these groups, the impact on their children's education is bound to be quite marked. Only fragmentary information exists on the issue of educational exclusions, which do not explain the realities for children, their families and their subsequent social exclusions. It is necessary to consider the impact of exclusions on such groups and comparative analysis and research is necessary. The work of the Social Exclusion Unit set-up by the Labour Government in Britain, may be a useful mechanism to reduce educational exclusions, by focusing on broader social exclusions.[10]

However, issues of racism in education and measures to implement intercultural education require long-term inclusive strategies and inter-ministerial and multi-agency strategies. There are a range of issues, which may appear to be similar, but which do not at the present time have any similarities in the ways in which they are formulated. For instance, in Canada and the US during WWII, the Germans, Italians and Japanese were considered as enemies of the state, and yet largely it was only the Japanese who were interned in Canada and the US.

Despite differing levels of discrimination of Germans and Italians, their social integration and higher educational achievement have been reasonably smooth. Subsequent migrations of poorer Italians from rural areas do demonstrate the continuing existence of a working-class population in many American cities. However, the life chances of those who fought for Britain and France have not seen a marked improvement of educational performance for their children or grandchildren. Hence, Magrebian children in France and colonials who fought for Britain in WWII after their settlement in Britain have seen a major setback of their children's futures. Two to three generations of descendants of those who fought for King, Queen and Country cannot say that they are now equal citizens. This remains an educational mirage and the formulation of institutional racism directed at non-Europeans is a serious phenomenon requiring detailed analysis and action, and differences in educational performances due to racism and xenophobia require deeper and more critical understanding. Although research into racism in education, including strategies for all 'white' schools, is fairly advanced, practice is still not optimum.

Practice has not always followed research in this field. There may also be a need to further examine whether racism and xenophobia are different and affect children in different ways.[11]

School and The Community

The issue of the differences between cultures of the home and cultures of the school also raise issues which require serious consideration. A simple construction made by some researchers in the past about 'ethnic cultures' which were distant from the cultures of the school is not necessarily the appropriate formulation of the question. For instance, in France, children of Italian, Spanish, Belgian and German origin do better at school than poorer French children, amongst certain sections of the population. Most of these researches tend to exclude the voice of the youth and, in intercultural contexts, a whole range of complex relationships and antipathies have been lost sight of. Educational policies, which include these voices, would be more useful. Research by Roger Hewitt in Greenwich suggests that 'the reproduction of adolescent racism did not seem to be the family but the peer group'.[12] While girls and mothers could be as racist, there are divergences between the way in which different genders manifest racism. This requires more rigorous investigation, especially as cultures of young people in the European context have similarity as well as differences, and the gang structures may have changing patterns on racial, ethnic and gender basis.

Given that many young people do bring some positive survival skills, cultural understandings and linguistic repertoires that are crosscultural into the school, how can the school and the education system build on these in a productive way? A cooption and a muting of youth resistance is obviously bound to fail. There has to be a genuine attempt to educate these young people because evidence demonstrates that the young reject schooling and the misplaced low expectations of teachers.

It is possible that, given the stresses and strains on the modern family, the school cannot rely on the biological parents to provide the appropriate educational support. Paradoxically, communities have been fragmented by the economies, technologies, fundamentalisms and ethnicities of modern times. A researchable question which needs to be addressed is: what is the core of life-long learning which can assist adults and young people to learn? Racist and fundamentalist adults can undo the antiracist and interfaith work of teachers and schools. Also, as the African adage suggests that it takes 'a whole village to educate a child': how and what type of policy and practice can allow life-long learning and teaching to take place, particularly at the community level, as communities have fragmented. To obviate discrimination it may be the majority adult populations who may need anti-discriminatory and intercultural education.

Fourthly, autonomous peer group cultures may not be in the best interests of the youth. These peer cultures needed to be mediated by adult cultures of parents, teachers, youth workers and others to ensure that young people are able to develop multidimensional and complex understandings of their current and future predicament.

The problem is highlighted by recent research which suggests that youth may subscribe to racial equality in the school. In the playground and the street, whites were being called 'honkeys' and blacks 'niggers'. Research by M. O'Donnell and S. Sharpe also suggests that religious bigotry amongst the young existed and that the journal antiracism of the school was not sufficient to end racist attitudes and behaviours.[13]

Constructing Broader Frameworks

Dealing with racism and attempts to develop intercultural strategies requires a more reflective, historical and contemporaneous analysis. The current problem, deficit and disadvantage models of analysis are not sufficient.

Many English speaking countries have merely focused their research on immigrants, from largely non-dominant, non-European origins. Such an analytical framework can include categories of language, religion, social class and territorial or regional groups. While, historically, most European states have been multicultural societies, there is very little analysis by historians and social scientists to construct a holistic, meaningful and mainstream research into the implications of this for effective anti-discriminatory and intercultural education. Devolution in Britain has recently seen the development of a Parliament in Scotland and an Assembly in Wales. Therefore, European states cannot assume that they are established, integrated and developed and that only 'developing' countries need policies of national integration, especially in education. The complexity of developing anti-discriminatory policies within Scotland and Wales are as important as in the dominant English nation. The integration processes in Germany, especially after the integration of East Germany and the rising levels of racism, is relevant to other European countries.

In Australia, the Aboriginals; in Canada, the Inuits and Indians; in the US, the Indian populations; in Sweden, the Samish and all over Europe, Travellers and Gypsies: all are excluded in developing meaningful anti-discriminatory intercultural educational policies. In Britain, the Scottish, Welsh and English as dominant groups in the devolved polities may not include themselves as in need of intercultural education to enable the development of genuinely anti-discriminatory, inclusive and intercultural frameworks. The immigrant focus thus remains largely intact. What is the situation in other countries? For instance, in Sweden does intercultural education include the Finno-Swedish, the Samish, as well as focus on immigrants, or is it the perspective of the dominant nationality on the immigrant groups which is seen as constituting legitimate intercultural education? In the devolved Catalonia, do the Catalonians provide for the education of languages and cultures of immigrants in Catalonia? The real educational question and issue is how to develop genuinely integrated frameworks of education which have historical/contemporary dimensions. This type of complex understanding would suggest a more genuine inclusive intercultural education and provide quality education to all citizens – however defined. The development of analytical disciplinary based research as well as multifactorial, multisector and multidisciplinary policies are obviously challenging directions which require further analysis, focus and implementation. At another level, these more critical foci might genuinely deal with issues of racism without racialising intercultural policies.

One of the critiques in some countries is that intercultural education waters down the curriculum and lowers educational standards. In fact, what has not been researched is how genuine anti-discriminatory practices and intercultural education that is rigorous and provides equity and quality can be developed and implemented. Policies which develop intercultural education and explore issues of quality and equality do not exist at the present time.

Another issue which requires analysis emanates from the way in which certain intercultural issues have been construed by conservatives and radicals in Britain and the US. The notion of interculturalism as leading to the fragmentation or balkanisation of societies is certainly not the intention of a number of researches in this field. Yet, the construction of questions and issues in this way does present a major hurdle to redressing these substantive problems. It is to be hoped that the tackling of discrimination and of intercultural education in the European Union will not become construed as to do with divisiveness. The issue of religious diversity also presents a major challenge within education systems in Europe. There are increasing conflicts between religious and secular aspects of society.

In terms of values, one of the challenges in European countries is how to strengthen the secular basis of modern societies, in which the school can develop a shared and common value system. The first precondition is that discrimination is disallowed and is made illegal and that the schools are safe and democratic institutions. What would constitute the core values of such a project to inject dynamism and shared democratic values in the public domain. How can private lives be seen to be part of the personal domain, and for the school to critically engage in developing inclusive values within the public domain. For instance, there has been an enormous amount said about the rise of fundamentalisms, whether Christian, Muslim or Jewish. Tackling such developments would enhance interculturally acceptable notions of citizenship, within the context of a democratic civil society. Yet, in interactive terms, what are the elements which constitute such a civil society that is able to build on differences as a strength? Following on from a number of issues raised above there is the problem of young people seeing others as not being part of 'their school', or 'their community'. The Report by the Commission of Racial Equality in Britain[14] demonstrated how racism is used to bully children who are seen to be, and constructed to be, different. Some effective school policies and practices have lessened racist behaviour. Increasingly, these issues intersect with religious issues and raise greater challenges for ecumenical work and interfaith education.

A more difficult question is, how and what educational strategies can be developed to focus on the imaginations of children in a school or a local area who exclude those who are constructed by so-called 'belongers' as 'the other' or 'the outsider' as those who do not belong?[15] The role of nurturing and developing positive imaginations and powerful ideas of creativity have not been explored fully.

There are obvious ways in which cultures have coexisted. As an example, architecture in cities represents a complex story. The Tower of London for instance, acquired different meanings at different times because of its changing functions. In the thirteenth century it was used to intern Jews, and subsequently it was used to protect Jews from rioting mobs. Buildings, squares and streets can therefore present very poignant and meaningful issues for learning and teaching, thus making them a site for understanding the complex architectural and material histories of a polity. Yet, there is a need to ensure that such aspects are researched adequately and seen to be part of a mainstream intercultural history and social studies curriculum at local, national and European levels.

Non-Centric Curricula

An entitlement to education cannot be met if the curriculum either remains Eurocentric or Anglocentric.

The issue of intercultural curricula is an issue within the public domain, and has been inadequately discussed or developed to negate discrimination in education. This is an important issue for the academy and not something which schools or universities could or should reject out of hand by labelling it an issue of political correctness. In order not to slip into the acrimonious debate which has raged in the US, issues ought to be critically examined to institute prophylactic action and make strategic interventions.

If certain education systems were to take a lead in this field, such action would have reverberations internationally, and in Europe, institutions like the European Racism and Xenophobia Monitoring Centre in Vienna may be able to play an active role. There is, however, little conceptual or theoretical work in this field, although increasingly more literature in various domains of knowledge has surfaced.[16]

The first issue that needs to be raised is that oppressed groups who have experienced exclusion of their knowledge and unequal educational outcomes are making separatist demands in polities which embody various indices of diversity, yet continue to be governed by hegemonic state apparatuses. This has set in motion what one might call a 'politics of recognition'. At one level, the demand for separate black or Islamic schools demonstrates this phenomena. The next step has been to demand a 'curriculum of recognition' – which has included courses like 'black', Irish, south Asian and women's studies. It is time to reappraise what the impact has been from these courses on the single disciplines, or on knowledge systems as a whole. This ought to then enable schools and universities to establish more inclusive courses which assist in developing a more common and shared understanding of the past.

The marginalisation through the under-resourcing of such courses has led in some instances to demands for Afrocentric or Islamocentric knowledge to counteract Eurocentrism. In other words, binary oppositions are being set up. E. Said, it would seem, correctly states:

> The whole effort to deconsecrate Eurocentrism cannot be interpreted, least of all by those who participate in the enterprise, as an effort to supplant Eurocentrism with, for instance, Afrocentric or Islamocentric approaches. On its own, ethnic particularity does not provide for intellectual process – quite the contrary.[17]

This is partly the case because separate schools or curricula do not assist in bringing about intercultural understandings. Within complex societies, the need to develop cross-cultural negotiations and learnings are an important issue. While it is important for minorities to know about their cultures and histories it is more important that other groups, and especially dominant groups, understand this issue. This is partly the case because there is an urgent need to develop common and shared core civic values with the public domain. The role that a rigorously selective but intercultural curriculum can play in helping to shape such values is fairly critical. The potential of such developments in strengthening civil democratic societies in Europe is enormous, especially if such institutions can become more inclusive. It is also important that in the current climate of stability, progressive changes can be made prophylactically and not reactively, as in the case of states like Yugoslavia which have disintegrated with disastrous consequences for all Yugoslavs. Such ethnicisations, xenophobia and chauvinism are not a preserve of states east of the Elbe, because they can spill over across boundaries and destabilise the European region as a whole. These issues cannot be seen as issues about minorities which can be contained or ignored by current national states through the principle of subsidiarity, but a matter for the EU at the broadest level.

One of the problems of devising what E. Said calls, a 'many-windowed house of human culture as a whole'.[18] is that such proposals do not carry much weight within systems. The serious question is how such proposals should be presented so that they will be seriously considered and implemented.

Part of the problem is that issues presented in the field generally described as 'multicultural' are seen to relate to immigrants, as the work of the European Union and the Council of Europe hitherto has demonstrated. Because these groups constitute a minority, or are seen as marginal groups in the European context, demands for action emanating from such quarters, particularly in a political climate of conservative restoration, has continued to be ignored. In the context of devolution the histories, literatures and cultures of the locally dominant groups can become privileged and those of other minorities excluded.

In socially diverse societies, a narrowly defined curriculum can only lead in reactive terms to ethnic, religious and narrow nationalistic values. A more substantive issue for social and political scientists is how to assist in devising a shared civic culture in a civil society which would ensure the rights and responsibilities of all individuals and groups in a secular society. Yet, there is very little being done within either the humanities or social science disciplines to ensure that the 'public square' is non-discriminatory and that inclusive values are being validated and nurtured. The question here is how can a changed curriculum be structured for intellectual and academic work as well as assist towards actualising these societal needs and demands? How does one respond if academics argue that it is not the function of curricular change or academic institutions to engage in issues of secular democratic societies and issues of human rights within them.

The threat to secular politics by Christian fundamentalists and Islamic and Hindu revivalists in Europe is something which cannot be ignored. While a secular polity can protect the sacred at the private level, in the European context the issue is how to cross-fertilise ideas from other civilisations with European thought and knowledge in order to develop new multiple or syncretic identities. At the national level, would such developments not lead to the strengthening of the dominant national identities, society and language without the reactive and narrow nationalistic and racist overtones?

The Inclusive Values and the Curriculum

Liberal education, itself at time of a change, can lead to a battle between the Ancients and the Moderns. There may be a need to effect a creative truce to establish a rationale for change rather than the setting up of barricades.

As Samir Amin points out after 1492, with continual Europeanisation of the globe, Eurocentrism became crystallised as a global project. This Europeanisation of the globe bears within it a de-universalisation of knowledge. Not only do Eurocentrists have a theory of world history, but they also have a global political project. From this perspective, the so called western thought and philosophy emerges from Greece and is based on 'rational principles' while the 'Orient' does not seem to move beyond 'Metaphysics'.[19] The curricular question is how can the university help to liberate universalism from the limits of Eurocentrism. The current habits of thought within some university faculties inhibit such a development and this tends to reinforce the notion of a 'Fortress Europe'. To reinstate 'this voice' of the disenfranchised would require a great deal of deep thinking and implementation with delicacy, diplomacy and sophistication, particularly if the desired changes are not to be relegated to the margins of educational and academic life. A Eurocentric curriculum leads to greater levels of xenophobia and racism, and is also nurtured by deep forms of racism which the academic institutions disguise in sophisticated ways.

To take one curricular example would have to suffice. In order to teach art history, western dominance needs to be displaced in knowledge terms, because it has succeeded in suppressing the past and artistic history as part and parcel of human knowledge. As an example of one particular discipline, art history is not located in any one civilisation. It is multifaceted and multifocal in its origins and developments, which are unfortunately not allowed to surface by academic neo-colonialism. In the eighteenth century the discipline had an intercultural outlook which needs to be reinstated by art historians. Indeed, art historians would be reclaiming a territory which became ethnocentric in the nineteenth and twentieth centuries, with the rise of racism, anti-Semitism and colonialism.

As dominance of Europe over other civilisations became entrenched, collecting became formalised as part of ethnology. Ethnographic Museums were opened (Copenhagen 1841; Berlin 1856; Leiden 1864; Cambridge, Mass, 1866; Dresden, 1876 and Paris 1878) where utensils, implements and sculptures from Polynesia, Melanesia, New Zealand, North and South America, and Africa were displayed. This was done so that visitors could determine, as Edward Tylor, Department of Anthropology at Oxford put it 'the relation of the mental condition of savages to that of the civilised man'. To fit these arts into the canon of art appreciation, a new category, 'primitive art', was created.

The great international exhibitions of the nineteenth century displayed the cultures of the world with a similar assumption. The Crystal Palace Exhibition of 1851 was supposed to exhibit the collective output of humanity. In describing the Indian exhibits, the catalogue stated that while some techniques had started in India they had matured in Europe.

To the 'primitive Art' category there has now been added the 'ethnic arts' for the work of the current minority communities in Europe. Such categorisation obviously excludes the Europeans as having an 'ethnicity'. In attempting to reinstate bodies of knowledge into the mainstream curriculum, some difficult questions are raised, including ones about the aesthetics of understanding these arts and literatures.

Issues of this type need to be examined across the curriculum to ascertain substantive questions about exclusion, which have clearly nothing to do with political correctness. One of the issues presented here is how to develop a literary and artistic aesthetic which will not be constructed from a very narrow reading. Both in the study of literatures as well as art history, the question of developing an appropriate noncentric, inclusive and intercultural intellectual perspective and aesthetic is an issue of priority. Otherwise, students would reject texts and artefacts which are unfamiliar. If universities attempt to become universalistic, such a project would necessitate the development of academic staff embarking on such a project.

Issues of intercultural knowledge and understanding by tutors within higher education can be undertaken, initially at least, at two levels:

1. The intercultural dimensions of humanities, social sciences and natural sciences which students need to learn about from different domains of knowledge. (scientists about social responsibility and social scientists about technology)
2. The intercultural dimensions from a cultural point of view of each discipline and domain, which then can inform the undertaking of cross multidisciplinary and interdisciplinary work. Such developments require academic structures to facilitate this work. In this context, students may themselves do original and useful research which would inform the field better.

Such initiatives would not replace the learning of the significant with the study of the trivial, but broaden and enhance our understanding of what is universally significant. The educational policies to enable this to happen have not yet been devised in any structured or meaningful way and can be considered as a matter of urgency. Such educational policies need to have both intellectual and educational rationale, as well as for the political, societal stability and peace in the European Union. They also hold the prospect of developing democratic inclusive values and futures for the polities in Europe.

This chapter has explored the complexity of educational strategies within education systems to tackle discriminatory practices. Discrimination not only has racist dimensions but also features of linguistic and religious exclusions which are relevant to education. To negate such complex discriminations necessitates an examination of Eurocentrism as an issue and especially its relevance to reforming the educational curriculum and institutional structures and policies in general.

Notes

An earlier version of this chapter appeared in *Comparative Education*.
1. 'European Journal of Intercultural Studies' (EJIS) (19940 Vol. 4, No. 2, 1993 and Vol. 4. The name of the journal was changed to 'Intercultural Studies' in 1999.
2. *Journal of Ethnic Development*, (1993) Vol. 2, No. 3.
3. The *Economist*, 24.8.96.
4. Jonathan Freedland, the *Guardian*, London (3.9.1997).
5. The Guardian Education, London (10.9.96) describes the anger of the Afro-Caribbean community against Asians in Leicester. Asians were accused of leading to the lowering of educational performances of black children.
6. G. Ezorsky. 1991.
7. Report of the Linguistic Minorities Project. 1983.
8. The *Guardian*, London (7.9.96).
9. The *Independent*, London (26.12.2000).
10. The *Guardian*, London (1.4.2000).
11. Chris Caine. 1995.
12. Roger Hewitt. 1996.
13. Research by M. O'Donnell and S. Sharpe, reported in the Independent, London (26.12.2000).
14. Commission for Racial Equality. 1988.
15. Central Race Equality Unit, LB of Greenwich and International Centre for Intercultural Studies. 1992.
16. Thyge Winther-Jensen, ed. 1996.
17. C. McCarthy, O.W. Crithlow. 1993: 311.
18. E. Said. 1993: 312.
19. S. Amin. 1989: 91.

Bibliography

Amin, S. 1989. *Eurocentrism*. London: Zed Books.
Caine, C. 1995. *Still no Problem Here*. Stoke-on-Trent: Trentham Books.

Central Race Equality Unit, LB of Greenwich and International Centre for Intercultural Studies. 1992. *Sagaland*. London: CRE.
Commission for Racial Equality. 1988. *Learning in Terror*. London: CRE.
Ezorsky, G. 1991. *Racism and Justice : The Case for Affirmative Action*. (Ithaca: Cornell University Press).
Gundara, J.2000. 'Issues of Discrimination in European Education Systems'. In *Comparitive Education*, Vol. 2, 223–234.
Hewitt, R. 1996. *Routes of Racism*. London: International Centre for Intercultural Studies.
Linguistic Minorities in England. 1983. London: University of London Institute of Education and Tinga Tinga Press.
McCarthy, C., Crithlow. O.W,. 1993. *Race Identity and Representation in Education*. London: Routledge.
Said, E. 1993. *Culture and Imperialism*. London: Chatto and Windus.
Winther-Jensen, T. 1996. *Challenges to European Education*. (Sonderbruck: Peter Lang), Jagdish Gundara 'European Integration and Intercultural Curricula'.

What Interculturalism Could Bring a Solution to Racism?

Rik Pinxten and Marijke Cornelis

Introduction

It is to be expected that Europe will continue to become mixed or multicultural in the next generation or two. This can either lead towards a heightened movement of racism and exclusion, or toward new and humanistic approaches of 'interculturalism'. In the wake of a new segmentation with new exclusions in the unified Europe, two unforeseen tendencies can be pointed at: (1) Traditional lower classes are drifting into situations of low opportunities (Bourdieu, 1994) and hence resort to racist and exclusivist opinions, while at the same time the poor immigrants join them at the bottom of the European society. At the same time, middle-class groups join them in order to protect their supposed privileges in rich regions of Europe. (2) Other groups of well to do Europeans and foreigners see the richess of new consumption and culture in multiculturalism while neglecting to deal with the shifts in power balance (Friedman, 1999).

Stating all this implies that the terms of discussion on racism and antiracism have to be looked at very carefully, and what was obvious a few decades ago (with a clear left against a recognisable right position) seems to become a hindrance for just understanding and action today. We think it is time to more radically take into account more the cultural dimensions of life in Europe, complementary to the socioeconomic factors. Issues of identity and cultural roots are rock-bottom issues in political decision making nowadays, and not just side issues or secondary aspects. If this is true, then it follows that policies to fight racism and to promote interculturalism have to become 'realistic' about cultural issues. In practice, this means that the deep-rooted provincialism and orientalism in Europe must be taken seriously and not considered a mere by-product.

Using an approach that enables us to map out in some detail the identity dynamics of different communities in Europe, and combining the results of this research with a short list of so-called 'sins' of extremism and expected 'virtues' of interculturalism, we propose a multi-layered and somewhat 'federal' model of the organisation of interculturalism. We think it important to safeguard at the same time a foundation of universalistic Enlightenment structures and principles, and allow for maximal autonomy of cultural groups and communities at the more specific levels of experience and action. So, instead of condemning universalism or relative autonomy of cultural communities, we seek to propose a combination of both. The final argumentation could be ethical-political (like decency in Margalit 1996) or intrinsically cultural (Sahlins 1999).

The Europe that is Emerging

After the Second World War, the European Union grew out of initial economic collaboration units (on steel, coal and agricultural goods). Belgium, the Netherlands and Luxemburg (Benelux), joined by France, Germany and Italy, formed a political union in the 1950s, gradually abolishing the borders between them. After several years, the rest of western Europe joined, expanding to Sweden and Finland to the north, and to Portugal and Greece to the south. The EU is the encompassing organisation comprising several institutions. The one which is best known and has the greatest economic power is the political entity of the fifteen member states at present, governed by the Commission. The group of fifteen is primarily an economic union, moving towards a genuinely political federation (since 1999, with a nucleus of common foreign policy and defence policy, for instance). The political decisions for the EU are taken by the government leaders of the fifteen nation states which form the Council of the European Union. Every six months, a different country presides over this Council. The Parliament basically controls the Commission and (to a lesser extent) the Council. The Council of the European Union (that is, of the fifteen member states) is formed by all ministers of a particular competence (depending on the agenda: foreign affairs, public health, etc.) and sets a long-term political agenda for Europe.

Over the past 50 years, a second organisation, comprising, for the latest decade, 41 member states, has been in existence: the Council of Europe. Since 1996, Russia is part of this organisation, as well as such muslim countries like Albania, Turkey, Cyprus and Bulgaria. All former Eastern European countries are part of it. Since the Vienna Declaration (1993), the Council of Europe not only guards 'democracy, rule of law and the human rights' within the EU and investigates whether these principles are fully shared by candidates for membership, but also starts to develop programs against racism and a positive 'plan of action' for the protection of national minorities. In that sense, the Council takes stands on wider political issues than the merely economic ones. For example, the Council decided that the European institutions should develop laws and implementation bodies to guard 'democratic security' and to actively combat 'racism and intolerance' (Vienna, 1993).

The role of the European Union (i.e., the union of the fifteen states) as a guarantee for peace in this part of the world became ever more prominent. The role of economic power is undeniable, especially since the start of the introduction of the Euro as monetary unit. From 1999–2000 onwards, negotiations are going on with possible new members of the Union on the eastern border: the so-called Eastern European countries like Poland and Slovakia, for instance, but also 'oriental' nations like Cyprus and Turkey. With the introduction of the latter as possible members, we think a move might be made to realise the larger political unit which would eventually span all sides of the Mediterranean sea. After the fall of the Berlin Wall (1989) we witnessed a decade of tremendous dynamics in the Council: since the Vienna Declaration most of Eastern Europe has joined, including the four muslim countries mentioned. In a decade, a diplomatic territory has thus been covered, a feat which was thought impossible for centuries. We understand from our personal communications with Spanish, Portuguese, Maghreb and Israeli friends that an expansion to the south coast of the Mediterranean might be considered in the future, and certainly carries the hope of many. The realisation of the integration of north African (Maghreb) and Asian parts (Israel, Turkey, etc.) into the Union would offer a unique opportunity to establish durable peace in this part of the world. At the same time, a solid economic power would emerge with a sufficient labour market and a vast exchange market. Of course, this expansion is not realised yet, but it is our 'educated guess' that we are moving in that direction (since talks with Cyprus and Turkey got started) and that Europe will have to develop that way or else yield 'Fortress Europe in conflict with muslim countries'.

In this paper, we subscribe to the 'visionary' hypothesis that the expansion sketched will be the goal for the next generation or so, and ask ourselves what will be the likely manifestations of racism and exclusion which will emerge during that process, especially because of the integration of muslim populations in the Union. Some of these manifestations are already surfacing now, and we speculate on the ways to deal with them in this contribution. A factor which can not be underestimated in this complex, is that of the historical basic intuitions in 'christian' European countries and 'muslim' new members and the antagonism between them that has existed over the centuries. We propose to analyse any possible policy on racism in Europe from now on while taking this long term perspective of the larger EU and at the same time granting that habits and ideas within populations change rather slowly or die hard. That is to say, that antiracism policies should not just mend results of crises and offences, but that they should evaluate actions and structures from a deeper and a more longitudinal perspective.

The European Union (EU) does not have a finished political structure, and consecutive rounds of talks are being organised to discuss what the future structure should be and how the larger Union can function: suggested plans range from a loose confederacy of nation states to an integrated sociopolitical superstate. The historical legacy is important, of course.As it is, the EU grows out of nation-states, each of which have existed for at least a century, often pursuing bloody wars against each other. This implies that citizens within these nation states have been raised in some form of nationalistic ideology for generations, often looking upon the subjects of other nations as enemies who can be held responsible for the death of relatives during war campaigns. Not only the German-French or German-English antagonism is relevant here, but the long term nationalistic propaganda between Greece and Turkey, or Israel and its neighbours offer examples of the difficulties to be overcome before the peoples of the whole area would consider to live peacefully in one union.

Concepts

In order to sketch what is happening in the EU we need a few concepts and terms that we can work with.

In the first place, we use 'multiculturalism' and 'interculturalism' in the way they are generally understood now in research on intercultural education: 'multicultural' is a descriptive term pointing to the factual given that a population is mixed, comprising groups from more than one cultural origin. Europe and the US are multicultural societies in that sense. 'Intercultural' refers to ways the groups from different origins organise communication and interaction across initial cultural borders, as a constructive means to cope with diversity. One can easily see that intercultural forms can be refused (as in the ethnic cleansing and the monocultural option) or that they can be promoted through education, cultural and social policies and so on. Interculturality demands skills to deal with diversity in long-term monocultural areas like Europe, a willingness to be open to others and cognitive, behavioural as well as emotional categories (instead of anxiety) that enhance the fitness for a mixed context.

In the second place, we need a viable concept of *freedom*. The (neo)liberal ideology which is rampant today has it that freedom is all we need to have a decent society which will allow a place to everybody, enough food and housing, etc. This is the negative notion of freedom: freedom from slavery, freedom from tutelage by the state, freedom from others. The so-called free market would then have its own laws which organise the world in an optimal form, once it can be deployed freely. (That the notion of free market may be an ideological fraud, which covers actual oligopolies of corporations (Korten 1995) is not our focus here).

We think a positive notion of freedom can be invoked which comprises the one outlined above and adds the criterion of equivalence. Freedom would then mean freedom of choice within a context that guarantees equal opportunities to all. In that case, freedom of all is only feasible when at the same time a redistributive equivalence obtains. The decent society in that case is not simply that of free individuals and a free market, but a society which makes choices for the good of everyone and makes a certain amount of rules and principles coercive for everybody. In a sense freedom is not just 'freedom from', but also 'freedom to'. This distinction might still be too simple: e.g., Giddens (1998) states that freedom + equal opportunities is still a 'neoliberal' ideological stand, and hence does not qualify as European tradition (but rather as a USA format) for him. Instead, the 'Third way' he advocates as an alternative for European integration stresses freedom + responsibility and solidarity, and an active participation in the state by critical citizens. Of course, this debate is far from closed. It suffices to indicate we are aware of the discussion and we take a particular stand.

To clarify the notions we encounter we propose the following conventions: Neoliberalism takes for granted that human beings are intrinsically free individuals. Any external constraints should hence be eliminated as they would hamper the intrinsically good and selforganising power of freedom. In practice, this view allows for severe and self-justifying inequality, in a corporation ruled world (the 'dual' society). In terms of culturally diversified societies and racism, it may yield so-called 'consumptive interculturalism' (just buying the products from others) and political segregation at the same time (type 'Fortress

Europe' or the exclusion of the poor and of others by the rich). Without corrective sanctions this leads to structural racism. The old socialist perspective held that human beings are free, but that a 'good' society will only emerge when such freedom is severely controlled and guided, in the end even programmed by structures which are compelling and are installed from above. The pessimism in this view holds that a third party (the state, the socialist party) should sanction the egotist tendencies in individuals. In terms of our focus on racism, the socialist view held that, with the economic well being of all, racism might disappear with time (Giddens 1998).

The communitarian perspective, which is mostly found in new extreme rightist parties at the present, states that community rights and community identity come first and override both the individual freedom and individual rights on the one hand, and the state rights and laws as well as Human Rights on the other hand. In terms of racism, it justifies exclusion of the other, because of so-called cultural particularities and constraints (de Benoist 1998). In our view, the cultural factors have been underestimated by both socialist and neoliberal programs, which start from rather exclusive views on human beings and society. On the other hand, the communitarian ideology is partly false and partly outdated, but grants some role for cultural issues. However delicate the question may be, we want to confront this complex head on.

The third concept is 'essentialism': every person wants to belong to a group or community. In that striving, one identifies with a group or community, which means that one's own identity (partly and temporarily) overlaps with that of the group or community. When people invest in an essentialistic identity, they claim and experience the identity adopted as unique, fundamentally unchanging, everlasting and inalienable. The 'Blut und Botem' version is the better known expression of this view on identity. Scientifically speaking, this essentialism is nonsensical, but politically it continues to have a great appeal (Pinxten & Verstraete, 1998). Essentialism is double-edged: it defines one's own inalienable identity and projects a similar unchanging complex onto the Other. The Other is constructed as a community with a different static identity, which at the same time creates a deep divide between them and us. These static identities turn the intercultural program and the integration of others in our dominant culture into an impossible endeavor.

Trends

Keeping in mind these conceptual distinctions, we see, at the least, two important trends emerging within the EU over the latest decade or so. That is, since the fall of the Berlin Wall and the collapse of the USSR, globalisation of 'wild capitalism' attacks old political structures and causes fear in sections of the population who live from older industrial labour.

In the political consciousness of Europeans we see three main effects. One trend is the hesitant and rather badly coordinated development of interculturalist society: some better situated European subjects travel, read about other cultures, sit on mixed boards, eat 'ethnic' from time to time, and so on, and consider the growing presence of the 'others' an enriching experience, provided they 'integrate'. With the rise of the ideology of freedom, this trend in fact turns out to be a mild 'laissez faire' in sociocultural matters, coupled with a factual dual society. The ideology of contemporary social liberalism (in the UK and on the European continent) seems to capture this, if it has a clear contents at all. Conservatives, christian democrats and socialists throughout Europe embrace this point of view. In an intriguing conversation between G. Grass and P. Bourdieu on Arte television (December 1999), the latter took the stand that neoliberalism is in fact in power, even in the guise of social democrats like Blair. Neoliberalism implies the demolishing of the power of the workers unions, the uncontrolled flow of capital in an uncontrolled stock market, the preaching of individual freedom as the highest virtue (unhampered by community rules and sanctions), and the reduction of the welfare state facilities for the needy. In all EU nations the statement that freedom should be enhanced by diminishing the state power is the basic stance of governments.

Within this context, different sub-trends can develop: factual multiculturalism can be matched with shallow interculturalism. For example, groups can opt for a strict internal monoculturalism (with white neighbourhoods, a safe and policed inner quarter of well to do people, etc.) and 'external interculturalism'. The latter means that one can visit the places of the other cultures as a tourist, abroad or in one's own country. 'Integration' on the part of the other-cultural subjects then means that they will know their place and stay there, not to mingle with the natives. They should remain in their country or in the designated neighbourhoods away from the richer citizens, away from the better schools, from the centres of power, and so on. The wealthy citizens are then 'free from' the others, and can visit them as tourists do. The opportunities are not equal for all parties: the others have no free choice like the better situated natives have. An essentialistic interpretation of one's own identity can easily supplement this freedom discourse. In our perception this sort of political situation obtains when rich parts of Europe such as Austria, Denmark or Flanders recognise themselves in the identity propaganda of extreme rightist parties.

It is interesting to note that socialist thinkers and politicians are attempting to correct the neoliberal trend in Europe by invoking the so-called 'Third Way': not the state-controlled soviet system, nor the individualistic dual society of the US, but a highly redistributive European system with a considerable social security and educational system to fight new exclusions (Giddens 1998). This 'Third Way' would combine freedom with equivalence and solidarity. Moreover, the citizen would become an active agent in the democratic functioning of the political structures. However, for the time being this is a theoretical construct. In practice, we witness an uncontrolled expansion of the free market ideology and a reduction of old solidarity structures. The better situated European gains from this evolution: goods and services are more easily available and cheaper at times. The poor European is excluded in new ways (Bourdieu 1994).

So, it is our conviction that beyond the material and economic basis of inequality, and within the generalised trend of expanding freedom, a new territory for racism and exclusion is growing. In the year 2000, rich small countries such as Austria, Switzerland, Denmark and Belgium have seen tremendous growth of extreme rightist parties in elections, and it is our conviction that the (neoliberal) ideology of freedom coupled with an essentialism on identity may yield for large groups of 'have somes' a justification of a segregated society and of a 'consumptive' interculturalism. This, together with protectionist ideologies in 'small countries' would partially explain the success of new xenophobia. Our suggestion is that we are confronting a cultural formatting here, which should be taken seriously in itself. The simple hope that 'better economic circumstances will dissipate racism' is a dangerous misperception, in our view.

A second trend is manifest in the lower classes or the groups of people who are excluded from the wealth society. They live in 'bad' neighbourhoods, feel abandoned by their political representatives, have their dreams of a better life scattered by unemployment and stagnation of opportunities, and live in the worse parts of the cities or on camping grounds. Violence is growing here, and policies such as 'zero tolerance' police actions openly repress any protest. These groups turn more and more towards extreme rightist parties, rejection of democracy, and a xenophobic view on society. The political establishment, the intellectuals and the European Union are seen as the enemies, and a neofascist ideology of communitarianism is embraced. Populist rhetorics is on the way up, helped by mass media such as television. The extreme right parties in Europe feed on this discontent as is clearly seen in their political grip on 'poor neighbourhoods' in cities (Spruyt 2000, and our field work in Belgian cities). In our view the ideology of new extreme right parties rejects the project of a large Union in favour of a smaller community to which one can belong, in which a certain fixed order and lack of freedom is defined, and interprets freedom as laxism and lack of safety and care. This trend is vastly underestimated (e.g., by European political parties), and its development seems not without ground. That is to say, at all levels of the functioning of the nation state (justice, police, taxes, urbanisation offices, social services, housing policies, etc.) more and more lower opportunity groups are excluded: they are loosing their job because they worked in 'old' industries (such as the automobile industry), or in radically changing businesses (such as banks, telephone or media industries) with ever growing 'flexibility' of job structure. Not only handworkers lose their jobs and get rapidly 'outmoded', but also lower clerks, and, in general, older employees are licensed. Also, coloured people and/or immigrants and refugees get the worst and most insecure jobs or no opportunities at all. The extent of this new structural exclusion is becoming clear in the beautiful collection *La Misère Du Monde*, which gives a unique fresco of the span of this trend (Bourdieu 1994). Looked at from the point of view of the Maghreb immigrant, the book by the late Sayad (1999) is a must. The feeling of rejection by the state and by the European Union (which is a 'big money union' with tremendous bureaucracy there) is getting firmly installed in the minds of this growing population of the have-nots. Their alternative is to fight the state and Europe and to vote for those politicians who take up these negative points in their programme and promote primordialism as an alternative: all extreme rightist parties in Europe. The claim is, then, that local communities have rights and privileges over and above the rights of the state and that of 'universalistic' levels such as Europe or the UN. The populist slogan of primordialism and the ideological claim of the sanity of 'ethnic cleansing' and cultural separation is the alternative that is presented as a utopia here: the community would have a (local and particularistic) identity which should be the basis of any recognisable and local political structure.

If the two trends exist next to each other, and simultaneously, they should be analysed carefully. For one thing, policy making cannot continue to be (as it often is now) an activity of the representatives of the better situated groups or of the big corporations over the heads of the other population and apparently (in their experience at least) installing control against the latter. The isolation and condemnation of the frustrated groups who vote for the new extreme right, as well as the denial of the right to vote for immigrants is in conflict with the democratic principles of European states and appears more like 'looking away' from the problem than actually taking it into account. Not looking at these trends in detail might turn them into a time bomb for Europe.

A third group of citizens presents a rather scattered minority. They are aware of the changing identity dynamics and take them seriously. They appreciate the multicultural character of Europe as a new given and seek to offer new solutions for this phenomenon. It is this minority that is exploring the nature and potential of interculturalism. What particular capacities should citizens show to deal with cultural and social diversity in a positive way? How can peaceful and durable coexistence of diverse groups and communities be allowed for, and what sanctions are effective to promote intercultural procedures for conflict avoidance and resolution? What educational strategies and what socialisation programs are to be preferred? In intercultural studies these and other questions are central, albeit for a small group of people at the present stage.

It is obviously beyond the limits of this contribution, and beyond the competence of the authors, to discuss this whole complex at once. Rather, as we want to point to deep policy solutions, we emphasise a few often forgotten cultural factors which should be taken into account if durable interculturalism is sought. We do not deny that socioeconomic initiatives are needed to allow for a society with just opportunities for all, but we claim that the role of cultural traditions is often underestimated in the antiracism discourse and policy. The new extreme rightist stresses fear of the other, protection of one's own property and cultural heritage, and the right of exclusion because of possible contamination of one's civilizational core. These more or less irrational attitudes and convictions are rooted now and will not simply go away with economic development. It is, at the very least, indicative that the richer regions of Europe (Austria, Denmark, Flanders, North Italy, Switzerland) produced a substantial following for extreme rightist political movements.

Cultural Essentialism

The European Union grew out of nation states which have been promoting their own identity and coherence for the past two centuries, often against neighbouring nation states. Within these states, the right of violence was delegated by the citizen to the state, which used patriotic and/or nationalistic identity processes to produce loyal citizens: education in history was national and not European for at least ten generations, and law, jurisdiction, language policy, the media and other public life instances were developed in the frame of the national boundaries. At the present time, a rapid change is sweeping over these nation states; the territory of legislation and of economic competition is suddenly defined as the EU with its 370 million inhabitants, twelve languages, and many lifestyles. Deregulation and free market rules demolish social and job securities of the past and dwarf many national and regional cultural and political entities, causing anxiety and a feeling of loss of identity in many. With the nationalistic and/or nation state ideology of the past in mind, it is to be expected that two alternative nationalisms are explored. One could be an ideology which strives for European nationalism against, for instance, American nationalism. We do not see how this desire could be realised, because of the history of strong nation states in Europe and the lack of unambiguous levers for European nationalism. The other way to 'reapply' the nationalistic frame of thought is to identify regional monocultural entities and promote the subjacent exclusivist and primordialist principles over the restricted population and territory. By defining the cultural features within a region as essences, that is as inalienable and everlasting organic characteristics, extreme rightist movements in Europe counter the fears among these communities and justify an exclusivist policy because of so-called cultural roots. This process strongly resembles what Gellner (1996) identified at the end of the Habsburg empire.

In the literature, anthropologists investigate these recent shifts in culturally inspired political practice. Friedman (1999) stresses that 'European countries have a negative attitude to immigration. Evidence ... is that integration is not occurring and that enclavisation and conflict are serious and growing' (1999: 681). The nation state as a cultural-historical construct in these parts, is anti-multicultural, and hence hinders changes. The urban anthropologist U. Hannerz adds that citizenship notions redefine national adherences in cultural terms (and often within regions instead of states) leading to a situation where 'the politics of exclusion in Europe now often takes the form of cultural fundamentalism rather than racism in the strict sense' (1999: 689). In an intercontinental context Appadurai (1996) stresses the point that transnational (or postnational) 'Others' are appearing in influential jobs and places, often accompanied by violence and exclusivist refusal by nationalists. It suffices to mention the immigration of high tech graduates in the US and Europe from Asia over the last years, leading to the growth of international businesses producing hyphenated identity groups like African-Americans, Afro-Europeans, Turkish-Europeans, Maghrebo-Europeans, and so on.

The definition of a (new and engaging) European identity in terms of one culture, one language, one history or one religion as was the case in the nation state ideology, becomes ever more threatened by such developments in the eyes of many fearful locals. In our view, the threat and the fear are only felt in this way as long as communities and groups keep clinging to the essentialism which is intrinsic in the communitarian form of (extreme) nationalism which new rightist movements promote. In our view, then, this essentialism is a continuation of the old nationalistic form which was implemented through education and propaganda for generations by the nation states and inertia redirects it to define regional or communitarian identities at a moment when the nation states are fading in the European political structure. Simply condemning this reorientation of essentialistic identification will yield more frustration, and with successful populist political figures (in the extreme right parties of Italy, Austria, Flanders, etc.) it might attack the difficult and vulnerable democratic structures and movements. The risk is especially serious in a period of political and cultural shifts and a need for mental reorientation such as we are experiencing now: after the fall of the Berlin Wall and the collapse of the Soviet Union, an antisocial free market 'fundamentalism' has conquered the political arena, accompanied by a relocation of power in nontransparant centralised (and hence intractable) Big Government bureaucracies and multinational corporations. So, the possibility of appeal to political representatives is diminished in the eyes of the common citizen, while at the same time society is slowly but steadily sliding towards a dual society, at the expense of the less privileged. The old state infrastructure is functioning less than adequately throughout the states of the EU, and larger groups of the population feel abandoned. In the cities, new ghettoes emerge: Friedman (1999: 685) mentions the phenomenon of ghettoisation in European cities, where over 50 percent of the population in the 'bad neighbourhoods' are unemployed, while a mile further down in the financial district vast profits are made daily on the stock exchange.

What should be concluded from the foregoing paragraphs?

1. One point is that extreme rightist and new manifestations of racism engage in *essentialistic* identity construction, where 'us' is seen as an inalienable and unchanging entity which is opposed to a structurally similar 'them'. The two cannot mingle and hence neither durable peaceful coexistence nor intercultural relationships are feasible.
2. A second point is that both the discourse on identity and difference and the construction of a self-image (like in communitarianism) are phrased in terms of 'culture'. Hannerz speaks of 'cultural fundamentalism' in extreme rightist thinking, stressing the fact that one's local culture is superior to all other forms and needs to be protected from contamination by outside influences. We need to develop this point in some detail.

Cultural Diversity

The point that anthropologists seem to agree on at the present moment is that the globalisation movement in the economic world did not necessarily entail the disappearance of local cultures. Put differently, the growing economic globalisation has not led to the evaporation of the cultural dimension, nor of cultural differences. The latter would have meant that universal rights and customs would have become the factual culture of humanity. Sahlins (1999) looks back on the twentieth century research in this realm and comes to the conclusion that old hypotheses proved to be wrong. One theory from the 1960s predicted that 'small cultures' which were gradually being encroached upon by western civilisation would be harmed by contact and become 'despondent'. Sahlins cites many examples of 'small cultures' which have been revitalised over recent decades and define an interesting challenge to globalisation adherents: cultural diversity is not going away, and modernity is adapted to local culture, rather than the other way around. In the words of Sahlins: 'Many of the peoples who were left for dead or dying by dependency theory we now find adapting their dependencies to cultural theories of their own' (1999: VI). In other words, we witness an indigenisation of modernity at the end of the century. His European colleague specialising in urban studies generalises this so-called 'culturalist' point in a rather bold statement: 'There is now a world culture, but we had better make sure we understand what this means. It is marked by an organisation of diversity rather than a replication of uniformity' (Hannerz, 1990: 237).

Taking these analyses seriously, we claim that antiracism and democratic policies, which would aim at fighting extreme rightist manifestations, should deal responsibly and adequately with the cultural dimension. This is a rather delicate issue since the older ideological analyses (and its recent manifestation in globalisation theories) had it that cultural aspects either did not really matter in the light of economic trends, or could be discarded as 'rightist culturalism'. Our perspective stresses that cultural factors do matter, and that denying their impact in human affairs is a sort of ideological dogmatism rather than scientific honesty. Once this point is made, it is important to distinguish different uses and understandings of the cultural dimension. One such use is, again, ideological and scientifically untenable: the new manifestations of racism in extreme rightist movements in Europe defend an essentialistic view of cultural identity. This view is historically wrong and sociologically nonsensical (see Verstraete & Pinxten 1998 for an overview) and the social scientist should never stop saying so. At the same time, it is clear that 'culture does not go away', that is to say, that individuals, groups and communities seek to define and redefine their identities in terms of cultural features. Hence, any policy which aims to combat these new manifestations of racism and extreme rightist exclusion will have to confront these cultural identifications if it aims to have impact. That is the important emphasis the social scientist wants to add. Furthermore, insights into the workings of these identity dynamics can teach us how we can safeguard democratic opinions and practices against the re-emerging exclusivist tendencies.

Towards a Constructive Antiracist Policy: Three Foci

The intercultural colouring of European citizenship should focus on several points at the same time. We want to present these foci as normative criteria for good interculturalism, which can be used to test and evaluate the degree of interculturalism in any society, and at the same time should allow for the production of better or alternative measures to enhance intercultural attitudes and structures within a community.

'Decent Society'

Europe should adopt the conceptual frame and the behavioural rules of the decent society. This notion was developed by A. Margalit (1996), an Israeli philosopher of law who lives and works in the context of multicultural and conflict-prone Israel. He aims at developing a just and respectful society, within the complex multicultural setting that is growing. The central category he proposes is that of decency. He states that individuals can live in a civilised society, but still humiliate each other. When this occurs the individuals can be sanctioned. However, societies as such can be humiliating to their subjects. In that case, the institutions humiliate the citizens, and the society is characterised as an indecent one. Decency, at the institutional level, might be thought to justify members of a society to treat each other with respect. However, Margalit demonstrates that such a 'morally inspired' attitude is without foundation. First of all, respect is a given and cannot be justified in any consistent way. What can be justified, he argues, is the foundation of avoidance of humiliation. Avoiding humiliation is sensible, and the cases where humiliation is structurally and institutionally organised show convincingly why it is not a durable or even a viable alternative. On that basis a respectful or decent society can be presented as the preferable format.

How does humiliation work? Margalit states that institutional humiliation means that the individual person is rejected by the society, entailing a loss of his means of basic self-control. The better known version is the authoritarian society which decides on all and everything over the heads of and even against the individual person. In actual practice, Margalit distinguishes a set of institutional behaviours which express humiliation:

1. The institution can deny or demolish a person's privacy, rendering him or her a person without rights and without freedom of choice or opinion. In other words, it can install control which is pervasive and precludes privacy (cf. Nader, 1993).
2. The institution can depersonalise individuals by denying them individual identity or reducing them to mere numbers.

This is best known from the effect of bureaucratic institutions, which have linear rules which prevail on personal features at all times.

1. Welfare, poverty and unemployment are in themselves humiliating, certainly when they are structural and escape is more impossible the longer they last. When applying this to the issue of interculturalism, it is clear that social and political exclusion of newcomers, refugees and immigrants from the dominant society will be indecent.
2. Charity has a humiliating effect, implying that the well-meant activism of churches and humanitarian aid groups can at the most be tolerated as a temporary answer to cope with a crisis situation. It can never be structural as a solution for interculturalisation. It is important that the permanent character of volunteer charity vis-à-vis the newcomers and the excluded is certainly characteristic in neoliberal and communitarian approaches to the EU: the newcomers are not treated as equal human beings who would thus have equal opportunities, but they are considered a 'problem' for the native community and should benefit, at the most, from special measures for integration.
3. Exploitation and punishment are humiliating. Exploitation should be combated and sanctioned, while alternatives for mere punishment should be installed where possible. Punishment in itself is not re-educating or bettering a person, while alternative measures (such as social work) may have this effect.

Looking at all these points, any policy against racism and exclusivism should aim at recognising features of indecency. It should also strive for the enhancement of the decent society. This should not be done because of some idealist ideology, but because the decent society is the only durable one, in that it prevents humiliation and hence frustration of its members. Moreover, and most importantly, it is the only one which is consistent with its own principles of democracy and equal rights. How this is compatible with the emphasis on cultural particularities which we advocated before will become clear in the second focus. For now it is important to understand that culture and cultural identity dynamics are not indecent in themselves, but rather that the subjects involved in them should be treated with respect. The condition of the decent society is that the identities promoted in such processes should be of a sort that can be integrated in a political project of democracy as explained below. We then speak of 'cultural' federalism, as distinguished from the established notion of territorially defined political federalism which are used in the EU construction so far.

Universalism and Cultural Particularity at the Same Time

The discussion, if you can call it that, between so-called 'materialists' and so-called 'culturalists' has the first deny a substantial role to cultural features (because they would be derived) and has the second claim that cultural identity is the main force that drives people. We call this the mono-causality fallacy: we think it unlikely that the complexities we are dealing with are characterised most adequately by identifying one and just one cause. Several codetermining factors are at work, and we highlight some in this contribution. So, at a sociological level, we see a relative autonomy of structural or institutional aspects on which policy makers can, and should, focus.

Apart from the decency of a society and the criteria to test it, the policy maker should negotiate a particular format for society which is binding for all parties. Any democratic rule is to be negotiated, and the skills to negotiate with knowledgeability should be part and parcel of any civil education in democratic societies (one which is not fulfilled at present). Taking for granted that cultural peculiarities and intricacies are important and cannot be reduced to a mere by-product of economic or other factors, it is the task of the politician to design a format for the multicultural society. In our view there are not many suggestions around. One is that of ethnic cleansing, primordialism or outright apartheid, where the community in power declares itself to be superior and forces the others out or demands that they assimilate (e.g., de Benoist 1998). Cultural differences are felt to be annoying or even threatening and should be abolished in favour of the culture of the dominant group. Although the diagnosis that cultural changes and the coexistence of different profiles can be felt to be threatening is right, the solutions proposed are anti-humanistic and exclusivist, resulting in so-called 'cultural fundamentalism'. In a democratic society this perspective has to be combatted.

The (neo)liberal view on society claims that the individual is the primary agent and the laws of the free market will regulate whatever needs to be regulated. In practice, this leads to the supremacy and the absolute power of the haves, where the corporations are running the society, decide what tastes and preferences will be marketable and what is accessible or not. There seems to be no guarantee that such a society develops in the direction of equality or equal opportunities for have-nots or have-somes. Over recent decades, new exclusions seem to be based on categories such as gender, race or culture. A democratic and multicultural political perspective runs into trouble with such a deregulated or uncorrected (neo)liberal society. Racism, apartheid and cultural cleansing are likely to appear as spontaneous 'solutions' in such a political context, and policy makers should be aware of it and react to it.

Another possibility is to confront the multicultural nature of present day Europe straight on and seek for a re-adaptation of the monocultural view on society. In the nation state period, territory and the national history became the core of political identity, eventually expressed in one language, one culture and/or one religion. With the gradual influx of large groups with different languages, cultures or religions, the monocultural national identity construct came under attack. With the internationalisation and globalisation of businesses (by the international corporations), the relationships between universal or culture-neutral political structures and the political recognition of cultural differences are up for reconsideration. In line with the Enlightenment belief in the European tradition we propose the following unambiguous political construct for a society, in which interculturalism would be a real asset for durable interhuman relationships.

The European Union and its member states should define a binding, but minimal universal political foundation for all and every state in the Union and for each citizen. The existing European Declaration of Human Rights can serve as a minimal basis of opinions and practices on which any community or group and any political structure in the Union can operate. It clearly defines rights of individual citizens and of states, and subordinates community rights to this universal frame. Any individual, group or community and any political or economic structure should comply with this basic criteria of Europeanness. We want to expand this legal frame with a political instrument. On top of and beyond the level of the EDHR individuals, groups and communities within the EU should learn to adopt a 'federal' attitude, granting freedom of identity dynamics and its expressions in sociocultural and political manifestations without reserve, provided the common and universal foundation is safeguarded in the process. Thus, we want to pit cultural federalism against cultural fundamentalism (Hannerz 1996). Cultural federalism means that it is an inalienable right of each and every individual, group and community to live by the moral, religious, linguistic and other cultural standards they care for within the EU, provided their way of living does not contradict or hamper or threaten the minimal uniform foundation of the Union. It is clear that our notion of 'cultural' federalism differs from that of political federalism in the EU, which refers to the collaboration of independent nation states within the larger Union. It also differs from the other territorially expressed form of federalism which can be recognised in the Europe of the regions. Both forms of federalist thinking in existence now have, as a basic referent, territorial adherence and territorial claims: the citizenship of the nation state is defined over a particular territory, and the federalism of the regions within the EU defines regional relative autonomy over a territory combined with a language or descent line. Cultural federalism takes the idea of relative autonomy one step further, but it is clearly opposed to either territorial or descent definitions of autonomy (and hence to Blut und Botem ideologies). Instead, it grants the cultural identity dynamics of populations and allows them to live and express these within the universally binding context of the uniform political structure of the EU. So the territory is that of the European Union as a whole, and within that context citizens can express their belonging to a cultural community by embodying a relative autonomy in culture, language, religion, etc. E.g., diaspora peoples, nomads (such as gypsies, but also new transnationals) and so on, but also settled populations should have the right to live these identities on top of and within the territory and the political structure of the encompassing EU. Buddhists, islamic subjects, catholics, but also Basques, Hungarian Germans, and so on can have the right to live their community identity, but only in full respect of the uniform European political structure every citizen in the EU subscribes to. Probably, the nation state is or was more opposed to and could cope less with cultural federalism than the EU, since the territoriality notions have played such an important role in nation state history. In practice, this means that assimilationism is out of the question (it humiliates groups and communities institutionally), but also, that cultural fundamentalism should be sanctioned by the political authorities (Friedman 1999). This means that cultural federalism could grant relative autonomy to communities (as the communitarians are now the only ones to claim) on the basis of cultural identities, but at the same time exclude territorial and descent definitions of identity expression. Such a proposal is not idealistic, but rather might be forced upon European rulers in light of the rapid multicultarisation of the EU.

Cultural fundamentalism amounts to the position that one's cultural forms are held to have an essentialistic character and to be superior to any other ones and that hence no common ground beyond or apart from one's own culture can be accepted. It entails that the way of living of any other tradition should be adapted to one's own, or eventually refused or chased. In an expected way, it wants to express identity in terms of a separate territory for one's 'cultural community' and eventually defines its autonomy by reference to bloodlines or ethnic history. Both auto-ghettoisation within and by some immigrant communities (who form 'villages within the foreign city') and ghettoisation of minorities by a dominant community (as in extreme rightist movements in Europe presently) fall within this category. In our view, both should be treated as in violation of the federal political structure, and urged to reorient. We know it is unusual to group extreme right autochthonous movements with some minority groups, but as social scientists we believe the similarities between some of these groups are striking: the islamists who abuse the democratic means of Europe to abolish that democracy are very similar in their treatment of the political structures to the extreme right parties who only use the election system to seize power and break down freedom of speech once they get some power (cf. press delicts and cultural conflicts in present day Austria and with extreme right parties in Flanders who claim cultural fundamentalism on any occasion). Even the simplicity of political analysis and of the solutions proposed are very similar.

The political authorities should be very clear about the minimal common foundation of civil society which is binding for all, and should unambiguously sanction any individual, group or community who denies it or threatens to demolish it. A workable and clear law on racism and discrimination could be an important instrument here, but the existing proposals seem, at present, rather powerless. The withdrawal of funding from organisations which obviously and purposefully abuse the foundational rules or undermine them is to be considered, as well as the sanctioning of types of populism which, at the most mislead, and at the worst create a climate of fear and fraud. We know that these phenomena are not well understood, and hence serious research on them is in order: the democratic project needs and deserves this, lest it will once again allow for self-destruction as has happened several times in the past. The famous dictum that fascism can be democratically elected to power in order to then eradicate democracy, may cause uneasiness with democratic minded people, but it is clear that it is more than just a slogan.

In the historical perspective that we have now it is important to devise democratic means to defend democracy, while keeping in line with the principles of democracy. This means, as mentioned earlier, that political structures and their rules should be negotiated, but also that the citizen should be educated in order to become skilled in negotiation and in conflict management. Both the decent society view and the mixed format of a universal foundation combined with the federal organisation of cultural diversity are invitations to think along this path.

Enhancing Intercultural Competence

A final emphasis we want to see in political work and political judgment is that concerning the world of experience of the citizen. Some of the reactions of people in the 1990s, with the growth of populism and extreme right voters, have been explained by fear, inability to adapt to rapid changes and anxiety about the loss of security The apparent lack of adequacy of conflict handling and conflict resolution procedures is an interesting entry in these matters (one of us, M.C., is working along these lines). Given that the conflict resolution procedures that European citizens and groups have employed in recent generations stem basically from the monocultural, mostly christian and national background that citizens have been educated in, it is to be expected that the inadequacy of these procedures in the context of a globalising economy, the waning of nation state power and structures, and the 'multiculturalisation' of one's world would cause fear and thus protectionism. With the lack of alternative capacities, skills and attitudes to deal with these changes as challenges, it is the task of the political authorities to actively intervene in this area, provided we want to combat new manifestations of racism in a durable and effective way. Only then will the citizen have an alternative to fear and exclusion and be able to cope with the sudden growth of diversity. The emerging programmes on intercultural education are important means to be developed here. Persons and groups should be taught procedures to cope with diversity and resolve their disputes in ways that differ from the former monocultural line. Although, finally, the initiatives to develop intercultural education were taken in the 1990s, not much ground has been covered. The European Journal of Intercultural Education is a start, but the lack of clarity on concepts and on strategies over and across national boundaries is striking. A tremendous amount of study on educational curricula, and on teaching and learning styles needs to be done, and fast. Educational material needs to be developed that goes beyond the nation-centered or even beyond the eurocentered scope that is still prevalent (Pinxten 1997, Sierens 1998). Most of all, national governments should enforce intercultural education and replace the nation state focus in the curricula and thus build the minimal foundation of europeanness. Finally, cultural and political cooperation should be positively sanctioned.

Conclusions

In this contributions we sketched how Europe is growing into a multicultural society which remains ideologically chained in nation state mentalities. Interculturalism is seen as a way out. We propose three foci for the political authorities who need to confront new manifestations of racism in Europe today:

1. Actively strive for a decent society, which goes against institutional humiliation.
2. Define a uniform foundation of rights, practices and institutions to be shared by all in the EU, on top of which, diversity can be integrated in a federal structure. Cultural federalism is pitted against cultural fundamentalism.
3. Deepen and broaden intercultural education and cooperation.

Bibliography

Appadurai, A. 1996. *Modernity at large.* Minneapolis: University of Minnesota Press.
Bourdieu, P. 1994. *La misère du monde.* Paris: Ed. Minuit.
de Benoist, A. 1998. 'Communitarianism and liberalism'. *TEKOS,* 1–12.
Friedman, J. 1999. Rhinoceros 2. *Current Anthropology,* 40: 679–694.
Gellner, E. 1998. *Language and solitude.* Cambridge: Cambridge University Press.
Giddens, A. 1998. *The Third Way.* Cambridge: Polity Press.
Hannerz, U. 1990. 'Cosmopolitans and locals in world culture'. In *Global culture.* M. Featherstone, ed. London: Sage. 237–51.
Hannerz, U. 1999. 'Comments'. *Current Anthropology.* 40: 689–691.
Korten, D.C. 1995. *When Corporations Rule the World.* London: Earthscan.
Margalit, A. 1996. *Decent Society.* Cambridge, Mass.: Harvard University Press.
Nader, L. 1993. 'Controlling processes'. *Current Anthropology.* 34.
Pinxten, R., and Verstraete, G. 1998. *Cultuur en macht.* Antwerp: Houtekiet.
Pinxten, R. 1997. 'INand ICE as a means to promote a New Personhood in Europe.' *European Journal of Intercultural Studies,* 8: 151–75.
Sahlins, M. 1999. 'What is anthropological Enlightenment? Some Lessons from the Twentieth Century', *Annual Reviews in Anthropology.* 1999: I–XXIII.
Sayad, A. 1999. *La double absence. Des illusions de l'immigré aux souffrances de l'immigré.* Paris: Seuil.

Sierens, S. 1998. 'Intercultureel onderwijs vanuit een pragmatisch perspectief'. *Cultuurstudie* 3: 130–178.

Spruyt, M. 2000. *Wat het Blok verzwijgt*. Leuven: EPO.

Verstraete, G., and Pinxten, R. 1998. In R. Pinxten and G. Verstraete: 4–79.

NOTES ON CONTRIBUTORS

Campani, Giovanni has prepared a Ph. D. in Ethnology, University of Nice (France) (1988) on *Family, Village and Regional Networks of Italian Immigrants in France*. (2000), *Genere, etnia e classe*. *Migrazioni al femminile tra esclusione e identità*, ETS, Pise; (1996), *La rosa e lo specchio*, Ipermedium, Naples. As editor: (1998) with Besalu, Palaudarias, *Educacion intercultural en Europa. Un enfoque curricular*, Pomares Correcor, Barcelona; (1997) with Verma, Woodrow, Trindade, *Intercultural Education: Theories, policies and practices*, Ashgate, London.

Cornelis, Marijke is an assistant in the Department Comparative Study of Cultures at Ghent University Belgium. She graduated with an ethnographic research on the effects of intercultural education in adolescents in Flanders.She is preparing a PhD on the intricacies of racist thought and attitudes in city dwellers in Europe, communautarian ideology and multicultural policy.

Fortman, Bas de Gaay holds a Master of Law degree (*Magister Iuris*) as well as a PhD in Economics, both from the Free University of Amsterdam, the Netherlands. Until 1991 he was also Senator in the Netherlands Parliament. In 2000 he was appointed to the Chair in Political Economy of Human Rights at Utrecht University. His recent books include *God and the Goods. Global Economy in a Civilizational Perspective*, Geneva: World Council of Churches Publications 1998; and *Where Needs Meet Rights. Economic, Social and Cultural Rights in a New Perspective*, Geneva: World Council of Churches Publications, 1999 (both together with Dr Berma Klein Goldewijk).

Greskovits, Béla, is a Professor of Political Science and Head of Department of International Relations and European Studies at Central European University, Budapest. Bela Greskovits's major field of interest is international and comparative political economy. His current research examines the role of economic sectors and state institutions in Eastern Europe's transformation and European integration. His recent publications include numerous articles on the social response to economic hardship in Eastern Europe and elsewhere in the world and a book The Political Economy of Protest and Patience. East European and Latin American Transformations Compared. CEU Press, Budapest, 1998.

Gundara, Jagdish Singh. In addition to a wide range of articles and international conference papers, Jagdish Gundara's publications include the World Year Book of Education on Intercultural Education (Kogan Page, 1997), Racism, Diversity and Education (co-ed., Hodder and Stoughton, 1986), The History of Blacks in Britain (co-ed., Gower 1992), European Intercultural Social Policies (co-ed., Avebury 2000) and author Interculturalism: Education and Inclusion (Paul Chapman 2000).

Hentges, Gudrun, Dr. phil. University of Köln, Germany studied political science, sociology, philosophy and French at the Universities of Marburg and Paris. Currently "wissenschaftliche Assistentin" at the Social Sciences Seminar, Political Science Section of the University of Cologne. Publications: *Antisemitismus. Geschichte Interessenstruktur –>Aktualität* (edited with Guy Kempfert and Reinhard Kühnl). Heilbronn. 1995; *Medien und multikulturelle Gesellschaft* (edited with Christoph Butterwegge and Fatma Sarigöz). Opladen 2000; *Politische Bildung und Globalisierung* (edited with Christoph Butterwegge), Opladen 2001.

Lerner, Natan, teaches International Human Rights at the Faculty of Law of Tel Aviv University, from which he retired a few years ago. He also teaches International Law at the Interdisciplinary Center Herzliya. He is the author, i.a., of 'the UN Convention on the Elimination of All Forms of Racial Discrimination in International Law', The Hague, 1991, translated into Spanish, and 'Religion, Beliefs and International Human Rights', New York, 2000.

Maier, Robert, senior researcher at the University of Utrecht, the Netherlands; research themes: (1) argumentation and debate and (2) forms of identity and exclusion. Authored and/or edited books include: Sociogenesis re-examined (New York, 1997), Gestion des risques et citoyenneté (Paris, 1998). Recent articles and chapters in books include: 'European identity: construct, fact or fiction?, Discourses of globalization and worldviews', and 'Types of debate'.

Pinxten, Rik is professor of cultural anthropology and the comparative study of religion in the Department Comparative Study of Cultures at the University Ghent, Belgium. He has done extensive research in cognitive anthropology, in theoretical anthropology and in the comparison of religions. He is editor of Cultural Dynamics (Sage), and author of several books: *Anthropology of Space* (Philadelphia, 1983), *When the Day Breaks* (Hamburg, 1997), *Goddelijke fantasie* (The Creation of God, Antwerp, 2000).

Räthzel, Nora is senior researcher at the departement of sociology, University of Umea Sweden. She works in the areas of racism, gender and ethnic relations, youth and migration. Her publications include: 'Germans into foreigners: how anti-nationalism turns into racism'. In Floya Anthias and Cathie Lloyd (eds:) : *Rethinking antiracism, from theory to pratice* (London,2000). Forthcoming. *Living Differences: Ethnicity and Fearless Girls in Public Spaces.* (In: Social Identities).

Schuster, Liza is T. H. Marshall Fellow in the Department of Sociology at the London School of Economics. She was previously a Research Fellow in the Faculty of Humanities and Social Science at South Bank University, London, UK.

Solomos, John is Professor of Sociology in the Faculty of Humanities and Social Science at South Bank University, London, UK. Before that he was Professor of Sociology and Social Policy at the University of Southampton, and he has previously worked at the Centre for Research in Ethnic Relations, University of Warwick and Birkbeck College, University of London.

Verkuyten, Maykel is an anthropologist and social psychologist by training. Currently he is an associated professor at the faculty of social sciences at Utrecht University, the Netherlands. He also works as a senior researcher at the European Research Center on Migration and Ethnic Relations (ERCOMER) at the same university. His main research interests are on ethnic identity and interethnic relations in particular amoung young people.

Verlot Marc holds a masters in history, a post-graduate diploma in social and cultural anthropology as well as a doctorate in comparative science of culture. He is currently a lecturer at the Ghent University in Belgium and head of the Centre for Intercultural Education at the same university. His main interests are institutional anthropology, anthropology of policy and educational anthropology, all of these in relation to the topic of multiculturalism.

INDEX

A

Abeles, J., 36, 41
acculturation, 140, 178
ADL, 49
affirmative action, 78, 194–95, 209
Ágh, A., 146, 159
Alston, P., 69n. 25
Amin, S., 206, 208n. 19. 208
Amos, V., 11, 24
Annan, K., 68n. 9
Anthias, F., 11, 24, 235
antiracism, 23–24, 46, 74, 138, 174, 176, 179, 190, 201, 211, 214, 220, 223, 235
anti-Semitism, 5–6, 12, 44, 47, 49–50, 57–58, 60, 64, 69nn. 12–13., 75, 86, 88, 90, 145, 206
apartheid, 5, 14, 80, 82, 168–69, 226–27
Appadurai, A., 221, 231
assimilation, 136, 178
asylum, v, viii, 15, 23, 58, 105–12, 114–24, 125nn. 12, 21., 126n. 50., 127n. 54., 127–29, 156, 198

B

Back, L., 10, 24, 33, 40n. 5., 42, 44–46, 52, 54–55, 77, 80, 82n. 4., 83n. 31., 84, 132, 138, 140
Bade, K., 126n. 44., 127
Balibar, E., 7, 12–13, 17, 24, 26, 91, 101, 184
Balkova, 114, 125n. 20
Banks, J., 177, 179, 184–85
Banton, M., 29, 40n. 3., 67, 70n. 40
Barker, M., 6–7, 24, 101
Bauman, Z., 15–16, 21, 25
Baumann, J., 126nn. 42, 52., 127, 172
Baumgartl, I., 45, 54
Beck, M., 26, 123, 126n. 50., 127
Beckstein, G., 122
Benoist, A. de, 7, 25, 216, 226, 231
Berend, I., 145, 159
Bernheim, J., 69n. 19
Betz, H., 152, 159
Bhatt, C., 53
Bhavnani, K., 26
Billig, M., 54, 140
Binet, A., 168
Bjørgo, T., 45–46, 49, 54–55

Blair, T., 217
Blommaert, J., 27, 40n. 1., 41
Bonnett, A., 138, 140
Bourdieu, P., 34, 184n. 3., 217, 231
Bowling, A., 49, 54
Bozóki, A., 153, 159
Brah, A., 26
Branscombe, N., 134, 140
Brennan, P., 179, 184
Britan, D., 37, 40n. 14., 41
Broca, P. de, 168
Brolman, G., 69n. 18
Brunsvick, Y., 184
Bulmer, M., 29, 41
Busch, H., 124nn. 9, 11., 127
Butler, C., 49, 54
Butterwegge, C., 125n. 28., 126nn. 36, 41, 43., 128–29, 234

C
Caine, C., 208n. 11., 208
Cambi, F., 173, 184
Campani, G., vi, 166, 185, 233
Carby, H., 11, 25
Carey, G., 198
Carmichael, S., 5, 25, 31
Cashmore, E., 29, 31, 40n. 3., 41
Castles, S., 174, 184
Cavalli-Sforza, L., 4, 25
Cheles, J., 45, 54
Chen, K., 25
Chennault, M., 45, 55
citizenship, viii, 26, 95–96, 101, 166, 175, 178–79, 182–83, 191, 198, 221, 224
Claessens, H., 158n. 3., 159
Coetzee, J., 80, 83n. 29., 83
Cohen, D., 5, 17–18, 25, 45, 54, 184
Cole, D., 76–78, 82n. 5., 83nn. 16., 19–21, 24.
Cole, J., 86, 91–92, 101
Cole, P., 25
Collins, P., 11, 25
colonialism, 5, 10, 12, 131, 169, 206

Commission (EU), 60, 64, 68, 74–75, 83n. 11., 87–90, 101, 106–7, 114–15, 122, 203, 208n. 14., 209, 212
Communitarian(ism), 216, 222, 225
concept of race, 4
Conquergood, D., 132, 140
Cornelis, M., vi, viii, 211, 233
Council (EU), 42, 57, 62, 64, 70n. 33., 68n. 1., 84, 88, 101, 115, 175, 180, 184, 205, 212–13, 233
Cox, O., 5, 25
Crithlow, O., 208n. 17., 209
Csurka, L., 150, 152–55, 159nn. 8, 10., 160
cultural federalism, 228, 231
cultural fundamentalism, 221, 228–29, 231
cultural racism, 6, 53
culturalism, 180, 223

D
Dannenbeck, C., 132, 138, 140
Danzin, A., 184
Davis, A., 11, 25
decency, 212, 224, 226
Demirgüc-Kunt, A., 159
democracy, viii, 21, 88, 97, 145–46, 150, 159–61, 171, 182, 218, 226, 229–30
democratisation, 145–46
deportation, 35, 108, 111–13, 118, 123, 125nn. 19–21., 126n. 50., 127, 129
Deslé, E., 27
devolution, vi, viii, 187, 190, 194, 201, 205
Diederichs, O., 124n. 9., 128
Dietrich, H., 125nn. 15,17., 128
Dietz, G., 40n. 16., 42
differential racism/racisme différentialiste, 6, 169
Dinstein, Y., 69n. 18

Index

discrimination, viii, 5–6, 10–11, 24, 29–32, 34–38, 40nn. 5, 11., 41, 57–68, 68n. 10., 69nn. 16–17., 70n. 40., 72–75, 77–79, 84, 86–90, 94, 101, 131–32, 134–37, 140–41, 143, 165, 168–69, 174, 177, 183, 188–89, 191, 193, 195–96, 198–99, 202–3, 209, 229, 234
diversity, 23, 32, 36, 39, 40n. 1., 41, 55, 74, 133, 136, 140, 166, 170, 174, 178–79, 182–85, 191, 196, 202, 204, 215, 220, 223, 230–31, 234
dominance, 139, 206
Donoghue, A., 179, 184
Du Bois, W., 43, 54
Dublin Convention, 109, 125n. 12., 128
Dworkin, R., 81, 83n. 33., 84

E
egalitarian, 8, 12, 32, 37–38
Eherlich, J., 41
Ekiert, G., 149, 160
Elgar, E., 84
Eliaspoh, N., 40n. 4., 41
Elliott, J., 174,176
Epps, E., 134, 140
equality, 7, 15, 59, 77, 79, 81, 88, 91, 168, 173, 177, 182, 183n. 1., 189, 191, 195–96, 198, 200, 202–03, 208nn. 14–15., 209, 227
Erdheim, M., 17, 25
Essed, P., 30, 41, 137, 140
essentialism, 216, 218, 220–22
Esser, F., 140
ethnic cleansing, 70n. 35., 215, 226
ethnic minority, 50, 131–34, 136–37, 139–41, 197
ethnic relations, vi, 41, 55, 131, 138, 140, 235

ethnicise, 99
ethnicity, viii, 9–10, 12–13, 25–26, 49–50, 52, 59, 61, 65, 86, 93, 141, 151, 173, 175, 185
ethnocentric, 35, 45, 206
ethnocentrism, 41, 165, 168, 183, 183n. 2
Eurobarometer, 86–88, 96, 101
Eurocentrism, 101, 204, 206, 208
European Court of Justice, 115
European Union, vi, vii, 22, 26–27, 37, 39, 83n. 13, 85, 87–88, 97, 101, 112, 114, 146–48, 160, 182, 187, 189, 194, 196, 202, 205, 208, 212–14, 218–20, 227–28
Europeanisation, v, 105, 107–9, 122, 206
exclusion, vii, 35, 49, 53, 77–78, 96, 101, 116, 136, 157, 190, 194, 198–99, 204, 207, 211, 216, 218–21, 225, 234
exclusivist, 211, 221, 224, 226
extremism, 107, 153, 157
Ezekiel, I., 45, 54
Ezorsky, G., 208n. 6., 209

F
Fanon, F., 6, 24–25
fascism, 5, 9–10, 16, 54, 166, 171–72, 229
Favell, A., 45, 54, 101
Ferber, D., 49, 54
Ferguson, J., 45, 54
Finkielkraut, A., 9, 25
Fortman, B. de Gaay, v, viii, 71, 82n. 6., 83n. 7., 84, 233
Frankenberg, R., 10, 25
Freedland, G., 208n. 4
Friedenberg, E., 83n. 18., 84
Friedman, J., 221–22, 231
Fuchs, D., 95, 101
fundamentalism, 227–29, 231
fundamentalist, 9, 17, 23, 145, 200

G

Gagnon, F., 185
Garcia, R., 177, 184
Gaserow, V., 126n. 45., 128
Gates, N., 49, 53–54
Gellner, E., 166, 184, 221, 231
Geneva Convention (GCR), 105–7, 111–12, 118–19, 124, 129
genocide, 4–5, 16, 51, 58, 62, 69, 86
Gentile, G., 166
Gergely, J., 159n. 10., 160
Gerhards, J., 101
Giddens, A., 215, 231
Gilman, S., 4, 15, 17, 25
Gilroy, P., 10, 25, 54
Glatz, P., 159n. 10., 160
globalisation, vi, vii, 7, 19–20, 22–23, 25, 129, 143–44, 147–48, 151–52, 156–58, 183, 217, 223, 227
Goldberg, D., 15, 25, 44, 46–47, 54, 140
Goldewijk, B., 83n. 7., 84, 233
Grahame, P., 40n. 12., 41
Grant, C., 177–79, 185
Grass, G., 217
Greskovits, B., vi, viii, 143, 159n. 9., 160, 234
Griffith, J., 79, 83nn. 27–28., 84
Grinter, E., 175, 184
guest workers, 94, 97–98
Guillaumin, C., 11, 25
Guillemin, M., 168
Gundara, J., vi, viii, 187, 209, 234
Gurin, P., 134, 140
gypsies, 4–5, 13, 58–60, 112, 181, 201, 228
ypsies, 66; 294

H

Hainsworth, D., 43, 54
Hall, S., 10, 24-25, 44, 54
Hamilton, C., 5, 25, 31
Hamm, E., 52, 54

Hannerz, U., 221–22, 231
Hansen, P., 22, 26
Haraway, D., 8, 26
Harvey, R., 140
hate speech, v, viii, 43–44, 48, 52–55
hatred, 13, 24, 44, 49–50, 52–53, 58–63, 65–68, 76, 145, 170
Henkin, L., 69n. 25
Hentges, G., v, viii, 105, 125n. 28., 126nn. 36, 41, 43, 51., 128–29, 234
Herzfeld, M., 28, 35–38, 41
Hewitt, R., 132, 138, 140, 200, 208n. 12., 209
Hickman, M., 26
Hilliard, A., 177, 185
Hirschberg, D., 4
Hirschfeld, M., 26
Hoffman, D., 179, 185
Höfling-Semnar, B., 125n. 30, 128
Hohmann, M., 121, 126n. 47, 128
Holmes, J., 43, 54
holocaust, 16, 25, 58–59, 62–63, 68
Holzberger, M., 125n. 28., 126nn. 36,41., 129
Hooks, B., 11, 26
hostility, 61, 66, 145, 147–48, 151, 156
Huizinga, H., 159
Hull, G.,11, 26
human right(s), v, vii, viii, 21, 58–64, 67–68, 68n. 10., 69nn. 10, 12, 15, 17–19, 21, 23., 70nn. 33–34., 71, 73–75, 77, 80–82, 83n. 11, 84, 88, 97, 109, 116, 123, 127, 129, 181–82, 188, 205, 213, 216, 227, 233–34
Hutnik, N., 140

I

identity, ii, vii, viii, 16–17, 20–21, 26, 36, 39, 40n. 16., 42, 47,

58, 82n. 6., 84, 91, 93–96,
    101, 113, 121, 132–34,
    139–41, 176, 179, 193–94,
    209, 212, 216–228, 234–35 ;
Iganski, N., 52, 55
immigrant, vii, 21, 33–34, 39, 40n.
    9., 41, 44, 57, 65, 98, 115,
    141, 146, 168, 175, 190–91,
    196, 201, 219, 229
immigration, 15, 26, 39, 40n. 8.,
    50, 55, 101–02, 110, 114,
    119–22, 129, 171–75, 183,
    221
inclusion, 96, 157, 158n. 5., 195,
    234
inclusive, 34, 63, 145, 171, 190,
    192, 199, 202, 204–08
inequality, 15, 53, 59–60, 76, 83n.
    19., 97, 100, 102, 140, 148,
    176, 183, 196, 215, 218
Ingles, J., 66, 68n. 17
insecurity, 76, 100, 139, 148, 157
institutional racism, v, 27, 31,
    35–36, 38–39, 138, 189, 194,
    199
intercultural education, viii, 175,
    177–80, 182–83, 187–89,
    199–202, 230–31, 233–34,
    236
intercultural, 174–77, 179–82,
    188–89, 194–95,
    198,200–204, 207, 208n. 1.,
    209, 215–16, 220, 222, 224,
    230, 233–34
interculturalism, vi, 174, 179, 190,
    202, 211, 215, 217–18, 220,
    224–25, 231
inter ethnic, 119, 235
internationalisation, 151, 227
intolerance, 28, 57–58, 60, 63–64,
    67, 68n. 1., 69n. 10., 74–75,
    213
Irving, D., 62–63
islamophobia, 181
    islamophobic, 37

J
Jacobs, D., 95, 101
James, R., 177, 185
Johnson, C., 195
Jong, W. de, 137, 140–41
Jowitt, K., 145–46, 149, 158n. 2.,
    160

K
Kalpaka, A., 19, 26
Kaplan, D., 45–46, 49, 55
Kehoe, J., 178, 185
Keith, M., 45, 49, 53–54
Kessler, R., 134, 140
Kincheloe, M., 45, 55
King, A., 11, 25–26
Kohn, D., 46, 55
Koonz, C., 10, 26
Koopmans, J., 46, 55
Korten, D., 215, 231
Kubik, I., 149, 160
Kushner,D., 55
Kymlicka, W., 185

L
Laferrière, M., 193
Lamont, 45, 55
Lange, A., 9, 26
Lawrence, S., 52, 54–55
Lay, C., 133, 140
Le Pen, J., 146, 155
Lee, H., 140
Leicester, M., 55, 175, 185
Lerner, N., v, viii, 13, 58, 69nn. 14,
    17–18, 22, 24, 27, 29., 70n.
    35., 234
Lesthaeghe, R., 40n. 1., 41
Leuninger, H., 128
Leur, W. de, 141
Levi Strauss, P., 168, 183nn. 1–2.,
    185
Liauzu, C., 168, 171, 185
liberalisation, 147, 149
Linquist, S., 172, 185

Lipstedt, D., 63
Loenen, 84
Losch, H., 140
Lovell, P., 72, 82n. 2., 84
Lugard, D., 80
Luther King, M., 174, 176
Lynch, J., 184–85

M
MacAndrew, M., 180, 185
Mac an Ghaill, M., 132, 138, 140
MacEwen, M., 83n. 22., 84
Maier, R., v, viii, 85, 95, 101, 234
majority, viii, 10, 13–15, 18–19, 24, 93, 122, 132–38, 150, 170–71, 182, 195, 200
Margalit, A., 212, 224–25, 231
Marshall, H., 132, 140, 235
Marx, K., 173
Maryknoll, K., 69n. 10
Matsuda, H., 49, 55
McCarthy, C., 208n. 17., 209
McCrudden, C., 83n. 26., 84
Memmi, A., 6, 26
meritocracy, 194, 196
Merz, F., 120–21, 126n. 46., 128
Mickelson, K., 140
migrant, 5, 7, 9–10, 22, 50, 98–100, 109, 174, 177–78
migration, 8, 41, 45, 55, 92, 98, 100–101, 111–15, 125n. 20., 127–29, 141, 172, 174–75, 184, 192, 197–98, 235
Miles, R., 4–5, 7, 26, 29, 40n. 3., 91, 101
Miller, M., 174, 184
minority, viii, 10, 14, 27, 32, 34, 38–39, 45, 50, 64, 69n. 20., 86, 129, 131–36, 138, 141, 145, 177, 179, 188, 195, 205, 207, 220, 229
modernity, 11, 15–16, 19, 25, 36, 51, 91, 165, 167–68, 223, 231
Mogdil, C., 184–85
Moluccan, 134

Montesquieu, de 173
Moodley, K., 176, 185
Morin, E., 180, 183n. 1., 184
Morley, D., 25
Moroccan, 77, 133–34, 184n. 5
Mosse, C., 44, 46, 49, 55
Müller-Funk, W., 25
multiculturalism, 22, 54, 140, 171, 174–75, 177, 184n. 6., 185, 197, 211, 236
multiculturalist, 8
multi-ethnic, 55, 184
multilingual, 190–91, 197–98
Murrell, P., 147, 160
Murrell, P., 192; 209n

N
Nader, L., 11, 225, 231
nation state, 11–14, 18–21, 23, 33–34, 36, 40n. 8., 87, 91, 97, 99, 158n. 7., 166, 170–71, 173, 182–83, 219, 221, 227–28, 230–31
nationalisation, 153–54
nationalism, 7–8, 12–13, 33–34, 41, 45, 50, 54, 145, 166, 170–71,173, 175, 184, 198, 221–22, 235
Nazi, 47, 51, 121, 165, 168, 170–71
Negrouche, N., 83n. 13., 84
neofascist, 44–46, 49–51, 218
neoliberalism, 20–21, 215, 217
Nguyen, T., 133, 140
Nicholson, L., 26
Nijhoff, 68n. 10
Noiriel, G., 124nn. 1–3, 5., 128
Noordhoff, 68n. 10

O
O'Donnell, M., 201, 208n. 13
Offe, C., 145, 148, 158n. 1., 160
Ogbu, J., 133, 141
O'Neill, B., 40n. 12., 41

Index

orientalism, 212
Ost, D., 145, 149, 160

P
Paech, N., 127n. 55., 128
Pagé, M., 185
Palidda, S., 41
Panayi, M., 49, 55
Parliament, 32, 87, 88, 101, 107, 109, 115–16, 127, 158n. 6., 187, 201, 212, 233
Parmar, P., 11, 24
Paulston, Ch., 179, 185
Perlmutter, P., 178, 185
Pettigrew, J., 50, 55
Pincus, F., 29–30, 41
Pinxten, R., ii, vi, viii, 41, 211, 216, 223, 230–31, 235
Pölöskei, F., 159n. 10., 160
Pomian, K., 166, 185
populism, 144, 149, 152–53, 155, 159, 229–30
Porrot, D., 168
postmodernity, 51
postsocialist, 142–44, 151, 153, 156, 159n. 10
poverty, v, viii, 21, 71–73, 76–77, 80, 82, 148, 225
power, ii, viii, 5, 11, 13–14, 16, 18, 20, 25, 31, 35, 42, 44, 46, 53, 73–74, 78–79, 81–82, 94, 96, 100, 119, 127, 132, 134–39, 145, 148, 151, 156, 176, 181, 187, 211–13, 215, 217, 222, 226–27, 229–30
Pred, C., 44, 52, 55
protoracism, 165–66, 185
Przeworski, A., 146, 160

R
racialise, 99, 195
racist discourse, 13, 47, 141
racist policy, 28, 34, 37

racist practice, 3, 10, 24n. 2., 35, 37, 64
Rea, A., 101–102, 127
refugee, v, vii, 105–106, 109, 112, 114–15, 118, 123–24, 128–29
Remmer, K., 157, 160
Renan, E., 168
Rey, V., 180, 185
Richman, H., 37
right
  extreme right, vii, 45, 48–50, 54, 150, 152, 155–57, 218–20, 222, 229–30
  new right, 7–9, 65, 97, 99, 116, 128, 155
  right-wing, 23, 48–50, 52, 54, 97, 99, 146, 152–53, 155, 159
Robinson, N., 69n. 18, 21
Rodriguez, P., 45, 55
Roller, E.,7, 95, 101
Rommelspacher, B., 10, 26
Roosens, E., 133, 141
Roth, C., 69n. 13., 125n. 28., 126nn. 36, 41., 129
Rousseau, 173
Ruggiero, K., 135, 141
Rushdie, S., 9

S
Sachs, J., 146, 160
Sahlins, M., 32, 41, 212, 223, 231
Said, E., 204–205, 208n. 18., 209
Sarigöz, F., 126n. 43., 128, 234
Saul, J., 170, 185
Sayad, A., 33–34, 40n. 7., 41, 219, 231
Schengen, 20, 107–16, 120, 124nn. 10,11., 128
Schily, O., 118–19, 122, 126n. 42., 129
Schlögl, K., 119
Schmitt, M., 140
Schröder, G., 120, 122
scientific racism, 4, 5, 10
Scott, 11, 26, 70n. 34

Seddon, D., 145, 161
Sedelmeier, U., 160
segregation, 29–32, 34, 40nn.5–6.,
    53, 76–77, 215
Seifer, N., 177, 185
self-esteem, 134–35, 141
self-worth, 134
sexism, 11, 13, 31, 178
Sharpe, S., 201, 208n. 13
Shore, C., 42
Sierens, A., 230–31
Silverman, M., 6–7, 26
Simons, H., 140
Slayden, D., 49, 54–55
Sleeter, C., 177–79, 185
Smith, B., 11, 26, 160
Solomos, J., v, vii, 29, 40n. 5.,
    41–46, 48–49, 52, 54–55, 77,
    80, 82n. 4., 83n. 31., 84, 235
Spruyt, M., 218, 231
Stallings, B., 160
Staples, H., 95, 99, 101
Statham, J., 46, 55
status, 12, 34, 64, 73, 82, 92,
    95–97, 99, 101, 105–106,
    116, 127, 132, 134, 137, 139,
    157, 194
Steniberg, D., 45, 55
Stenner, P., 140
Stern, D., 168
structural racism, vii, 27–29,
    31–32, 34–35, 38–39, 138,
    176, 216
subordination, 11, 18–19, 23–24,
    139, 155, 159n. 10
Sükösd, M., 153, 159
Swanson, G., 40n.15., 42
system blame, 134
Szacillo, M., 112

T
Tabory, E., 69n. 18
Taguieff, P.,7, 26, 86, 91, 101, 165,
    167, 169, 181, 185
Tajfel, H., 132, 141

Taylor, D., 135, 141
terrorism, 52, 107
Thornberry, D., 69n. 18.
Tocqueville, A. de, 76
Todorov, T., 180
Todorova, M., 158n. 7., 161
tolerance, 9, 27, 40n. 1., 41, 119,
    144, 157, 218
Townsend, E., 40n. 12., 42
Tribalat, M., 92–93, 101
Troyna, I., 31
Tudor, C., 150
Turkish, 95, 127, 133
Turkish, 129; 165; 176

U
universalism, 12, 74, 166, 173,
    182–83, 206, 212, 226
universality, 12, 168
Uremovic, O., 26
Uwer, T., 126n. 40., 129

V
Valier, L., 42
van Boven, T., 74–75, 83nn.
    10,12., 84
van de Calseijde, S., 141
van der Linden, J., 84
van Dijk, T., 11, 26, 137, 141
Várhegyi, E., 158n. 3., 161
Vaughan, C., 45, 54
Venner, M., 9, 26
Verkuyten, M., vi, viii, 131–32,
    134, 136–37, 140–41, 235
Verlot, M., v, vii, 27–28, 34, 40nn.
    16, 17.,42, 235
Verschueren, J., 27, 40n. 1., 41
Verstraete, G., ii, 216, 223, 231
violence, v, 43–45, 48–50, 52–55,
    57–58, 61, 65–68, 77, 87, 107,
    145–46, 157, 168, 218,
    220–21
Virdee, 52–55
von Bebenburg, P., 129

Index 245

von der Osten-Sacken, T., 126n.
   40., 129
von Pollern, H., 126n. 34., 129

W
Wallerstein, I., 13–15, 24, 26, 101,
   165, 167, 169, 176, 184–85
Walton, J., 145, 161
Ware, V., 10, 26
Waters, M., 133, 141
Whillock, 49, 54–55
Wiener, A., 85, 101
Wieviorka, M., 30, 42, 44, 55, 86,
   91, 102
Williams, J., 31, 140
Wilson, O., 98, 102
Winant, H., 82n. 1., 83n. 23., 84
Witte, E., 40n. 1., 41, 45, 48–49,
   54–55
Wodak, R., 11, 26
Wood, C., 72, 82n. 2., 84
Wrench, J., 44, 45, 48, 55
Wright, S., 42
Wynn, C., 177, 185

X
xenophobia, 16–17, 40n. 9., 47,
   54, 57–58, 60, 64, 74, 86–90,
   96, 101, 143, 145, 148,
   151–53, 156–57, 199, 203–04
Xenophobic, 35, 59, 87, 89, 92,
   97–98, 144, 149–53, 156–57,
   158n. 6, 218

Y
Yuval-Davis, N., 6, 11, 24, 26

Z
Zack, N., 11,26
Zoltán, M., 153, 159n. 10

About the Evens Foundation

Operating since 1996, the Evens Foundation owes its existence to the generosity of Mr. Georges Evens, a businessman of Polish origin, a philanthropist and supporter of European unity.

The Evens Foundation develops its activities in the intercultural field. The artistic component is our second core activity.

The Foundation awards the 'Evens Prize for Intercultural Projects' to a project deemed to have made an outstanding contribution to the European social integration in the field of intercultural education. This is based on our mission statement: 'To enhance the respect for differences in Europe'.

The Foundation is setting up an Evens Art Prize to support contemporary artistic research/practice relating in a renovating way to society.

The Evens Foundation coordinates and supports pan-European intercultural projects in Belgium.

The Foundation supports academic initiatives aiming at analysing growing tendencies of new exclusions from society and racist ideologies in an increasingly multicultural world. In particular, it sponsors international conferences in this field, focusing on research and possible alternatives for action.

The Evens Foundation copublishes this series 'Politics and Culture'.

Corinne Evens	Christine Castille	Ellen Preckler
President	Director	Project coordinator